ARTHUR STANLEY SMITH, better known as Neddy Smith, has been a long-term resident of Sydney's Long Bay Jail. As one of Sydney's most notorious criminals in the 1970s and 1980s, he enjoyed extensive police protection.

In 1992, after being provided with an indemnity from prosecution, he gave detailed evidence to an inquiry on police corruption. Smith suffers from Parkinson's disease. He is serving two life sentences for murder.

TOM NOBLE, is a journalist at *The Age*.

He is the author of two bestselling books, *Untold Violence: crime in Melbourne today* and *Walsh Street,* the story behind the shooting of two young constables in a cold-blooded revenge killing in 1988.

The life and crimes of Arthur 'Neddy' Smith

NEDDY

An autobiography with Tom Noble

crime books

First Published 1993
Second edition 1998
Reprinted 1998
Third edition 2002
Published by Noble House Enterprises Pty Ltd
Printed with the assistance of Kill City Crime Books
226 Chapel Street
Prahran, Victoria 3181
Tel (03) 9510 6661

© 1993 Smith Family Trust
© 1993 additional matter, Tom Noble
© 2002 Noble House Enterprises

This book is copyright. Apart from any fair dealing for the purposes of private study, research, criticism or review, as permitted under the Copyright Act, no part may be reproduced by any process without written permission from the publisher or the recording of Copyright Agency Ltd under their rules for use.

Cover design by Combined Media Services Pty Ltd
Typeset by DOCUPRO, Sydney
Printed by McPhersons, Melbourne

Distributed by TOWER BOOKS in Australia

National Library of Australian Cataloguing-in-Publication data:

Smith, Arthur Stanley, 1944–
 Neddy
 3rd Edition

ISBN 0-9580996-0-X

1. Smith, Arthur Stanley, 1944– . 2. Crime–New South Wales–Sydney.
3. Criminals–New South Wales–Sydney–Biography.
I. Noble, Tom, 1964– . II. Title.

364.373092

*To my three children,
Jaime, Darren and Daniel,
to my three beautiful
grandsons
Raecin, Jordin and Kaed
and to a special friend
Donna Brotherton.*

Chapter twenty Nine.
The Bus Depot Robbery.

████████ invited himself to lunch with me and Harold, not only did he invite himself but when he arrived he brought with him, four of his friends. "other detectives."
████ had plenty of front but i didn't mind as they may come in handy one day in the future.
It was my policy to try and have all the police on side, even if you never had reason to call on their services. "One day you might need them."
████ had some information to sell, it was very important, those were his words.
As it turned out the information that ████ had was older than last weeks bread.
████ told me that another special task force had been formed to try and find out what Rogerson and i were up to and to do their best to arrest us.
The task force was made up of both state and A.F.P....the reason for the mixture was because there weren't enough state police that were not on my payroll to make up a squad, so, they invited the A.F.P. to join them.
That was ████'s version but the real reason for mixing the two police forces was so that the A.F.P. could keep an eye on the state police.
It was quite obvious to everyone but ████ that there was a leak in all the other task forces that had been formed to investigate us and now they were doing their best to plug the leak.
I let ████ think that he was doing me a favour and i gave him $1000 for his trouble....he was very quick to pocket that.
Roger was already facing several charges at this time but i never had a worry in the world.
The lunch turned into a show ground for ████, he likes to boss his team mates around infront of Harold and i.
He was ordering them to do this and that, "go and ring him..go and do that". He was unbelievable the way he behaved, now i knew why he wasn't accepted by the dodger and his gang.
The drinking got out of hand after about three hours and Harold ended up trying to strangle ████ on the floor.
I was blind drunk at the end of the day and ████ insisted that i should not drive myself....i was driving a grey rolls at the time.
It ended up with ████ telling one of his younger detectives to drive me to where ever i was going and to stay with me and to look after me.

Facsimile of Smith's original typescript entitled Thank Christ for Corruption, *1992*

Contents

	Editor's Foreword	9
	Introduction	11
1	The Fuzzy Blue Line	13
2	Home Boy	22
3	In the Nicks	38
4	Looking down the Barrel	57
5	Easy Money	66
6	Double Bay Days	77
7	Educating Neddy	86
8	The Bangkok Business	106
9	The Green Light	118
10	With a Little Help from my Friends	127
11	Mixed Fortunes	137
12	Back with Abo	160
13	Blood on the Streets	170
14	Doing Business	190
15	A Spot of Robbing	207
16	Broad Daylight	220
17	Going to Work	231
18	The Life of Riley	246
19	Stinks	265
20	Losing Control	278
21	Betrayal	289
22	Back Inside	300
23	Payback Time	310
	Postscript 1	318
	Postscript 2	320

INDEMNITY

WHEREAS the Independent Commission Against Corruption is investigating possible corrupt conduct by present and former police officers, including serious criminal activity, pursuant to the Independent Commission Against Corruption Act 1988;

AND WHEREAS one Arthur Stanley Smith has provided information to the Independent Commission Against Corruption and may be required to give evidence at a hearing to be conducted before the said Commission, to adduce all the facts known to him relative to such corrupt conduct by present and former police officers; and may be required to give similar evidence in ensuing prosecution hearings;

AND WHEREAS, as a consequence of giving such evidence, the said Arthur Stanley Smith may render himself liable to prosecution for an offence or offences under the law of New South Wales arising out of his actions in concert with certain police officers, including robberies, unlawful payments to police officers, and drug offences;

AND WHEREAS I, Peter Edward James Collins, Her Majesty's Attorney General for the State of New South Wales, being satisfied that for the effective conduct of the investigation now being conducted by the said Commission, and for the due administration of justice, it is necessary to have resort to the evidence of the said Arthur Stanley Smith and for that purpose, the said Arthur Stanley Smith should be indemnified as hereinafter appears;

NOW THEREFORE, I, the said, Peter Edward James Collins do hereby undertake that no criminal proceedings shall be had or taken against the said Arthur Stanley Smith, in relation to any part had by him in the commission of any offence, other than homicide, which any member of the New South Wales Police Service, past or present, aided, abetted, counselled or procured, of which the said Arthur Stanley Smith hereafter gives evidence whether before a Court or before the Independent Commission Against Corruption;

PROVIDED that the said Arthur Stanley Smith gives his active co-operation including the giving of evidence truthfully and frankly and without embellishment and withholding nothing of relevance in the proceedings aforementioned.

Dated at SYDNEY this 24 day of October, 1991.

<u>ATTORNEY GENERAL</u>

Facsimile of Indemnity granted to Smith

Editor's Foreword

If you think there is a can of worms being opened up in Queensland in the Fitzgerald inquiry, then you can take my word for it you have a container full to deal with down here . . . compared with a sardine can full of corruption up in Queensland, New South Wales leaves Queensland for dead.

David Kelleher,
to a Sydney court, mid-1980s

This is an extraordinary book, not just for what it says, but for what it is.

For two decades, some of Australia's leading journalists have written about crime and corruption in Sydney in the 1970s and 1980s, a time when politicians, magistrates and police have been jailed for corruption.

Here, in this book, however, is a wealth of material from an insider. And not just any insider, but one of Sydney's biggest and most enduring criminal figures.

Neddy Smith's confessions have already prompted a massive inquiry by the Independent Commission Against Corruption (the ICAC), an inquiry that has become New South Wales' biggest probe into police corruption.

Smith's allegations have been extraordinary and his revelations have repeatedly made front-page headlines. Many will be made public for the first time in this book.

The question of how accurate these allegations are is one that will be debated for a long time to come. My view is that they have been thoroughly investigated by a team of trained professionals from the ICAC—who have excellent access through subpeonas and the like to various material—and they obviously believe there is a good deal of truth in Smith's stories, otherwise the matter would have been ditched more than two years ago.

It must be said that Smith has been coy about some matters in this book, notably his knowledge of murders and of drug trafficking. Because he has an indemnity on crimes committed in New South Wales, he has been extraordinarily frank about these—confessing to many crimes he would never otherwise have been associated with. But his indemnity does not cover murder or activities that cross state or international borders, hence there are passages in this book that—clearly signalled for the most part—reflect the limits of that indemnity.

Another notable change to Smith's orginal manuscript is the deletion or amendment of peoples' names. Much of this has been done on legal advice.

Apart from that, however, Smith's story is very similar to when I first read it. While I have acted as editor and researcher, the flavor and style of the book are very much that of the original manuscript, entitled 'Thank Christ for Corruption'.

Throughout his life, Smith has been fit and healthy, a man who has never smoked or used the drugs he sold—his diet is vegetarian. Yet he is an ill man. He now takes 36 pills each day to stem the effects of Parkinson's disease. For a man who was once very fit, he can manage only 20 minutes walking a day. Yet Smith wants no sympathy. Refreshingly, for a book by a criminal, Smith does not seek to justify his actions, engender sympathy or protest his innocence. As he says, he chose his course and he must go where it takes him.

Tom Noble
Sydney, May 1993

Introduction

I'd like people to know what they've really got in this country. Most of the public are like sheep. They don't look up, they don't know what's going on—and they don't want to know. It's about time they found out.

Smith, on his reasons for writing this book

In Victoria, there isn't much corruption. They kill you down there. They certainly don't do too much business.

Queensland's not bad for gambling and prostitution, but they don't let you do armed robberies.

But when I was working in New South Wales, just about everyone was corrupt and anything was possible. Late 1980 was the beginning of a decade of crime and corruption within the New South Wales police force that will never be equalled.

There has always been crime and corruption within the NSW police force, but nothing like it was then. And I was in the middle of it.

At least a dozen different squads tried their hand at catching me without any luck. They formed special task-forces to try and catch me. They suspected me of numerous crimes, but couldn't catch me doing anything.

How could they, when I had the other half of the police force helping me avoid being arrested by their mates? It was like a game.

I had police organising crimes for me to do, then keeping me informed as to how much—if any—progress was being made in the investigations. I had what is commonly known within criminal circles as the 'Green Light', which meant I could virtually do as I pleased. Nothing was barred, with one exception—I was never to shoot at any member of the police force. But apart from that, I could write my own ticket.

I bribed hundreds of police and did as I pleased in Sydney. There was no limit to what I got away with. I could never have committed any of the major crimes I did, and got away with them, without the assistance of the NSW police force. They were the best police force that money could buy—believe me, because I bought them hundreds of times.

There will no doubt be some people who will ask: 'Why are you telling this story? And why are you telling on the police?'

I will explain my reasons in greater detail later, but essentially, the police set me up with the intention of having me killed when they decided I knew too much. I survived, and maybe I will even the score with my revelations in this book.

The NSW police have had it their own way for too long now. Along the way they didn't care who they hurt. They verballed [*compiled false evidence against*] anyone who got out of hand—or should I say anyone who would not pay them. They stamped [*extorted*] people for the money they earned, then would still put them in the nick. They loaded [*planted evidence on*] those who would not cooperate with them. They even stooped to pinching your wife or your girl, to get you to sign up [*admit to the crime*].

The worst part about all these things was that the judges all knew what was going on—and they condoned it without as much as a 'how-do-you-do'. The only ones who were safe from these arseholes were the few like me who had the Green Light.

Well, it's payback time now, which means there are going to be a lot of very sorry police out there. But they should not blame me entirely. They should blame their mates for being greedy and trying to get rid of me.

When police fall by the wayside over the ICAC inquiry it won't be my fault, but the fault of those arseholes that wanted to set me up and have me put out of the way. Apparently there is no retirement plan for criminals who work with the police.

Neddy Smith
Long Bay Jail, 1993

1
The Fuzzy Blue Line

But it is not the place of the Police to convict guilty men as it is by them they get their living ...

Ned Kelly, *The Jerilderie Letter* 1879

[*A police officer Smith names*] invited himself to lunch with me and Harold. Not only did he invite himself, but he brought four of his friends with him. Other detectives.

[*The police officer*] had plenty of front, but I didn't mind: his friends might come in handy one day. It was my policy to try to have all the police on side, even if I never needed to call on their services. He had some information to sell. It was 'very important'.

As it turned out, the information was older than last week's bread. He told me that another special task force had been formed to try and find out what Roger Rogerson [*a Sydney detective, now a convicted and jailed criminal*] and I were up to and to do their best to arrest us. The task force was made up of both state and federal police. Because there weren't enough state police not on my payroll to make up a squad, they invited the Feds to join them: that was [*the police officer's*] version. (The real reason was so the Feds could keep an eye on the state police.) I let [*the police officer*] think he was doing me a favor and gave him $1000 for his trouble. He was quick to pocket that.

The lunch turned into a showground for [*the police officer*]. He liked to boss his team mates around in front of Harold [*Smith's criminal partner*] and me, ordering them to do this and that. 'Go and ring him ... Go and do that ...' It was unbelievable the way he behaved. Now I knew why he wasn't accepted by The Dodger [*former Detective Sergeant Roger Rogerson*] and his gang.

After a few hours the drinking got out of hand and Harold ended up trying to strangle [*the police officer*] on the floor. I got blind drunk and [*the police officer*] insisted I shouldn't drive. It ended up with him telling one of his detectives to drive me wherever I was going. A young cop drove me to the Covent Garden Hotel and parked the car for me in the car park across the road. I had a grey Rolls at the time. When I left the hotel that night I ended up smashing the Rolls into the car park wall, trying to back out of there.

The next day Harold and I had terrible hangovers and were out and about looking for work. We had no luck that day, but in the evening I got a call from [*police*] arranging for me to meet them. At the meeting, at the Regent Hotel at Kingsford, [*a policeman*] came straight to the point:

'Waverley bus depot. I have a contact there that will help us with any information we might need. It's worth over $200,000.'

He said the payroll came fortnightly, delivered by Armaguard at about 7.30 on Thursday mornings.

'The armored van drives in the front gate on the main road, out to the back where the buses exit, and pulls up at the gate. Two guards get out and take the money up the fire-escape stairs. At the top they turn left and there's a short hallway. At the end of the hallway there's an armor-plated door with a bullet-proof glass piece in the door so they can see whoever comes to the door.'

Harold and I listened. We didn't want to interrupt.

'There is an alarm button installed in every desk that goes straight to the police station. But that won't be a problem. There is a main key just inside the front door. As you go in you can turn it off. It cuts off every button.'

He told us exactly where the key was located.

'There is a large walk-in vault in the office that you can lock everyone in. There is an alarm button in the vault, but it only goes to another office. It was only installed in case someone got locked in the vault by mistake.'

It sounded very interesting. We showed interest, but I couldn't give an answer until we had looked at it. [*The policeman*] said his contact at the bus depot could help with further information, but wouldn't help during the robbery.

After a few cold beers, [*the policeman*] had to get back to the office, so he left us there to discuss the bus depot between ourselves.

Harold and I talked about the details and decided to have a look at the bus depot straight away. We knew it wasn't the day that the payroll was delivered, but there were other things we could look at and decide on. We were anxious to get into this one.

The depot was a huge place, although it didn't take long to locate the pay office. Harold went up the back stairs like the pay guards would. A couple of minutes later he came back and said everything was as [*the policeman*] said it would be.

After that, we had time on our hands. We had to watch the van actually deliver at least twice before we could even consider going on with the robbery. Even then, there was a lot more work required. This one presented a challenge to us. If we pulled it off and showed the hold-up squad we were the best there was, then there would be no stopping us. We went into this robbery with that thought in our minds.

First, we had to get through the armored door without raising suspicion and without any noise. If there was any commotion, one of the staff was sure to set off the alarm to the police station. Then we'd be fucked. We also had to get to the door without anyone noticing us. That was another problem: all the pay office windows looked out on to the street and were tinted black. They could see out, but no one could see in. There would also be all the people hanging about waiting for their pay.

So before we could even think of doing the robbery, we had several more meetings with [*the policeman*], fishing for any little detail that could assist us. But he had nothing more to give us. We just couldn't come up with a way to get through the front door. We couldn't smash our way in, as the alarm would be raised before we got inside. The answer came to me one night while I was drinking with a few detectives at a pub in Balmain. Why not get hold of a few cops' uniforms and go in disguised as uniformed cops? Surely they wouldn't challenge two cops knocking on their door. Without arousing the suspicions of any of the cops I was drinking with, I dropped a question: What did they do with their uniforms when they became detectives?

'Oh, they're hanging up somewhere at home,' they all said. I let it go at that. No one mentioned it further that night. That was it: our way in. We knew it was a winner. All we had to do was find two uniforms. I knew plenty of police, didn't I? Surely they had a spare uniform hanging around somewhere that I could get hold of.

I mentioned my idea to The Dodger. He was keen. He also saw the funny side of it. 'Just be arrogant. Act like pigs and you will have no problems getting in.'

A meeting was arranged with [*a senior policeman*] for the next day. The meeting was set at a hotel out in the outer suburbs. This cop didn't want to be seen with us too often. The guy was starting to give me an inferiority complex.

When I turned up at this out-of-the-way pub, where no one was supposed to know us, Roger was waiting, but the other guy hadn't turned up yet.

We got a beer at the main bar. The men at the bar were staring at Roger all the time and when we went to get another drink they all said 'Hello' to the pair of us. So much for going to the outer suburbs where no one would know us.

[*The policeman*] arrived late. When he got there he went straight to business: 'What's so important that you have to see me?'

I thought about cracking a joke with him, but decided against it.

'I want to discuss an idea I have for doing this next robbery at the bus depot.'

He wasn't real happy about it at all. 'Let's hear it, I don't have a great deal of time.' I explained the problem we had getting into the office with the door and all and I told him about my idea to use police uniforms to gain entry.

'That is up to you—how you do the job. I don't really want to know the details. Can't you operate through one of the others? I'm sure you won't have a problem getting some uniforms.'

Before he left I thought that I could see the faint sign of a smile on his face—I could hardly believe it.

This particular policeman wasn't one to socialise with us, certainly not one of the 'Barbecue Set' as we crims and cops were later known. Maybe he thought that he was too good for our company. Roger and I talked about where I was going to get hold of the uniforms for a few minutes and then we left the hotel and went down to the Rocks and had some lunch and got on the drink, forgetting all about the robbery for the rest of the day.

The next day I 'ordered' two complete police uniforms. Several days later I picked up a brown paper parcel containing the uniforms at the Three Weeds Hotel in Rozelle. I had to get alterations done as one pair of pants was too long and the other too short. The police shirts were short sleeved, so I had to go out and buy identical wind jackets to those the police wore. Then I had the police badges taken from the shirts and sewn on to the jackets. There were other minor alterations, but finally I had the uniforms ready to try on. Harold and I put them on and, I have to admit, we looked good.

Meanwhile, we continued to watch the depot every chance we got. One Thursday, we were in Centennial Park, dressed in tracksuits making out we were training while we watched the van deliver the money, when I saw a guy taking a more than casual interest in us. I motioned to Harold to make like we were doing callisthenics and he walked away. (After we'd done the robbery, that guy gave the police a detailed description of us and related to them how we were acting like we were training. He hadn't missed a trick. You can never be too careful.)

Transport for the getaway presented a problem, too. By now I was right into playing police, so I told Harold: 'Why don't we go the whole hog and get a small police car? It will give those people looking out of the windows something to think about. They won't know what to do, or where they are.' Harold agreed. I contacted the young guys that I always used for my transport and discussed it with them. Police car or Holden bomb, it made no difference to them as long as the money was there.

As the time drew near, I went out with the young guys to make sure they had no problems getting the police vehicle. That's when we hit our first hurdle: to steal a police car was no problem. The problem arose in storing it until we were ready. They would be looking for that stolen car everywhere and would have an all-points bulletin posted. We couldn't take the risk of being pulled over in a stolen car on our way to commit the robbery.

So I decided to get a civilian car identical to those used by the highway patrol, then add the fittings. That night we stole a car and put it away. The fittings were just as easy. There was a place in Glebe where they did maintenance work on all the police cars in New South Wales. They were always parking the cars on the road. So getting the police lights for the top of the car and the police signs was easy. The young guys had them within an hour. We put them on the car and it was an exact replica of a real police car. Then we carefully went over it to make sure we left no prints. We filled the tank and checked everything to reassure ourselves that it was in perfect condition. It was. Last, we 'rented' a truck. (For this, we paid someone—usually $500—with an average-looking face to rent a vehicle from one of the big car-hire agencies. The helper would use a false licence and pay for three or seven days rental in cash, depending how long we needed the vehicle. Once we finished with the hire-car or truck, we usually abandoned it.) On this occasion we got a truck with a roller-shutter door, so we could secrete ourselves in the back without too much trouble.

The day arrived and we were hot to trot. Early that morning we drove the false police car close to the bus depot where we could get into it when we needed without arousing too much suspicion. Then we went back to our base and put on the uniforms. We had everything that real cops had: we even had our scanners on our belts, instead of the walkie-talkies that the normal police had. Looking good. I was anxious to get on with this one. My nerves were playing up a bit.

We started to laugh at each other as we walked out to get into the back of the truck and pick up the police car. Harold had two stripes on his jacket and I was the shitman: I had only one stripe. We joked about this on the way to the depot. The driver was dressed in a suit to make himself look like a detective. Pulling up around the corner from where we had parked the police car we got out without anyone seeing us. We walked to the police car and the three of us got in. We started the car and moved off slowly. No one had taken the slightest bit of notice of us.

We drove slowly around to just outside the pay office, waiting for the van to deliver the money. It was a few minutes late, but we were not worried. We got out of the car and told the driver to signal us as soon as he saw the van leave the depot: it would then be time to hit the pay office. From where we had parked, everyone inside the pay office had a clear look at the police signs on top of the car. This would put them off guard.

Harold and I walked up the street looking like two cops walking the beat on their shift. We took our minds off the van for a matter of seconds and nearly missed our driver's signal. Across the road we walked and up the fire-escape stairs, taking our time. Harold was carrying a cricket bag for the money—and for safety's sake he had a pump-action shotty [*shotgun*] in the bag. My nerves were perfect. The adrenalin was pumping madly and I was feeling good.

Through the door, along the hall and up to the armored door. No one had seen us. I could see the small glass window in the door. I loosened my pistol in the holster as we approached. I banged on the door. A face appeared at the glass, looked at us, noticed the uniforms and smiled.

'Can I do something for you, officers?'

I said: 'Constable Baker. We are from Waverley. Open up. We want to check on the people to assure ourselves that all is OK.'

It worked like a charm. He opened the door for us. As soon as it was open I moved inside and rammed my gun into his guts, pushing him into the room. I began to round up the others and get them into the vault. I knew Harold was taking care of the key and the alarm system. Then he would bag the money.

Meanwhile, I had a small problem. A girl clerk became a little hysterical and started running around the filing cabinets, so I had to chase her. Finally I caught her, locked everybody in the vault and closed the door. There was a fellow standing at the pay window counting his money: 'What's the matter, officer?' I grabbed the money out of his hand as I went past him.

Harold had grabbed just about all the money when I spotted a heap of tins on the floor. Most were filled with silver, but [*a policeman*] had told me one had notes in it. I found the one with the notes in it, grabbed it and we took off. Three minutes had passed from the start. We still had one minute to go until we could expect company. We went down the stairs, moving quickly but not running. People were coming up as we passed them—they were wondering what was going on. I still had the gun in my hand. Just as we got to the 'police car', the scanner started its song: 'Robbery at the Waverley bus depot. Two police are said to be robbing the depot.' Into the car and around the corner to the truck, not more than 200 metres away. We jumped into the back and down came the shutter. It was pitch black inside.

I called out to the driver: 'Go straight back the way we came. We haven't time to go the other way.' He did exactly as I told him. We were moving. The scanner was still humming and it was nerve-racking in the back of the truck. Harold and I changed out of the police uniforms. There were still sirens going off all over the place. Some sounded quite close by.

It took us roughly seven minutes to get to our destination. Once there, we jumped from the truck with all that beautiful money and the rest of the gear. We were excited and rapt that everything had gone exactly as planned. Not a single error. That would give the police something to think about. They would really appreciate this one. It was textbook.

We shook hands all round, proud of what we had just pulled off. No one else could have done it. We had more than $200,000 in the bag and $20,000 in $2 bills in the tin. Not a bad day's work.

Our driver got back just as we were dividing the money into bundles to whack-up between us three. The police share—10 per cent of the total—and expenses had already been deducted; what was left on the table was ours to share. Our driver was overjoyed when he got his share. He had a few outstanding bills to pay and needed the money badly. We had a shower and shaved off the moustaches we had grown for the job.

We intended to really party on that night. We went to lunch, but we were too bloody tired to really enjoy ourselves. We had had very little sleep the last two days.

I still had to meet the [*police*]. I had arranged to see them at a brothel—we were going to have a good time and celebrate a job well done. It didn't work out that way. Harold and I fell asleep in the brothel's lounge. The news had been good from the [*police*]. The police force had no idea who had done the robbery. They were even blaming real police. Eventually they got around to blaming us, but not straight away.

I was pleased the robbery was over and done with. Maybe I was getting too bloody old for this type of work. That's what I told myself, anyway.

I didn't stay asleep long at the brothel. When I woke up I left them to enjoy themselves. Once out in the night air I was wide awake. I felt like a drink. I headed down to the Covent Garden Hotel—it was only early evening. As I walked in, I noticed there were a lot of cops drinking there—not unusual for a Thursday night, so I didn't take too much notice of them.

I was enjoying my first beer when two detectives I knew came up and bought me another beer. 'Good one, mate!' they said. Then they walked back to their mates. None of these police knew for sure that I had been partly responsible for the bus-depot robbery, but they suspected it, and word had gone round among the older-type cops. The old school were still around and liked it when a good one went off.

2
Home Boy

Every society gets the kind of criminal it deserves. What is equally true is that every community gets the kind of law and order it insists on.

Robert F Kennedy, *The Pursuit of Justice*

I was born at Sydney's Royal North Shore Hospital on 27 November 1944. I never knew my father. I was what people referred to in those days as 'a war baby', the name used for children fathered and left behind by the yanks who came to Sydney during World War 2.

My mother liked to tell a story about my birth that often got a laugh from her friends. The story goes like this.

My mother was lying in bed after giving birth when the nurse brought me in. My mother took me in her arms and smiled. Then she looked at my right hand, which was closed up in a little ball. After a few seconds she decided I had a deformed hand and started screaming: 'Doctor, my son is deformed!'

The doctor rushed in, picked me up and looked at my mother, who was pointing at my clenched fist. The doctor took hold of my hand and opened it. His watch was in my hand. My mother didn't know whether she was relieved or not. Afterwards she told friends: 'So, I always knew he would end up a thief.'

I was brought up by my grandmother in a small house in Redfern, which was then an inner-city slum south of the central business district. My mother was only young when she had me, and she dumped me on her mother. I don't dislike my mother for what she did—she was young, still enjoying life and would not have had much of a life had she been stuck with me. At the time, I may have disliked her for what she did, but now I understand her actions and can't fault her.

For some reason my grandmother hated me and I grew to hate her too. She used to flog me all the time and, as I got older, I used to fight back—and that seemed to stop her from hitting me. That was when I first realised that you had to fight for what you wanted out of life or let people walk all over you.

I had a half-brother called Edwin who was always trying to curry favor with my grandmother. For a long time he helped her bash me. That came to a stop one day when I was about 11.

Edwin was bashing into me and I had had enough. He was giving me a serve and smiling while he did it. He didn't smile for too long. I saw a long knife lying on the kitchen table, grabbed it, said, 'Fuck you, cunt,' and stabbed him straight through the hand. That fixed him. He never raised his hands to me again.

After that he hated me, and years later he tried to even the score by giving evidence against me in a series of well-publicised court cases. But more on that later.

It was decided that I was uncontrollable—I had stopped going to school and just roamed the streets stealing from shops—so, at the tender age of 11, I was sent to Mittagong Boys' Home. My case hadn't been helped by my grandmother, who used to ring the police and tell them my mother had dumped me on her and she was too sick and broke to look after me. Stabbing Edwin in the hand was the final straw.

The home was south of Sydney between Bowral and Mittagong. It is an experience that will always remain in my memory because of the kindness I was shown there.

I was housed along with 30 other boys in a huge mansion, like the sort I'd seen in movies. I'll never forget it. There was a family that looked after us, Boss Morgan, Matron Morgan and their daughter Vivian. They were English and they treated me very well.

It was the first real home that I had ever had. And not only did I discover kindness, I discovered that my first name was Arthur. Until then, I had always been just 'Neddy'. I spent just over a year at Mittagong and when the time came for me to leave, I was reluctant to do so. I'd felt safe there.

But I had to leave and things soon got back to normal. At Mittagong I'd continued my schooling. Once released, I was meant to go to Cleveland Street High in Redfern, but I rarely went. I last saw the inside of a classroom when I was 13. Instead, I ran around the streets, stealing to survive. I had no ambition at all. I was living from day to day, not caring what happened to me. It wasn't long before I was back before the courts. I received several good behaviour bonds before being sent to Gosford Boys' Home, 50 kilometres north of Sydney, for 12 months for stealing. This time I was 14 and Gosford was no Mittagong.

It was like a concentration camp. Hard labor was the name of the game. Discipline was very strict and I fell foul of the screws many times. They made us continually shovel dirt from one heap to another, then back again. It was senseless to my way of thinking, but I wasn't there to think, as they kept telling me.

Some of the boys used to act as screws. If a boy tried to escape they would chase him and bring him back. Never a day went by that you didn't have to fight for some senseless reason or other. They needed no reason to fight you if you had something that they wanted, or you looked at them the wrong way. That was enough.

I was only a skinny kid, so I came in for a fair amount of harassment and had more than my share of fights. I soon learned that it was a case of first-in best-dressed, so I always managed to get the first punch in. That soon put a stop to them picking on me.

I found out who the local heavy was and one day on work party I waited until I had him positioned and I hit him with the best left hook I had ever thrown. He went down and out like a truck had hit him. That soon became the talk of the place and I had no problems with bullies after that.

While at Gosford I made the mistake of getting tattoos. I did it because I was told not to. It was also done out of boredom. More tattoos were added when I was in jail aged 18. I regret getting them and have made attempts in the past to have them removed. These attempts were only partly successful.

I spent nine months at Gosford that time, before I was back on the streets again. I was nearly 16 and I thought I was some sort of big shot. Fucking, fighting and stealing, that's all I ever did or wanted to do. Nothing had changed.

I ended up at Kings Cross being a filthy rotten hoon [*pimp*]. At 16, I was living with a 26-year-old prostitute. I thought I was smart, but little did I know that hooning was looked down on as one of the lowest things a crim could stoop to. I make no excuse for doing it, but at that particular time it was the in-thing to do. Even today it's frowned on, even though some of our so-called big gangster fools do it on a large scale behind respectable fronts.

I was arrested and charged with living off the earnings of prostitution. I was sent to Gosford, again for 12 months. Before being transferred there, I stayed at the Albion Street Boys' Shelter in Surry Hills. It was a madhouse, a breeding ground for young up-and-coming toughs, thugs who wanted to make names for themselves. Standovers and bashings were a daily occurrence. Even the screws got bashed regularly. It was the survival of the fittest.

I met some very willing boys there. Billy Harrison was one of them. He was only small, but there wasn't a guy there that could fight like he could—his whole family were fighters. He punched like a heavyweight, was very violent to boot and was scared of no one. Anyone silly enough to try him out soon realised their folly.

Another guy I became friends with was Jimmy Finch, who went on to become one of the Whiskey Au Go Go bombers. [*The Whiskey Au Go Go was a Brisbane nightclub that was fire-bombed in 1973. Fifteen people died in the blaze. Finch and another man were subsequently convicted and sentenced to life in jail.*] He was a Doctor Barnardo boy from London. He too could fight and was very violent.

The three of us ended up at Gosford together. They split us up as we couldn't be controlled together, but that didn't stop us getting into fights every day. I think that we were trying to outdo one another to see who was the best fighter. Kid's stuff.

It was around this time that I was sent to the lowest place on this earth or anywhere else.

Tamworth Boys' Home was a real concentration camp. They treated the young boys like animals, with daily bashings and starvation. People treated their dogs better than they treated us at Tamworth. I've been to the notorious

Grafton Jail twice for a period of more than four years all told: I was systematically bashed daily, flogged into unconsciousness several times but, believe me, that was nothing compared with the treatment I got at Tamworth.

On my arrival at Tamworth Boys Home, in the Great Divide, about 300 kilometres north of Sydney, I was flogged by an arsehole of a man I'll call Jenkins. He told us that he was an ex-commando. He stood six foot six in bare feet, weighed about 19 stone and would get pleasure out of bashing and terrorising you. His favorite go was to throw you bodily around the room, bouncing you off each and every wall. He gave me some merciless floggings during the nine months I had to endure that hellhole.

The rest of the screws were no better. They didn't so much flog you—that pleasure was reserved for Jenkins—but they had other ways to make your life a misery. There was the non-stop screaming at us all day long; they made us do exercises all day without a rest; they would starve us for minor things like sniffing, a loose button or a loose shoelace. We were not allowed within two metres of another boy; we couldn't talk to anyone *at all*; we weren't allowed to look at another boy. If we did, they put us in solitary confinement on one slice of bread per day. If we wanted to ask a screw something we had to stand at attention and hold our hand in the air for 15 to 20 minutes at a time and, if you put your hand down, you were bounced—and that meant no meal for you.

That was their favorite go. They would drive you all day long, nagging you and yelling at you. Then when you were at your lowest they would smile and say: 'You're bounced.'

It drove me insane. They never let up on us for a minute. I only did nine months there but that was more than enough for me. Jimmy Finch was there at the same time as I was, as was another boy I knew, an Aboriginal called Bobby. We used to sneak looks at each other every now and then. The whole time we were there, we continued to try to get away with any little thing we could. That was our way of rebelling.

They had a special way of torturing us known as 'holly stoning'. Any boy that has been there will remember it. Each boy was given a 30-pound [*13.5 kilogram*] sandstone block and was forced to squat on his haunches and push this block back and forward for hours on end without rest. It kept the floors white—and kept us worn out.

This particular morning the three of us, Finch, Bobby and myself, were chosen for the holly stone job. We were taken to the clinic to do the floor there with one particular screw. He hated the three of us so he had deliberately picked us for the job. He told us all the time that he had been a pilot in the war and always used to say: 'I fought for scum like you, shitmen.'

Well, he was in for a big shock.

We were squatting on our haunches pushing these fucking holly stones back and forward when this screw caught us looking around at one another. He went off his head, screaming: 'You three are bounced. Now get to the grill.' That meant a flogging for us. We looked at one another. I remember thinking how skinny and stupid the other two looked and wondered if I looked the same to them. They were so thin and their eyes were bulging. Bobby and I looked at each other, we both smiled and we reacted together like clockwork. Bobby lifted up his holly stone and hit the screw over the head: I punched and kicked him as he went down to the ground.

We kept attacking him until the rest of the screws bashed us unconscious. We woke up in the pound black and blue. I can remember Bobby saying to me: 'This will get us out of this dump.' I hoped he was right about that. We knew that we were in for it this time, but we were hoping to get charged so that they would have to move us out.

But they didn't charge us. It caused an uproar because the screw was hurt pretty bad and, without us being charged, he couldn't claim compensation for his injuries. But it wasn't to be. They hushed it up and we were not charged with anything at all. They didn't want the public to know what went on behind those walls. It didn't get us out of Tamworth. I had to finish my time there.

I was released when I turned 18, out on the street again and so glad to be out . . .

Nothing much changed. I went back to the same lifestyle, same places and same people. I had no money and nowhere to live, so it was back into busts [*burglaries*] again. I ran into Bobby and we started working together, robbing anyone and everyone we came across.

Bobby used to steal cars and ram police cars just to get them to chase him. It was madness. He got his kicks that way (to each his own), but I wanted no part of it.

I was stupid and, aged 18, got married to this girl I had known only a short time. It failed miserably, we were both too young to know any better. I'm not sure how long it lasted, but it wasn't long. The divorce came through three years later when I was in jail. There were no children.

Before long I was arrested again and charged with numerous busts. I ended up at Long Bay Jail, refused bail.

I had finally hit The Big House. And let me tell you, I wasn't one bit impressed. It was a shock to the system to see the conditions we were expected to live under.

The police who charged me were real charmers: they kept telling me that when I got to the Bay I would get fucked by some big guy. I was a little concerned about it when I arrived but I knew I would kill before I would be fucked by anyone.

I soon saw a face I knew, a guy called Garry, who I'd met at Gosford Boys' Home years earlier. It was his first time in the Bay too, so we teamed up. One morning we were walking up and down the exercise yard talking, when a guy about 30 came up and offered me things like tea and coffee.

'No, thanks,' I told him.

He said: 'You will be moving into my cell after dinner. OK?'

'OK,' I said. But instead I got a steel shit-tub and smashed him in the skull a few times. That was the last time anyone tried to get me in their cell. But I was locked up for assault and given 14 days solitary confinement.

I eventually went to court over the busts and pleaded guilty. I expected about a year, no more. When I got a sentence of six and a half years jail I was shocked. I immediately lodged an appeal against the severity of the sentence. It was later reduced to four years.

Once I had been sentenced, I was put into One Wing, which was only for boys under 25. But I just couldn't keep out of trouble. I was always fighting and belting mugs for any little thing at all.

The screws hated us young guys and every chance they got they had a go at us. We gave as good as we got, but we always seemed to come out behind the eight ball, so to speak.

I started to have fights every single day. I was out to prove something—I still don't know what.

Jimmy Finch and Billy Harrison arrived there too.

At about the same time a guy called John Andrew Stuart was trying to run the Bay. He went around breaking people's legs with iron bars and the screws were too frightened to do a thing about it. A huge man, as strong as a bull, he was in jail for shooting Jackie Steele, an old school safe-blower and gunman. Stuart had the run of the jail and did just what he liked.

One morning he sent me a message telling me that I was next on his list for a broken leg. I sent back to him: 'Is that right?'

He used to try and psych you out first. He would see how you handled that before he did anything more. When it did nothing to bother me, he made a bad mistake. He told a guy: 'Tell Billy Harrison that I'm going to give him a serve also.'

Bill did the smart thing, he got in first. Bill was only very small, but he wasn't worried about anyone at all. He waited until Stuart was parading around, big-noting in the shower. Bill got a 20-inch blade from the kitchen and fronted the naked Stuart: 'Hey, cunt, I'm Billy Harrison. Want to see me?'

Before Stuart knew what was going on, Bill started stabbing him in the guts, over and over. Stuart made a run for it, but Billy chased him everywhere he went and kept on stabbing into him. Stuart was screaming for someone to help him, but no one did a thing. Billy kept after him, yelling: 'Stand still, you dog, I am going to cut your head off.'

Finally, a screw got Bill to give him the knife. They put Bill in his cell and rushed Stuart to hospital. He wasn't expected to live. The final outcome was that Bill was charged with attempting to murder the fool.

The police hated Stuart and they gave Bill drink and food and even a girl while he was at the cells. The police tried every way they could to avoid charging Bill, but he wanted to plead guilty to it. 'I wish I'd killed the cunt,' he told the judge. He received 15 years on top of what he was already serving.

But Stuart survived and teamed up with Jimmy Finch when he was released. They tried to take over the rackets in Queensland, with no luck. Their futile attempt was to result in 15 people being killed when they deliberately fire-bombed the Whiskey Au Go Go nightclub. Stuart was to kill himself in prison, maintaining his innocence to the end. Finch conned his way out of prison with the help of a journalist whom he convinced he was innocent. When he got back to England, Finch appeared on Australian TV and confessed to the fire-bombing. He big-noted how smart he had been in conning everyone into believing him. The police may have verballed him [*organised a false confession*] and planted evidence as Finch had claimed, but he was as guilty as anything.

Straight after Billy stabbed Stuart I was accused of stabbing another guy. Nothing happened to me. The guy never gave me up. The crims were solid in those days.

That incident stemmed out of nothing. I was working in 4 Yard folding lottery tickets all day, when a discussion got out of hand. I told this guy to shut up, or I would stab him. He said I wasn't game to stab anyone, so I stabbed him, just to prove a point. It was a stupid incident, although I should explain that in those days in jail you had to do the best you could, just to survive. There were daily pack rapes by men on those young kids that had shown that they could not defend themselves. Likewise, there were daily bashings. In this atmosphere, prisoners were always trying to test each other. Those who did not assert themselves or who showed any sign of weakness, just suffered. I make no excuses for my behavior in jail. I wanted to survive.

I teamed up with a guy called Barry. He was a tough guy, or he thought he was, yet he was to turn into a child molester. We went around flogging everyone in sight, we wanted to fight anyone that thought they could fight.

One evening mealtime some new receptions arrived. There were two brothers, real giants of guys, who started telling us what they wanted and what they would do if they didn't get it. Well, they got it, but not what they expected. We flogged them senseless the very next morning. We were locked up and confined to the segro yards (where they kept the troublemakers away from the other crims) to await the governor's pleasure. We saw the governor and he told us that the brothers were in hospital and we would be charged.

We were never charged, but we were shipped out to the notorious Grafton Jail that night.

There was Barry, myself and an Aboriginal guy named Pete. Pete had been to Grafton before. We were handcuffed and our feet shackled with chains, just like convict days. They took us by van to Sydney's Central Station and we went by train to Grafton in a cattle car converted into a cell. We were put in a cage with no space to move, our backs were up against one wall and our knees touched the other wall. They gave us a shit tub to keep us company but forgot to tell us how we could use it while we were shackled together. It was a long trip as they still used steam trains in those days. I think it took us about 24 hours to cover the 500 kilometres north. All the way there, Pete kept telling us all about how they bashed you as soon as you got there and he elaborated about the continual bashings we were in for each and every day. Pete took great pleasure in telling us about the place. 'The food is good,' he said. Some consolation!

He certainly put the wind up me. I was fucking terrified of the place and I hadn't even got there. As I listened to Pete's account I kept thinking to myself: 'This can't possibly be true. If they bashed you that often you would be dead in a week.' I told myself that he was just exaggerating to make himself sound tough.

It wasn't long before I found out that he was telling the truth. When we got into Grafton station we were dragged bodily out of the cabin and I was punched straight in the face for looking at a screw. That was the start of two years of hell for me. We were thrown into a van and headed for the jail.

When we got there I was not feeling too brave, in fact I was close to shitting my pants. I wasn't going to make one sound when they bashed me, no way would they get a peep out of me. They put us into separate yards. They then stripped me naked and attacked me with these huge batons, hitting me around the ribs, the kidneys and the back of the legs. I was thrown into a cell and, as a parting gift, I was kicked in the face. I just lay there thinking: 'How the fuck am I going to live through this?' There was no way anyone could cop that every day and live through it.

While I was lying on the floor contemplating my fate, the

door opened. 'Get on your fucking feet, cunt, and face the back wall.' I did what I was told. 'About turn, face the governor.' I walk over to the governor and look at him. That was a mistake. The governor hit me flush on the chin and I hit the deck.

'Don't you ever look at me, cunt, got that?' He left me locked up till the next morning.

Daylight came and I was up early folding my bed so as not to give them a reason to bash me. Well, the door opens and I'm facing the back wall. Four of those dogs attack me, hitting me in the back of the head and the kidneys. They are all yelling at once: 'Your blankets are all wrong, you haven't cleaned your sink.' Kick in the back.

I replied: 'No one told me how to fold the blankets, sir.'

A screw punches me right in the face. 'Shut up, maggot.'

I couldn't win.

They leave me alone for a short time, then it is on again. I can't take too much more of this shit. 'Quick march, left, right, left, right.'

I haven't a clue where I am being taken. 'Move it, cunt.' I'm beginning to think Cunt is my new name by this time. Eventually I get taken to a yard, being bashed all the way there. 'Inside, cunt.' There it is again, cunt!

Once inside I saw Barry. He wasn't looking too good either. There I was, 19 years of age, in a madhouse, getting bashed every time I looked sideways. All I could do was cop it sweet and do the best I could. There was nothing anyone could do.

The yard was about 20 feet square with a roof, three walls and bars on the front so the screws could see you at all times. In the yard with me was Kevin Simmons—he later hanged himself there—and a guy called Jimmy Thornton. They were smiling at me. I could see no reason for anyone to smile. They taught me the routine very quickly.

Simmons gave me a pleasant enough thought to dwell on: 'You either learn quick or they will end up killing you here.'

I did learn quickly, but apparently not quick enough for the screws, because the bashings continued. Thornton tried to settle me down by telling me that the floggings wouldn't go on forever, only a few months—only a few months!—until I learned the rules.

One Saturday morning there was a big Pommy screw on

relief watching us. This screw was standing there winking all the time, so I mentioned this to Thornton.

'Listen mate, he's a top screw. If he winks at you then wink back at him.' I walked a bit longer and he started winking, so I winked back and smiled at him. He went off his head, yelling at me: 'I'll kill you, you cunt.'

Thornton had conned me—the screw had an affliction in one eye. He took me up to the pound and flogged me for being a smarty. At the time I didn't appreciate it, but looking back I can see the funny side of it. We all had a good laugh about it later.

I was released from Grafton on 5 December 1965 after 19 months in that hellhole. They put me on a train going south and told me not to get off before I reached Sydney. I had no intention of getting off.

I arrived at Central Station at 7pm with £4 in my pocket. I had no idea what I was going to do or where I would stay. I hadn't kept in touch with anyone while I was in jail so I had no idea where my friends were. I felt lost. As I walked along I saw three people waving at me. As I got closer, I realised it was my half-brother Edwin. He was with two young boys who I didn't know.

Edwin grabbed me and said: 'This is Patty and Johnny, your brothers.' I couldn't believe how much they had grown. I hugged them both for quite a while. I'd always been very close to my two young brothers, and still am. We got into his car and drove to see my mother in Bondi. Once there, she started crying and all that shit. I thought to myself: 'She could have written or visited me.' I stayed at her home for about two weeks before I moved out with a friend.

I had made up my mind that there would be no more jail for me. I had done enough jail to last a lifetime.

But it didn't take me long to turn hoon again. (I hated it and I'm not proud of it.) I was the worst and the brokest hoon in Australia. I wasn't really interested in being a hoon, I just wanted the rent paid—I supplemented her income by thieving. At that time my only interests were to sleep with as many women and buy as many good clothes as I could.

While inside I'd become good friends with a guy called Robert 'Chapo' Chapman. When he was released from jail I drove to Bathurst and brought him back to Sydney. It didn't take us long to get into trouble once we got together. Our interests were the same: fucking, fighting and good clothes. Not much to build a friendship on, is it? We were out to prove something to ourselves and each other. We started carrying guns with us everywhere we went. I don't know why. We were just louts looking for trouble.

We went everywhere looking for girls and fights, it didn't matter which we found first. We attacked people for nothing at all. They didn't have to do anything wrong to get bashed. We were the best candidates for the nick I have ever seen, the way we went on.

One night we were driving around bored, looking for trouble, so we went in search of a victim. Anyone would do, it didn't matter who. We headed up to Kings Cross to see who we could find and the first person we saw was a police informer [or 'dog'] known as 'Buckets'.

We decided that he would do perfectly, so we grabbed him and put him in the car. He had no idea where he was going—nor did we.

We headed for Moore Park Dogs Home—we thought that was funny. Once there we accused him of all sorts of things—we had to rev ourselves up—then we attacked him, bashing him badly. I think a knife was produced, but I'm not sure. Chapo and I were out to outdo each other by seeing who was the most violent. Anyway, we finally dropped Buckets at St Vincent's Hospital—we just pulled up and chucked him out on the road in front of the hospital. It was childish, but we didn't care. Off we went, looking for another victim to attack.

South Sydney Juniors was our next stop. We parked outside waiting for a likely victim. We didn't have to wait long before a guy called Jimmy came along. He was another dog. He saw us and tried to run, but Chapo caught him. We escorted him to the dogs home, laughing all the way.

'What have I done wrong to you two?' he asked.

Chapo said: 'You are guilty of fucking our mate's girl while he is in the nick.'

That was good enough for me, so he got the treatment. The only difference was that we threw him out at the Rachel Forster Women's Hospital in Redfern. The next day the story was in the papers. On the front page was a picture of Jimmy in a woman's nightgown in the women's hospital. We killed ourselves laughing. He was the only male patient ever to be admitted.

We were both arrested over the attacks but beat the charges because Buckets and Jimmy were too scared to appear in court against us.

We carried on as though nothing had happened. A few nights later Chapo suggested we visit these girls that he knew. I knew one of them and had been to bed with her many times before. We arrived at the house at Crystal Street, Petersham, knocked on the door and a girl answered. We'll call her Ann. There were four of us and she let us in. I tried my hand at getting into Ann's pants, and she didn't seem to object.

I told the others to piss off for a while. They went and Ann and I got it off twice. We both enjoyed it—and I certainly did not force her to have sex with me. After we finished we made arrangements to see each other again—although I had no intention of seeing her again.

As I was about to leave, Chapo came in and asked her: 'What about me, sweety?'

She looked at me.

'It's up to you,' I said.

I then left them alone to do their own thing.

After Chapo and she finished, the four of us left. Chapo and I went home to our place and we thought that the other two went home, too. But it turned out that they went back and bashed her after we had left. I never raped that girl and the first time I heard a thing about any rape was when I was arrested for it.

We were arrested about two weeks later by two cops who went through the normal procedure, one acting tough and the other being the good guy. Everyone's been through it before.

One of the cops told me Ann said I had raped her.

'Listen you shithead, I raped no one, fuck you.'

The cop said: 'If you're that sure, will you front a line-up to see if she will identify you?'

I wasn't worried as I had not raped anyone. 'OK by me.'

I wanted to front the line-up and prove that I had not raped any girl. It was a bad move because the police had told Ann to say that I was one of the men that had indeed raped her. They put me in a trumped-up line-up. Not one of the other men resembled me in any way at all; they were all over 50 and most of them were drunks, and I was in my twenties.

'What is this? Some sort of joke?' I said. 'This is no line-up, this is a set-up.'

They push me into the line and in comes Ann. She walks straight up to me and pats me on the shoulder. Fucking unreal!

'That's one of the men.'

I couldn't help myself. I spat straight in her face, a bad mistake on my part. The cops dragged me upstairs and started bashing me. I gave as much as I got, and they came out worse than I did. One of the coppers started rolling up his sleeves.

'What do you think you are going to do, cunt?' I said.

The copper starts coming towards me. 'I'm going to teach you some manners, you pig.'

'Is that so, stupid?' I get stuck right into him and flogged him easily. He wasn't too happy about it, either. With the help of a few constables he managed to cuff me to the desk. Then he went away for a while. When he returned he put a gun on the table: 'See this? It's all yours.'

I said: 'Go fuck yourself.'

He laughed: 'You want to be a gangster, cunt? Then we'll make you one. OK, stupid?'

I was taken downstairs and charged with rape, assault and, of course, possession of the gun. They put me into a cell and I went to court the next day. I was refused bail and taken to Long Bay Jail. Before long I was sent on to Parramatta Jail and on arrival put into solitary confinement. No reason was given to me. I was not allowed to see anyone at all.

After a week I got a visit from Dorothy, the girl I was living with. She was pregnant with my eldest child, Nicole. She wanted to help me get out on bail. I was in plenty of trouble, I knew that. I needed a lawyer for starters, and for that I needed money. But lately money had been a stranger to me. Dorothy promised to get me a lawyer straight away. I was amazed when she came up with a lawyer *and* bail money and, before long, I was released.

Chapo and I decided we were not going to hang around to front court, so we jumped bail and went to Brisbane. We didn't last long there, and we were soon back in Sydney living at the same place as before. Stupidity!

Chapo was living with a prostitute, Toni. She caught him playing up and told him that she had taken 50 sleeping tablets and wanted to die. Chapo told her to die and then went to sleep, thinking she was joking about the pills.

Well, he woke up the next morning feeling horny. He tried to hug Toni and rolled her over to find that she was dead! He was shocked to say the least. He jumped out of bed and woke a mate of ours, Robert Donnelly, and they both had a look at her and saw that she was, indeed, dead. They both bolted out of the flat leaving her there. Halfway to my place they pulled up and reported it to the police.

A few nights later we were drinking at the Abercrombie Hotel in Redfern when in walked Jack Ryder from the consorters *[the police consorting squad]*. I tried to bolt but Ryder caught me and I ended up back in the nick again, refused bail.

I spent the next 10 months waiting for my trial to go on so I could get my sentence and kick along with it. My day came and we were found guilty, me on the rape and the assault charges. I was given 12 years with a seven-year non-parole period. A lifetime—I would be 30 when I got out of jail, an old man. Shit!

I gave the judge a nice pay (stupid me again) and he told my solicitor: 'Tell your client to close his foul mouth or I will not hesitate to increase his sentence by half again.' I clammed right up with fright.

Off I went to jail for seven-to-12 fucking years, thinking: 'How am I going to do 12 fucking years in jail, I can't manage it! I'm a lost cause, no good for anything.'

So, feeling sorry for myself, I started my 12 years in the nick. It took me quite a few more years to wake up to myself and change. It was 1968 and I was 23 years old.

3
In the Nicks

I know not whether Laws be right,
Or whether Laws be wrong;
All that we know who lie in jail
Is that the wall is strong;
And that each day is like a year,
A year whose days are long.

Oscar Wilde, *Ballad of Reading Jail*

My mind was in turmoil as I sat in my cell at the Bay on that first night. I cursed myself for wanting to be a tough guy.

The next morning I saw a few familiar faces, including Chapo, and started to feel better. But that didn't last long. The jail's governor, who had sent me to Grafton last time, immediately had me thrown into observation. Observation is reserved for real nutcases. I was welcomed by a screw who pushed me into a padded cell with a belt to the back of the head. Just what I needed.

The screws gave me the odd whack in the mouth, threw my food at me and deliberately spilt the shit bucket on the floor of the padded cell. It was two or three days before I got out of there and was sent back to segro.

While I was there, other crims used to look after me, sending over extra food and books. There were no TVs or radios in those days. The two guys who helped most were Ronny Feeney and John Regan. I didn't know them, but in those days crims used to look after each other a lot better than they do these days.

Feeney was a giant of a man, six foot tall and 19 stone. He was a singer and a frustrated gangster, but I couldn't fault him. He was good to me while I was in trouble. Feeney had been involved in the murder of Jackie Odder at Waterloo some years before, but avoided being charged. He died in jail of cancer.

Johnny Regan was to become a living legend in the Sydney underworld. He was a hoon with a lot of girls working for him—he made plenty of money out of it. People, among them the police, claim he killed a dozen or more people. Anyone who got close to him always seemed to go missing or was found dead. When I met Regan he was only doing a very small sentence, I forget what for. On his release he made a name for himself as the most feared man in Australia—he earned it, too!

Anyway, Feeney and Regan treated me well while I was in segro.

A month later I was moved to Bathurst Jail, west of the Blue Mountains, where the conditions were a lot better than the Bay. The screws were all bushies and I got on OK with them. I managed to get myself into a decent wing and attempted to settle down. I went along very quietly for ages until, one night, after we were all put away for the night, the boot shop—which produced boots and shoes for officers and prisoners throughout New South Wales—burnt to the ground. And guess who got the blame? Even though I was locked in my cell when it happened!

The following morning I was training on the weights when I was called to the front office. As soon as I got there I was grabbed and cuffed, thrown into a waiting car and taken to Maitland Jail, near Newcastle.

I spent about a year at Maitland, which was mainly for homosexuals and people that continually fuck up, before I was sent to Parramatta Jail.

When I arrived at Parramatta, I was taken to see the governor. He lectured me for half an hour about my past record and assured me that he would cop no shit from me.

At Parramatta I met up with Billy Harrison again. He was training every day and looking good, so I trained with him. Billy taught me how to throw a punch properly and how to hit harder. He knew just about all there was to know about fighting. I used to practise throwing punches over and over, not dozens of times but thousands of times every night until they were natural for me. This went on for years. I studied any books I could get hold of about fighting, about how to hit correctly and how to do the most damage. I learned where to hit to slow down, knock out or cripple my opponent. From my first fights as a child, I'd learned that I had to hit as hard and as fast as I could, without the other guy having a chance to hit me back, and I developed this technique. So most fights I had as an adult—if you can call them fights—lasted only one or two blows. I rarely got hit, which is why I kept my looks.

The crims were very cliquey at Parramatta. They wouldn't talk to young blokes. They thought that they were too tough and above us. We soon changed their minds about that.

Billy and I decided to see just how tough these older guys were and it didn't take us long to find out that most of them were living on their past reputations—they could not hold their hands up. We started to belt them, sometimes we would knock out two or three a day. We enjoyed taking their reputations off them. I had plenty of mug in me in those days. The old school, as they referred to themselves, soon complained to the governor about us. We were warned to pull up. We took no notice of the governor's warning and continued doing what we liked.

At breakfast one morning Billy knocked out this big guy called Ray Potts. He was six foot four and a good 16 stone. Potts never threw a punch; Bill knocked him out first punch. Potts gave Billy up.

So we went off to see the governor once more. The governor said: 'You listen to me, Harrison, lay one hand on Potts again and you're off to Grafton, get me?'

As we left the governor's office, Billy hit Potts on the chin and left him out cold on the governor's doorstep. Not to be outdone, I belted this other guy and broke his jaw. There were no more warnings for us. That night we were both cuffed and taken by car to Grafton. Boy, were we in for it when we got there.

It was a long drive and not a word was spoken to me by the screws. All the way there I was psyching myself up. I knew I would be flogged, but I was not copping it this time, no way. I was going to attack as soon as they took off the cuffs—first-in best-dressed. I knew that Bill would also have a go at the mongrels. I was concerned, but I knew that they couldn't kill me.

The car pulled up outside the jail, the big gates opened and we went in. This was it. Either they would break me or I would come out in front.

As the gates shut behind me, I felt the tension. I waited

for the handcuffs to come off so I could get a few in before they gave it to me. I was dragged from the car, still cuffed, pulled through a small gate and thrown against the wall. I couldn't see Bill, but I could hear him being moved. I turned to face the screws; there were seven of them, all glaring at me. I was still waiting for them to take off the cuffs so I could attack, but it didn't work out that way.

I remember hearing one particular screw's voice ringing in my ears: 'So, you're back, Smith!' With that, they started into me with their batons and fists—feet, too. I was still cuffed, so all I could do was cop it sweet and make sure I didn't yell while they were bashing me. The last thing I remembered was them flogging me, and Bill yelling for them to leave me alone.

When I came to I was cuffed to the front gate—just hanging there. They were giving it to Bill. I yelled out to leave him alone and got a fist in my face. Then they started on me again.

I woke up in a dark room. I couldn't move too well and my eyes wouldn't open properly. I was aching all over but I was still alive and kicking—and I didn't yell. I must have fallen back to sleep because I woke again to a kick in my guts and my breakfast tipped all over me. I couldn't move. By then I realised I was in solitary confinement. I was bruised all over.

They bashed us every time they fed us. After the third day I was starting to get to my feet when the door flew open.

'Get to the back wall. Move it!'

I tried, but I was too slow. The doctor came over to me: 'How do you feel, Smith? Any complaints?' He had to be joking, surely, I thought. I said nothing.

As soon as the doctor was out of sight, they got stuck into me again. I'd had enough of this shit.

I spat the dummy. 'I'm not copping any more shit, so fuck you all.' They took one last swing at me and slammed the door shut.

An hour or more went by.

Then I could hear them at the door again. I had to go on with them this time, I couldn't cop any more of this. The door opened.

'Get to the back wall and push your face against it.'

I start yelling: 'Get fucked, all of you!' Then I got right in the corner so they couldn't get a good go at me. Five screws came in followed by the governor. I knew him, he was the ex-deputy from Parramatta jail. He said: 'What's the problem, Smith?'

I blew up. 'I am not going to cop any more bashing from your stooges. I will kill the first one I get a chance to. I don't care how long it takes me.'

I was doing 12 years, so what the fuck.

'Come on now, Smith, calm down. There will be none of that here while I am in charge.'

'Don't bank on it.'

He sent the screws outside, then said: 'There will be no one touching you again. Calm yourself down, let me take you to the clinic.'

I decided to take him at his word.

'Come on Smith, let's get you cleaned up.' He took me to the clinic. On the way there he said: 'You will not be touched again, but you can expect no special treatment from me.'

That suited me fine.

'Just leave me be. You'll get no trouble from me.'

The governor was near retirement and didn't want trouble. He told the screws that I was not to be touched again. They hated me, but I didn't care less. From that day, they never laid a hand on me.

After being treated for cuts and bruises, I was marched to the yard to mix with the rest of the crims. The first ugly face I saw was Chapo. I didn't know he was there so it was good to see him. He started laughing at me.

'Let me in on the joke, cunt.'

He just kept laughing. I started to laugh myself, Christ knows why.

'You look like a zebra,' he said, referring to the baton marks on my body.

I often used to wonder if I would have tried to kill a screw? I believe I would, because at that stage I had nothing to live for, or so I thought. Twelve years felt like a life sentence. And Grafton was not worth living in.

At Grafton we spent four hours each day in the yards, where the only work available was sewing shirts by hand. The other 20 hours we spent locked alone in our cells. That was the biggest killer at Grafton, the boredom. They used to allow us only three books per week, no TV, no radio, no newspapers. All news of the outside world was cut out of our letters—if we got them.

Cell furniture consisted of one rope mat to sleep on, one large wooden stump to eat off and one very small shelf for our one possession—our toothbrush. The only noticeable change in the cells was that we now had sewerage instead of shit tubs.

They deprived us of everything possible to make us feel anything but human. There were no mirrors or toothpaste allowed, no shaving gear. A local crim had to shave us twice a week; we hadn't even the bare essentials to live with.

I was placed in a cell next to Chapman in the normal wing along with the rest of the tracs [*short for intractables, one of two groups of prisoners at Grafton: the other group was made up of inmates who were locals. The two groups were not allowed to mix.*]

Each night after our evening meal we were systematically searched. It was done mainly to humiliate us, nothing was ever found. It also gave these big brave screws a chance to show each other how tough they were. Some nights they would come in drunk and big-note about who they were going to bash. Then they would go looking for a crim who'd made a small mistake so they could justify bashing him. They were real brave cunts.

The search consisted of one screw coming into your cell with a ladder and a hammer to hit the bars of your cell to see if they were secure. Then he would rub his finger round the floor looking for dust—if any was found then that was their excuse to start bashing you. After flushing your toilet to make sure that nothing was hidden there, they would tell you: 'Gear off.' That meant that you had to take your coat and slippers off and throw them outside the door, then stand facing the screw. You couldn't look at him, you had to keep your eyes on the floor. Then came the dangerous part—you were pushed back against the wall by the screw and body searched. After that you had to lift each leg in the air for them to check your legs; that's when you got the odd uppercut or punch in face.

All of the screws had their own methods of trying to terrify us; some worked, some didn't. It was terror tactics all the time, that's how they had control over the crims—fear. That, and the bashings that went on every day.

Before long, Chapo and I were separated. I found myself in 4 Yard punching out braille texts for blind children. At least I had a change of scenery and some new guys to talk to. I knew two guys in 4 Yard, Keith Bonny and Jimmy Thornton.

Keith Bonny was a big boy, about 17 stone and tough. He was at Grafton for belting a screw at Goulburn Jail. Keith got more than his share of bashings. He used to just snarl at the screws, they didn't worry him one bit.

Jimmy Thornton was there for the second time. Apart from thinking he was a gangster, he was OK, but he used to scream and cry when he was bashed. He was very emotional and couldn't handle it there. He wanted out any way he could. Any opportunity to be transferred to the Bay.

One day Jimmy asked Keith and me to break his leg for him. Why not? We decided to do it on the weekend when the screws were at the far end of the yard. The plan was to drop a heavy stool on his leg and snap it for him.

On Saturdays we were given a hose to clean out the yard. We lifted the stool on its end and got Jimmy to lie down and stretch his leg in front of him. I told him to look and see if the screw was coming—as soon as he looked away I let the stool fall on his outstretched leg. It snapped like a twig. He let out this mad scream and screws came from everywhere.

'What's going on here, Smith?' said the screw in charge.

I explained that Jimmy was holding the stool, slipped and dropped it on his leg. The screw in charge said: 'You, lift the stool off his leg and drop it on his head.' He was looking at me.

'Are you talking to me, sir?' I said, being smart.

Keith piped up: 'He certainly isn't talking to me.' We were both in fits of giggling.

'It's broken,' I said, pointing to Jimmy's leg.

The screw said Jimmy needed a doctor. 'And so will you two cunts if you keep giggling.' With that he left.

About 15 minutes later he returned with a towel full of ice. 'Put the ice on his leg, then put the towel around his neck and hang the cunt,' said the chief screw. He then left to get a doctor, or so we thought.

Keith and I put a little ice on Jimmy's leg. It was a hot day so we ate the rest of it. Jimmy was grunting and groaning on the ground.

Three hours later there was still no doctor. I asked the head screw when the doctor was coming: 'Shut up, cunt, or you'll need one, too.'

The doctor finally came and Jimmy got his wish—he was moved to the Bay that night. That was one way out of Grafton, but not for me. I'm a born coward—I would sooner hurt someone else, not myself.

After the incident with Jimmy's leg, I decided that I would exercise every spare minute I got, never resting or thinking for a second. It worked well. I didn't think of the outside much and I used to do push-ups and callisthenics every spare moment. I put on weight and grew in the right places. I was a growing boy and I ended up one of the fittest people in the country. Those weak screws shat themselves.

They couldn't work out how I was putting on weight—they weighed us every month and most of us lost weight through nerves.

The reason was that a young guy who was the cook managed to get extra food like eggs and bread in to me. I don't know how he did it—if they had caught him they would have half-killed him. That food was about the best I have ever had in any jail.

I had a few people writing to me. One was Robert Donnelly. We had grown up and been to school together. We were very close. One day I got this letter from him saying he was running around with two guys, Johnny Regan and Kevin Gore.

I got the shock of my life. Even though he helped me out earlier on, Regan was a lunatic. He killed all his friends; he even killed a little girl. Gore wasn't much better than Regan. He was the leader of a gang the media dubbed 'The Toecutters' or 'The Boltcutter Boys'. Gore first hit the headlines when he kidnapped Baldie Blair, one of the guys that robbed an armored car of over half a million dollars. Gore cut off Blair's toes with boltcutters until he revealed where the money was hidden.

I didn't want Robert involved with those two. I wrote to him straight away telling him to watch himself and to get out of those two madmen's company. Robert was due to visit me the following week, but I never saw him again. No one else has seen him, either.

Regan was completely insane. He had an impulse to kill everyone he could. He wanted more than anything in the world to be the most feared man in Australia. He got his wish all right! He also wanted to kill Gore, because Gore was feared by anyone who was anyone in the underworld. So, to improve his reputation, Regan formed a plan to kill Gore and become the man he so wanted to be. And the way to get Gore was through my mate Robert.

Regan tailed Robert around to get his movements down pat. He saw Robert borrow Gore's car. Now was the time to make his move. He placed himself where Robert would see him when he came past. Sure enough, Robert drove by, spotted Regan and gave him a lift. It was Robert's last mistake.

Stage One complete, Regan called to see Gore on some pretext or other, and asked Gore how Robert was. (No one realised that Robert had already been killed.) Gore said he was worried because he hadn't seen Robert or his car for two days. They talked for a while, then decided to try and find Robert (goodbye Kevin Gore). They called into Neville Biber's warehouse to see whether Neville had seen Robert. Once inside, it was all over for Gore. He, too, vanished without trace.

Biber knew about the murder before and after it happened, but could have done little. His only involvement was actually letting Regan use his warehouse to get rid of Gore. Biber was running a business dealing in fake brand name clothing and watches—and was being stood over by Gore and Regan. He probably thought he would be better off with one less person threatening him.

The police questioned Regan but, like all of his murders, nothing ever came of it. Regan went on to kill a few more people, including Jackie Clarke, a killer himself and close friend of Lennie McPherson [*a Sydney identity*]. Again Regan used his head: he got Jimmy Driscol blamed for shooting Clarke. Driscol was another killer who was a member of the boltcutter gang. Driscol was convicted of Clarke's murder and got sentenced to life in prison. He was fortunate to have the conviction thrown out on appeal years later. He was deported back to England.

Robert Donnelly was an innocent victim, but it was just another way for Regan to forward his career—so Robert went missing. Regan was eventually shot down by his friends and killed in a lane at Marrickville (right whack [*just desserts*] for a madman).

I spent more than two years at Grafton on my second visit. It was much easier the second time round. I coasted through it without any side-effects. Then I was sent back to Long Bay. It was a long way by car, and I closed my eyes and thought about my future. I wondered where I was going to finish and how I would cope back in the civilised world, among real people.

Back at the Bay, they didn't want any part of me so they stuck me straight into segro in 4 Wing. They threw me into an empty cell and took my clothes from me. Next morning I was escorted to the reception room with a towel wrapped around me, to get clothes.

On the way Chapo turned up: 'Hello mate.'

He gave me things like toothpaste and real soap, even clean underwear. (Shit, I was going well.) The screw had allowed Chapo to come to the reception room with me so we could talk. Chapo filled me in on what happened to Robert, plus all the scandal of the past two years. I was not destined to stay at the Bay for long. The governor had made up his mind before he even saw me. 'There's just no way I will allow you to stay in my jail and disrupt the routine,' he said. 'Get out of my sight.' It was nice to be wanted.

Back to the yards I went. After 10 days spent in segro at the Bay, I was taken out early one morning and put through the same routine—cuffed for another car trip, this time to Maitland Jail. On arrival at Maitland we were kept waiting outside the main gates; just sitting there waiting for more than an hour. Apparently my reputation had arrived at the jail ahead of me and the governor wanted no part of me either.

I asked the screw: 'What's the problem?'

He said they were ringing head office in town for instructions as to my fate.

Finally, after nearly two hours waiting outside the prison, they opened the gates and we drove in.

I was taken to the tracs section of the jail, a minature

Grafton, minus the bashings. Once there, this shithead of a screw told me to strip off. I did so; it was normal procedure.

Then the fool said: 'Bend over and pull your cheeks apart.' He had to be kidding. I said: 'You pull your own cheeks apart.'

The screw told me he could send me back to Grafton again.

'So?' I said. 'There are no lions or tigers there!'

They put me into the smallest cell I have ever been inside. All it contained was a bed. There was just enough room to stand between the bed and the wall.

After what seemed hours, I was presented to the governor of the jail. He talked straight. 'Look here, Smith. Your reputation has preceded you. Apparently they were terrified of you at Grafton and you somehow escaped the bashings. That's the talk going round the system.'

I just stood there listening. It was all bullshit, but if he wanted to accept it as the truth, then far be it from me to try to convince him otherwise. (Over the years my so-called reputation grew out of all proportion. It was ridiculous, but there were many times when my 'reputation' helped me do things that normally would not have been possible.) So I let him continue.

'You will be put into the normal routine of my jail—against my better judgment, I might add. But the decision has been taken out of my hands.'

I was allowed to mix with the rest of the crims for the first time in years. I knew a few of the guys there. Steve Nittes was one. He had robbed an armored car of over half a million dollars and then became involved in the infamous toe-cutter gang. I liked him, he had a good sense of humor, something people tell me I lack. We sort of teamed up while I was at Maitland. There was also Ronnie Thomas, Darrell Burke and Mick Marsden, all friends. I have always kept to myself most of my life, but these guys were top people and I enjoyed their company.

I was feeling better than I had in a long time. The screws left me to my own devices and I caused them no problems.

I spent a lot of time with Nittes. He used to tell me stories about when he had been the trump [*the boss*] over all the painters and dockers in Melbourne. The painters and dockers were a wild bunch at that time and they were always in the newspapers, so I was interested in what Nittes had to say. I believed I could learn a lot from him.

The very first—and most important thing—I learned was that you could not afford to trust anyone at all. 'If you want to survive,' Nittes used to say, 'keep your enemies close to you and your friends at arm's length.'

He constantly told me: 'It will be a friend that gets you if you're silly enough to drop your guard.' He has been proven right more times than I would like to comment on.

I never had a moment's trouble whilst at Maitland Jail, no one ever bothered me. I had been there for about 12 months when this guy came from Parramatta. He had been emptied [*transferred*] over a disagreement with another friend of mine.

He liked to think he was one of the old school. He never used to talk to us young guys, he thought he was too good for us. As soon as he arrived we got off to a bad start. He kept trying to outstare me and glared at me all the time. I was not having any of that crap.

'What the fuck's your problem?' I said.

He started yelling in front of the screw: 'Fuck you, you don't bother me one bit.'

I didn't want to start anything at that time or place, because it would be broken up too quickly. That's what he was banking on—he thought he could put on a show and save face, then the screws would break it up.

I quietly said to him: 'Don't big-note in front of the screws. If you're serious about getting on with me, then let's do it properly. Come down to the wing straight after lunch and we will settle it then.'

He couldn't back down. 'I'll be there. Count on it.'

'I am counting on it, believe me.'

I had my lunch, all the time thinking about the fight. The bell went for let-go and he walked past me.

'I'll be right back as soon as I muster.' He was certainly keen.

Muster over, he strolled down to the wing ready to have the stink. We went to the top landing so we wouldn't be disturbed by any screws and there would be no chance of anyone trying to break it up.

Once we got there he started to talk: 'Listen Ned, there's no sense in us fighting. We could be mates, good mates.'

I'd got him. He didn't want to go on with it!

'No way, mate. You had your say in front of all the crims and the screws, now it's my turn.'

My blood was pumping madly. I loved the feeling I got before a fight, it was like when you're scared. Anyway, I flogged him without getting hit.

Next day, I was off again, this time to Parramatta. Same old routine, cuffs and the whole works, including the tracs as soon as I got there.

As it turned out, the guy did me a big favor by getting me emptied to Parramatta. It was the beginning of a change in my life.

I arrived at Parramatta Jail late in the evening. Once more I was not really welcomed with open arms—they didn't want me, either. I was starting to feel like a leper. I went straight into solitary until the next morning when I saw the governor. He had already formed his opinion of me, before he'd even met me.

He laid down the rules: 'Act like a man and you'll be treated as such. Go on like a lout and you won't last here long enough for your feet to touch the ground.'

I just nodded, not wanting to open my mouth in case I put my foot in it.

'Is that understood?'

Again I nodded.

'OK, now fuck off and remember that your fate is in your own hands.' It was short and sweet. It also made me think.

I woke up the next morning in a cell in 5 Wing, looked around me and said to myself:

'Is this all that you want out of life? If it is, then you may as well neck yourself now and get it over with.' This was really when I decided that I wasn't coming back to jail ever again.

For the first four years of my sentence I had contemplated revenge against those that had put me away on the rape charge—for which I was innocent. My attitude was one of hate against society as a whole. Chapo and I had talked a lot about escaping and planned that, once out, we would kill everyone responsible for our convictions, then let the police kill us. Fortunately, the authorities learned about our plan and I was put into segregation for two years. And over time, my desire for revenge ebbed.

I looked at the men I had known over the years. They were always in jail. There were never any new faces. It was the same old ones all the time. I decided to change my attitude towards the screws, and the crims as well. It wasn't easy, believe me.

I'd read in a book somewhere: 'You cannot expect to control others if you cannot control yourself.' That stuck in my mind. I began trying to control my actions and emotions—and I spent the next few years reversing almost everything that I had been doing and thinking for the first 25 years of my life.

I started by speaking politely to everyone. I'd say 'Thank you' and 'Please' whenever I spoke to anyone. A lot of the screws thought that I was up to something and they watched me closely. It took a long time to get people on side. Then their attitudes towards me changed overnight.

I was being given extra time on visits and spoken to properly for a change—it seemed that you could achieve more with a smile than you could with a snarl. I still had three years to go before I was due to be considered for release on parole. I was already 27, time that I grew up and got on with my life.

I started to cultivate one of the screws, Keith Coleman. At first he wouldn't have a bar of me, but eventually I wore him down. He started to take time out to come and see how I was going and have a chat. I was staying right away from trouble and he liked to think that he was responsible for the change in me—and I let him do so.

They made Coleman deputy governor, which was great for me. He immediately had me put into the best job in the jail, in any jail for that matter. It was in the clinic as a sort of medic. I knew nothing about medicine, but that wasn't a problem. There were good perks that went with the job. For instance, I had access to the only phone and could get out at night to use it, if I wanted to. It was the only job where you had the use of a phone.

I lived in a clinic dormitory with my own kitchen and I cooked my own meals. This was definitely a step in the right direction for me.

The job wasn't hard. All I had to do was hand out medication and give injections to the crims and the occasional screw. The jails had only male nurses then and only in the daytime. At night, if anyone got sick, they would take me to see the person. If I couldn't do anything, then I would ring the doctor and get him to either tell me what to do, or he would come in himself. I had a rort going with the doctor. I would ring him at home at least twice a week, sometimes more often if he needed the money. (The doctor's dead now.)

I handed out the drugs (unsupervised) and I gave injections the same way. I used to stitch the crims up, too. I think I would have stitched 50 crims or more. The funniest thing I ever did was perform a small operation on one of the two male nurses, who was too tight with his money to pay a doctor to remove his piles. So, armed with an anaesthetic, a scalpel and penicillin powder, I did the job.

The jail's governor allowed me to run the SP betting while I was there. It had been running for ages and every governor allowed it as long as there was no trouble. Part of the deal was that I donated money and tobacco as prizes on sports day. In turn, I got a mate of mine called Billy McLain to run the SP for me as I had to work seven days a week in the clinic.

Billy and I had grown up together. He was doing 10 years for murder after a few guys that he thought were his friends cut off a guy's head while they were drunk. Billy could not read or write well, but you couldn't tell him anything about racing. He knew it all, and used to bring in about $600 per week, not bad for jail.

Through Coleman, I got Chapo a job in the clinic. The screws complained for weeks, but Coleman stuck to his decision. With Chapo working with me, I only left the clinic to train each day, preferring to avoid contact with the other crims.

One Saturday, we were drinking tea in the clinic when there was an attempted escape from near the visiting section. There were screws yelling and running all over the place. Coleman yelled to me: 'Ned, get up here quick, there is an officer hurt.'

I ran up to where Coleman was waiting by the visiting section gate. Through we went. He took me inside an unfinished building and I saw an officer lying on the ground with blood all over his head.

'How is he, Ned?'

I just shrugged.

'Will you have a look at him and see?' He was panicking a little bit.

'Of course,' I said. I looked him over. I didn't need any medical knowledge to know he was dying. His brain was hanging out of his head. 'Get an ambulance right now. No good getting the doctor.'

I didn't want to say he was dying because the officer was looking up at me, just staring straight at me. He had that pleading look.

The screws were still running around everywhere looking for the escapees. They hadn't caught them.

I attempted to assist the officer. I went and got some bandages and a blanket. I tried to push his brains back into his skull, but it did very little to help, so I just wrapped him in a blanket and kept him warm until the ambulance came and took him to hospital.

The ambulance left and I was taken back and locked in the clinic. I asked Coleman what had happened. He said they had caught three men that had tried to get over the wall. I later found out that it was Raymond John Denning who had smashed the officer over the head several times with a hammer.

Denning was sentenced to life for the assault on the officer. [*Denning became a notorious escapee, a public figure in the cause of prison reform and a police informer. In May 1993, he was released into the witness protection program. Two weeks later he was kicked off the program. On the night of Thursday, 10 June, after dinner with his girlfriend, Denning began to vomit, had a seizure and then died in mysterious and controversial circumstances.*] The officer lived for some years but he was a vegetable the whole time.

A few hours later, Coleman took me in to see the governor.

'Sit down, Ned. The officer will live. Thank you.'

I was puzzled. 'For what?'

The governor and Coleman both came over and shook my hand.

'Thank you for what you did for Officer Faber.'

I told him the truth: 'I did nothing.'

I went back to the clinic. The next morning the doctor said he was recommending that I be released on licence because of the assistance I gave to the injured officer. The governor and Coleman told me the same thing. They had written reports to head office recommending my release.

What the fuck was going on here? Why was everyone trying to help me? I didn't know what to think. Could it be possible that I was going to be released?

The next morning, after a sleepless night trying not to think of the possibility of an early release, I approached the doctor and explained that I really did nothing to help the officer. He took me into his office and sat me down.

'Listen to me, Neddy. You are not really a bad boy, just misunderstood. You deserve a chance. Keith and I are giving you that chance.' I didn't know what to say. 'Just you keep your mouth shut and accept without question that some people want to give you a chance.' He also explained that every senior officer in the jail had put in a recommendation that I be released early because I had helped Faber.

I tried not to build up my hopes about being released, but it was impossible with all those people helping me. I had just about convinced myself that I was getting out. Three weeks went by and I was in a state. There was no word yet about the release. I was waiting for some news—any news would do, good or bad. I was still conning myself that I had some sort of a chance of getting out when the news came through.

I had been knocked back.

Paul Genner, who worked in the jail system, helped keep my spirits up. He was a good man who tried to help a lot of prisoners. Later, after I was released, I met him and took him to lunch. He was accused of doing something sinister with me. He did nothing sinister with me, nor did he do one illegal thing with anyone else. He considered that prisoners were not animals, but human beings. Everything that he did was above board. He was the one to introduce sporting gear to jail, helping men to ease the boredom and do something with their time.

One evening, Genner dropped into the clinic and sat down for a cup of tea. He didn't pull any punches: he told me I would be released in 10 days—three months before my minimum release date. I didn't believe him at first—but he was telling the truth.

I found out the next morning that the doctor and senior jail staff were so disappointed that I had not been released that they applied on my behalf for me to be released on a section six [*a clause in the Prisons Act that allowed the Parole Board to let you out up to three months before your parole date*].

I was so excited. Then I started to panic. I had thought of nothing else except getting out for the last six years and nine months—yet I still had no plans.

I was frightened, truly frightened, of what I was going out to. I had no home to go to. I hadn't kept in touch with my family. There were a few girls that had visited me while I was in jail. Maybe they would help me. I would have to find out.

I eventually got the courage to ring a young couple, friends of mine. I asked them, would they just say that I could live at their house to get me released on parole? They said they would be happy to have me for real if I wanted to stay there.

The next thing I had to do was to locate someone who would give me a job—or at least say that I had a job to go to. I contacted a mate of mine, and he arranged for someone to say I had a job and could start straight away.

Things were finally starting to look up for me, everything was working out. I rang Paul Genner and I explained to him that everything was in order and ready to go. 'Just try and sit back and relax for the next few days until it's time for the big day.'

The day before my release I went to check how much the Prisons Department would give me for the six years and nine months that I had done. The answer was $18. Wow. So I was fortunate that I had managed to accumulate just over $4000 from the SP. Inside the jail I had $600 cash, plus bags and bags of tobacco [*jail currency*]. I shared it out between Billy and Chapo. I thought they would continue the SP and keep themselves in comfort for the remainder of their sentences. I was wrong. They had one thing in common—they couldn't resist a bet. They would bet on anything at all and, as soon as I was out the front gate, that's exactly what they did. They both backed a rotten horse and did their money.

The big day finally arrived. I had not slept a wink. For most of the night Chapo and I discussed our plans for when he was eventually released. (It turned out to be a big waste of time, as the reader will see. Very few friendships last outside jail.)

Up bright and early, dressed in a nice new suit, I was ready for the outside world—or that was the impression I was giving everyone. In my own heart I was terrified of what was going to happen once I got out among real people. I said my goodbyes and walked through the gates.

I had never been in the Parramatta area before. I had no idea even which direction to take or who I was going to see. And I couldn't get a taxi because there weren't any around.

So I knocked on the bloody front gate and got them to ring me a taxi! The cab came and I gave the driver a girl's address. Her name was Dale and she had stuck by me through the whole of the sentence, visiting me and writing to me every week. I was nervous as the cab took off. I was out on my own.

4
Looking Down The Barrel

Anarchism is a game at which the police can beat you
George Bernard Shaw, *Misalliance*

Within a few weeks of my release I met 'The General'. I was introduced to him by Greg Johnson, a guy I knew from the nick. The General was running a very large SP business at the time. He and Greg picked me up and took me to get some clothes made and outfitted me with everything that I needed—nice folks!—and The General gave me a job. I will always owe The General. He looked after me off and on for the best part of 15 years. He never said 'No' when I asked for help, not once.

The SP work kept me in money for a while. I also made a few extra dollars collecting bad debts for The General, who introduced me to other people that needed money collected.

At first I had a few minor problems collecting—I was an unknown quantity—but once people got to know me, things changed. I had to be careful as I was still on parole and it wouldn't have taken a great deal to put me back inside. I learnt to be diplomatic—I found I could get better results by being nice to people than I could by sticking a gun in their faces and demanding money—and I soon became a very proficient debt collector.

I'd made up my mind when I was released—5 March 1975—that I was *never* going back inside again. *Never*. Not while my arse pointed to the ground, *no way*. I was 30 years of age, a free man at last and my mind was made up. Jail was for fools and I'd been a fool long enough. It was time to prove to myself that I could make it on my own, alone, in the outside world.

I also had to face facts. In jail I was someone—people knew who I was. They were frightened of me, they looked up to me, they even came to me for advice. But out in the big bad world of real people, I was just a nobody like everyone else. No one knew or cared one thing about me. I was just one of the millions of nobodies!

On my first day out of jail I caught up with some friends and saw my daughter, Nicole, who had just turned seven. (Her mother, Dorothy, had arranged a lawyer and put up my bail when I had been arrested on the rape charge. I had two other children, a son and a daughter, also born about the same time as Nicole, each with different mothers.)

I also bought some casual clothes. At first I was a bit afraid to go inside the shops. I had this awful feeling that everyone was staring at me all the time. Later that day I arranged to pick up a handgun from a guy I'd known for years. He turned up with a .22 target pistol fitted with a silencer. Just what the doctor ordered! He also gave me some money to help me out. I told him that I didn't need it, but he said: 'You will shortly.' I took it and we parted company.

Next stop was a hotel that I used to drink at before I went away—I thought I might run into a few guys I knew. I found my mother and two younger brothers there looking for me, so we exchanged gossip and had a few drinks.

Nothing spectacular happened for the next couple of weeks. My head was full of ideas—some good and some bad—and all I had to do was make them come to life. One of my first objectives was to get Chapo out of jail, because I had promised him I would do whatever I could.

I rang Paul Genner and invited him out to have lunch with me. I told him what I wanted to see him about. He couldn't make it for lunch but he said that he would try and help Chapo for me, but didn't hold out much hope of success.

A few days later Paul rang me and he told me that he had checked on Chapo. The very best he could manage to get off his sentence was one month. That was great—a month is like a year when you're in jail.

Chapo got his early release, one month off as Paul had promised.

We ran together for some time and committed shit crimes, nothing worth talking about. Chapo was married to a woman called Gail after being out of the nick only a short time.

I met this girl called Debra Joy Bell and started taking her out. She is now my wife and we have been together for 17 years and have three great kids. She is without doubt the best thing that ever happened to me.

[*Soon after meeting Debra, Smith made his first deal with police—the first of hundreds to come. It shows how criminals sometimes needed to commit additional crimes to pay the bribes demanded by police.*]

I was arrested by two cops stationed at an inner-city police station. Stealing was the charge. They made a big thing out of it and stamped me [*stamping: to demand money*] for $2000 just to get bail. (It was worth it simply because I was still on parole.)

Enter Brian Alexander, a law clerk and one of the lowest corrupt men I was ever to meet. [*Alexander, who often pretended to be a solicitor, was a bagman, ferrying cash between criminals and corrupt Sydney police. He disappeared in December 1981: more on his disappearance later.*] With a colleague, Alexander made arrangements for me to hand over the money to him so the cops could pick it up.

Chapo and I had been cutting into a few armed robberies together, nothing worth talking about, just small shit getting us no more than maybe $10,000 or $15,000 tops each one. The reason we did little robs was because we had this stupid idea that the police would think they were too little to pay any real attention to. (Before any of you get the idea that I am telling on Chapo, we have already been pinched on them.)

As soon as I was let out on bail, I had to cut into an armed robbery to get the money to pay the two coppers their $2000. We got it the same day I was bailed.

I paid Alexander the money and everything was sweet. Alexander promised to fix the stealing charge for a price to beat it in the low court. That was to be the first of many deals I did with the police—deals that are going to be made public and brought out into the open.

After my first deal came the first time I was accused of

murder. I was living with my wife and son at Rockdale, in Sydney's south. It was early 1976 and each Saturday I had to report to the police station on the stealing matter. I was sitting at home when there was a knock on the door. I answered it to find two cops standing there.

'Can I help you?'

They both glared at me. 'Are you Arthur Stanley Smith?'

I waited for them to continue.

'Well, are you?'

I told him that was my name. 'Who is it wanting to know?'

They produced their ID cards. 'I am Detective Benson and this is Detective Thompson.'

I stood there waiting.

'We would like to ask you some questions about the disappearance of a man named Robert McKinnon. Do you know him?'

'Yes.' That's all I was able to get out before Benson piped up again: 'We have reason to believe that you are responsible for his murder. Can we come in and look around?'

I was not having any of this. 'Pull up right there. You're joking, aren't you?'

'Can we come in?'

They had to be kidding! 'Not without a warrant you can't!'

Benson again: 'Got something to hide, have you?'

It was plain to see the cops hadn't a thing to back up their claim.

'No, I have nothing to hide. But if you two are serious about this then I have nothing to say to either of you without a solicitor present.'

'Are you cold, Mr Smith? You're shaking!'

'Why wouldn't I be shaking? You have just accused me of murdering a friend of mine.'

Benson again: 'Be at Kogarah police station at nine in the morning.'

They walked to their car and drove away. My wife was listening and wanted to know what was going on.

'I don't know yet, but I am going to ring Leon Goldberg.' [*Smith's solicitor*]. I got in touch with Goldberg and he went with me to Kogara police station the next morning to make sure that I wasn't verballed.

Benson and Thompson were waiting for me. I introduced Leon—they weren't very happy with me. I made a record of interview and signed it. Goldberg witnessed it. They gave me a copy and we left. That was the last I heard about it. I found out from being interviewed that Bobby McKinnon had gone missing and that a guy called Jimmy had gone to the police and accused me of the murder. The last time I saw Bobby McKinnon was at Chapman's wedding.

Chapo came to see me with a plan for an armed robbery. I was not really interested as he was in a hurry and wanted to do it without me seeing it—but he talked me into it. It was the Fielders Bakery payroll at Granville, out near Parramatta. A van with two young guys picked the money up from the bank at 9 o'clock every Thursday morning.

We got there and positioned ourselves, waiting for them to arrive. We waited—no van. Finally, a hotted up GT Falcon pulled up at the bank. 'That's them,' Chapo said as they walked into the bank. We planned to drive out and block the car as it tried to leave. I would stay in the car while Chapo would get out and grab the money.

Out they came. Chapo stalled too long, letting them get into the car, lock the doors and drive off. I tried to cut them off by pulling out in front of them, but they saw what I was up to and the driver cut over the median strip in the middle of the road. The next thing I heard was two shots ringing in my ears—Chapo had let go at them in futile anger. He jumped back in the car and we managed to get away without any problems.

We changed cars a few blocks away. And Chapo's wife, Gail, was driving the second car! His own car! We both got into the boot so it looked as if there was only a woman in the car. It turned out that Chapo's car had been spotted—not the number, only the color. That was Chapo's downfall. His own stupidity brought him undone—along with his wife and me. (If we had had cops on side we would have *known* what was going on.)

Chapo and his wife decided to report the car stolen. But he didn't report it stolen once, but three fucking times! Three times in the one night to three different police stations. Fucking insane.

Well, you don't need a college education to work out what happened next. The police saw this as a strange thing for a normal person to do, so they reported it to the hold-up squad. The hold-up squad quite naturally put the dogs [*surveillance police*] on Chapo's wife. They saw Chapo coming and going, found out who he was and, bingo, he was pinched along with Gail.

I didn't hear from him, but thought nothing of it for a few days. But when I tried to contact him, I found out he'd been arrested. I made a few inquiries (I had no police on side to check with) and discovered that he'd been refused bail, but Gail had been bailed.

I couldn't go and see her because I guessed they were watching her place. Not for one minute did I think that I had been nominated as the other guy.

My life went on as normal. A few times I felt I was being followed, but shrugged it off as paranoia.

Saturday came: time to report on bail on the stealing charge. I tried to get my solicitor, Goldberg, to come with me, but couldn't find him, so I decided to take my wife with me. It turned out to be a bad decision.

Before I went into the station I drove around looking for anything that was not normal. Finding nothing, I told Debra: 'I'm going to report. If I'm not out in five minutes, you leave and get me a lawyer straight away.'

I walked in. Everything looked normal enough. 'I'm reporting on bail, Sarge . . .' was all I got a chance to say before about 10 cops jumped me, threw me on the floor and cuffed me. There I was, flat out on my back with a detective just standing there, smiling, with this giant shotgun pointed at my head.

'Got you, Neddy!'

That was the first experience I had of Roger Rogerson. We often laughed about it later over a few cold ones, but let me assure you there wasn't even the hint of a smile on my face that day.

They took me to police headquarters and, as I walked in, I saw that Debra was already there, sitting in an office being interviewed. This was to be an experience I wouldn't forget in a hurry. Rogerson sat me down and cuffed me to a chair.

'Listen to me, Neddy, we know that you and Chapman attempted to rob Fielders Bakery. How do you think we got on to you?'

I just sat there thinking.

'Come on, Neddy. You're not silly. Chapman's wife has nominated you as the driver of the car. You can't deny that, can you?'

My mind was racing. He then said he would also charge Debra with the robbery unless I confessed.

I thought deeply and went the opposite way to normal. No smart-mouthing or trying to be a big shot. I knew these people wouldn't put up with my smart-alec tactics. Instead, I continued the innocent act.

'Look, I'm not going to cop any robbery that I didn't do. You'll have to charge Debra too, 'cause I'm not copping it sweet.'

'We have a clown here,' Roger said as another copper walked into the room.

For the next six hours they kept me cuffed to the chair. The threats came from Roger first, then other coppers. Occasionally, one of them would get me on his own, look around the room and say: 'Got any money? If you want to talk business now is the right time.' I never fell into any traps, I just kept pretending I was cold on the blue. Roger finally came in.

'Listen, Neddy, I'm out of patience. Either you come to the party or I charge her, along with you, with the armed rob and two counts of attempted murder. What do you say?'

I put my head in my hands and said: 'You'll just have to charge Debra.'

He really blew up: 'You weak cunt of a man, letting your wife cop the blue for you.'

He ended up charging me with armed robbery and shoot with intent to kill while committing an armed robbery. They didn't charge Debra. If it had come to the crunch, I would have ended up copping it, but it turned out all right for her. But Roger had to go one better on account of me refusing to talk. He loaded me with [*planted*] a gun. Low bastard.

Roger got me straight before a court. I was officially charged and bail was refused. I was in a state of shock. I was going back to the Bay. So much for all my nice plans.

Before I got to Long Bay, one of the coppers [*Smith names this policeman—for legal reasons we've removed his name*] came to the cell to see me.

'Listen, Neddy, do you want to do anything about this blue?'

'Look,' I said, still being nice. 'I had nothing to do with this robbery, you know that. Besides, even if I wanted to do any business, I don't have any money.'

He repeated his offer. 'Just tell me, yes or no. We will work out the details later if you agree.'

I thought it was a trap, but I had to take the chance. 'Sure, why not? But don't ask me to tell on anyone.'

'Someone will be out to see you for me in a few days,' he said. Then he walked off.

I arrived at the Bay and saw Chapo. 'Hello mate,' he said. 'What happened to you?'

I said: 'I thought maybe you could tell me.'

He started to go off his brain, which didn't impress me. I had known him too long to take any notice of his ravings. 'Do you think me or Gail gave you up?' he said.

I was confused. The cops always tried to cause friction between people charged—it made their job easier. 'I don't honestly know,' I said.

He wasn't impressed one bit. That was the beginning of our split-up, we hardly talked after that. We spent a few weeks at the Bay waiting to go back to court. We weren't very friendly during that time. I kept on accusing his wife of telling on me.

During this time I got a visit from Brian Alexander, the law clerk. His opening speech went like this:

'Neddy, you are a genius. Not many crims can get on the right side of [*a policeman*] that quick.'

I didn't come in. 'What are you talking about?' I didn't trust him too much.

'Someone has spoken to [*the policeman*] on your behalf. You are going to be all right.' I just looked at him stupidly—a natural look for me. 'Don't tell a soul about this or they will drop you like a hot potato.'

'What about Chapo and Gail?' I was curious to see if he'd managed to fix something up.

'Chapman and his wife are not concerned about you, they are doing something with Rogerson. You just look after yourself.' And off he went.

[*Much to Smith's surprise, when the case came to court a few weeks later, he was granted bail. One of the key factors behind bail being granted was the sudden 'appearance' of a record of interview between Smith and police, which fea-*

tured Smith denying involvement in the robbery—and his answers seemed to satisfy detectives. Bail was set for Smith and Chapman at $10,000 each.]

5
Easy Money

By right means, if you can, but by any means make money.

                    Horace, 65–8 BC

I had a sinking feeling. Chapo was walking out of court on bail, but I wasn't. Where was I going to come up with $10,000 for my bail? Debra was there, very happy that I got bail, but she was crying.

'Don't worry Ned, I won't leave you there. I promise I will get you out.' I knew she would try, but she had no hope. She knew no one with that sort of money to put up for my bail.

Back to the Bay I went. The next day I was sitting in my cell when a screw called out to me: 'Smith, to the office for bail.' Was he having a go at me? That's what I thought. He sent me to the general office to sign the bail slip, and then I knew he wasn't joking.

I still didn't know who had bailed me out. Papers signed, I was dressed, and they took me to the front gate. Debra was standing there! For a change she was smiling. 'I told you that I would never leave you in there, didn't I?' I found out later that Debra had asked a friend of her mum's to put her home up for me. Once out, we had no option but to move into my mother's. I was flat broke and had nothing coming in.

I tried to tell Debra what had happened, but she didn't want to know. She was still very gullible then and didn't believe that the police were corrupt. Most of the public are still like that today—they just don't want to know.

My main problem was that I needed money from somewhere to support myself and my family. We couldn't live on love. The question was where to get it without running foul of the law.

I had a sneaking suspicion that [*Smith names a policeman*] and his gang were watching me. There was no contact from [*the same policeman*] or anyone else for that matter, so I waited. I was getting paranoid. I knew they were watching me. Maybe they wanted to see what I would do and who I talked to. I didn't know.

Eventually I kicked a small goal and got a job—a sort-of job—working three nights a week at a pub called the Governor Burke in Glebe. Three guys had opened a disco there and were having problems with louts. Three of the previous bouncers had been badly beaten up.

First, I advised them to have no other bouncers, as they were only asking for trouble putting themselves on show standing by the door. They took my advice and never had any further trouble. I was only getting $100 a night, but it was more than I was getting sitting on my arse all day doing nothing.

I'd been working at the Governor Burke for only three nights when I met Graham 'Abo' Henry again. I knew him from Parramatta Jail. Abo [*so-named because of his dark complexion*] appeared at the pub one night and we got on the drink together. After a few drinks we were pretty pissed and decided to box on at a disco called Hazy Land at Surry Hills.

Abo was a very violent person, and I knew this. He had plenty of go in him and wouldn't cop shit from anyone. When he was a kid he used to love gangsters. His idol was John Dillinger. It was Abo's dream to be like him.

We got to Hazy Land and were there for half an hour or more, enjoying ourselves and minding our own business, when some clown had a go at us because we were having such a good time on our own. Well, I belted him and out he went, cold. I looked over to see what Abo was doing; he was arguing with one of the bouncers about something.

I went to see what was going on and as I got close I heard the bouncer say: 'I have a gun in my pocket.' He only just had time to finish saying it when out of the blue a knife appeared in Abo's hand and he stuck it in the guy's stomach several times. He said: 'The gun is no good to you in your pocket.' Abo was laughing as he did it. Blood was flying everywhere and I was covered with it. We left Hazy Land as soon as we could, before the cops arrived. Abo said as we left: 'Let's box on somewhere else, it's early.'

I thought by 'box on' he meant drink on. That's what I used to call it, anyway. We went to this disco around the corner from Hazy Land, Minnies. (Both are gone now.) As soon as we got there we were told by the bouncers that we couldn't come in. They had already heard about the stabbing at Hazy Land.

Now that was a bad mistake, telling us we couldn't come in. Abo and I attacked the two closest to us; they had no chance at all, it was over in seconds. Then, to show them we didn't give a shit, we walked into the place like we owned it and ordered a drink. We drank up and left, laughing all the time. By now I was starting to sober up and I wanted to get as far away from there as I could.

'Let's go somewhere else and box on,' said Abo.

No way was I boxing on any more that night! Abo was the worst drunk in the world, barring no one. Finally, Abo got into his car and I caught a cab to my mother's place, where I was still living. I started to think over the night's events and was certain that some arse would give Abo and me up to the police, so I showered and got rid of the blood-stained clothes I'd been wearing.

The next morning I rang The General. I didn't tell him anything about the previous night's events—I waited to see if he had heard anything.

'Hello, General, how's everything going?'

He recognised my voice. 'Don't say anything on the phone,' he said. 'Meet me at The Oak [*The Royal Oak Hotel in Double Bay*] at 4pm and be on time.'

I worried all day. I thought it had to be about the stabbing. Why did I go on like an imbecile? I cursed myself all day; I deserved to be pinched for stupidity.

It was too nerve-racking waiting to see The General, so I went to The Oak early, arriving at 3pm instead of 4pm. The General hadn't arrived, so I watched the clock, waiting. At last he turned up. We ordered a drink and he kept me waiting for the news.

Finally he said: 'I hope that you know what you're getting into.'

What was he talking about?

'What do you mean?' I said.

He looked at me.

'Be very fucking careful of these people.'

He then told me that he had been told to arrange a meeting between me and a guy called Kenny. I knew Kenny; I'd met him at Maitland Jail years before. He was [*a policeman*]'s dog [*informer*], everyone knew this. I realised that he was the contact from [*the policeman who asked me whether I wanted to do business over the armed robbery charge*].

The General told me to contact Kenny the next morning at the Rose Bay marina. 'He will meet you there. He will be cleaning his boat.'

I asked: 'Will you be there, mate?'

'No fucking way,' he said. 'That team is out of my league.'

I tried to sound out The General about Kenny, but he wouldn't come at a thing. He just kept telling me: 'Make sure you know what you're getting into with this guy, he tells [*a policeman*] everything.' But I already knew *that*.

I drank with The General until 7pm. He religiously went home at 7 o'clock every night and was up at 5 o'clock every morning running, regardless of how he felt from the previous night. I headed home to think about this meeting. A thousand thoughts went through my mind. Should I go armed or not? Could I trust him? The answer was no. But I decided to meet him. I had nothing to lose and everything to gain. I went armed.

I got to the meet early to have a look around, but Kenny was there before me, cleaning his boat. I watched him moving around. He was huge: about 19 stone and very fit. I waited a little, then proceeded down to the marina.

I asked one of the workers whether Kenny was about. He pointed out Kenny on the boat and called out: 'Kenny, someone here to see you.'

Kenny looked up and waved like we were old friends: 'Hang on, I won't be a minute. I just have to bring the boat in.'

It was a beautiful boat, a 25-foot offshore racer, a formula one. I was impressed. He brought it into the jetty, jumped off and we shook hands.

'I'm glad you decided to come,' he said.

We talked shit for a few minutes, then he said: 'Let's take the boat out for a run. We can talk better away from here.' I must have hesitated because he laughed and said, 'There's no problems, mate.'

I got on the boat and we went for a spin. We cruised around the harbour for 20 minutes, then he pulled into a cove and dropped anchor. 'No one can overhear us here. Let's talk.'

That was fine by me, and I said so.

'Do you know why I wanted to see you?'

I nodded.

'Well, [*a policeman*] asked me to see you on his behalf. You have a few problems that I can help you out with. Has anyone spoken to you about doing any business yet?'

'He mentioned something could be done, but that's as far as he went.'

'That's right, something can be done for you. But it will cost $20,000 to fix the blue.'

I just looked at him and said nothing.

Then, for a while, he told me about how he and [*a policeman*] had been good friends since school. He started to sound me out about the armed robbery.

'How did you get involved with a fool like Chapman? Armed robberies are for mugs.'

I told him that I was cold on the blue and that I had been loaded.

'Haven't we all?' he laughed. 'The main thing is that something can be done for you to beat the blue.'

'Kenny, I don't have that sort of money.'

'We'll worry about that later.'

'OK, what do I do?'

'I will fill you in on that later. Consider the blue beaten.'

'I can't find that sort of money, mate. It's no good saying that I can come up with it if I can't.'

'If you agree to come in with me, there won't be a problem getting the money.'

'OK. I will do just about anything at all to get the money.'

Kenny didn't mention what I had to do to earn the money. I just hoped it wasn't armed robberies—and it didn't sound like it was.

We reached a jetty at Watsons Bay, near South Head and

the entrance to the harbour. Kenny tied the boat up and said: 'Hang on, I won't be long.'

This was where Kenny lived. I made a mental note of the location.

He was soon back with a bag in his hand. 'Hold this for me.' He gave me the bag. 'Let's go and pick up my car and we'll call in to see about getting you a decent car.' We got into his car, a red Aston Martin. He'd impressed me again. The guy certainly had a quid.

'We're going to see a mate of mine who runs a car yard. We'll get you something, nothing too expensive. You can get whatever you want when you earn your own money. It won't be too far off.'

We pulled into the guy's car yard, got out and went into his office. Sitting there was this little fat guy in his 50s. Kenny introduced us. 'Billy McLaughlin, this is Neddy Smith.' We shook hands.

Billy said: 'I've heard a lot about you Ned, you have a top name.'

I just shrugged off the compliment.

Kenny said: 'What have you got in your yard that we can give Ned to run around in until he decides what he wants?'

'What sort of money are we talking about?'

'Come on, you old cunt, just show us what you have, then we'll talk money.'

Billy showed us around the yard. Kenny picked out a lemon-colored two-door Ford. It looked a good car. 'How much, Billy?'

'Ned can have it for what it owes me. Let's look at the books.'

Billy let me have it for $2500, a good deal. I couldn't understand how he could sell it so cheaply, but I didn't complain. Kenny paid Bill the $2500 and then we went across the road to the Regent Hotel for a few drinks.

At the pub, Kenny handed me another $3500. 'Get the phone connected as soon as you can. And ring me every morning about 9am. OK?' He then left.

I remained drinking with Billy for a few hours while he got one of his guys to do the paperwork on the car.

Billy and I became good friends over the next few years. I drove the car home to show Debra and got her to ring up and get the phone connected. Then I handed her $2000 telling her to pay some bills and spend $1000 on herself and the kids. The kids needed it. They had gone without for a long time. But there was no more going without for them. My kids never needed another thing for the next 14 years. Except for their father, that is.

I decided that I would go along with Kenny—so long as it suited my purposes and I had control over my own fate.

I rang Kenny every morning, but nothing was ever ready to go.

It wasn't hard to find out about Kenny and what he was doing for a crust [*a big-league heroin dealer*]. I didn't tell my wife. I didn't want her involved or worried about me. Or disgusted, for that matter.

Kenny started to take me everywhere he went, usually to Eliza's Garden Restaurant at Double Bay. In the end I was eating there every weekday for lunch or dinner. Two or three times a week I would go out with Kenny on his boat.

I was to meet plenty of people, all of them wealthy and some influential. I made plenty of contacts for the future. As well, I was starting to make a decent wage collecting for bookies and other people who had money owing to them.

The bookies' settling day was Monday, at The Oak Hotel in Double Bay. I made it my business to be there every Monday when they settled, and I picked up some good business that way.

One morning early, I received a call from Kenny: 'Do you have a gun? Meet me at Eliza's at lunchtime and bring a gun if you have one.'

I went to meet him, with a gun, wondering what he was up to. Kenny was waiting at the bar.

'Are you ready to earn the $20,000? We have work to do today, so let's get on with it. There is a green rent-a-car parked out front, you take that.'

He handed me the keys.

'Follow me everywhere I go and don't lose me. If anyone tries to stop me or run me off the road, do whatever you have to, OK?'

'What about police? Do I stop them?'

'Yes. Stop them. I can fix it up later. Just stop anyone!'

Kenny was also driving a rental car. I followed him to the North Shore, where we pulled into a car park near this big American car. An old guy of about 60 got out of the car and talked with Kenny for a while. I met the old guy later—he was Murray Riley, an ex-cop.

They were only talking for about 10 minutes when another car pulled up. Kenny waved to let me know that it was sweet. A young bloke, in his mid-20s, got out and went straight to his boot, where he took out a big suitcase and handed it to Kenny, who quickly put it in his boot. Kenny waved to me again and began to drive slowly out of the car park.

He then sped up and, at times, I had trouble keeping up with him. We got to Manly and he pulled up, got out and walked back to me.

'You did real good mate! You go now and wait at the Sheaf [*the Golden Sheaf Hotel in Double Bay*] for me. Just put the car in the car park and leave the keys under the floor mat on your side.'

I took off trying to see where Kenny was heading. I was trying to find out as much as I could about him in case he tried to set me up. He turned up at the Golden Sheaf an hour later and handed me $5000.

'That's yours. You'll get the rest next week.'

I was happy. This was the easiest money I had ever made in my life.

'I will be busy for a week, mate, so ring me on Friday.'

I waved as he went, then headed home to my wife and kids.

I was still working—if you could call it that—at the Governor Burke three nights a week. One night Kenny arrived. We had a few drinks then stupid me went to Hazy Land again. I always went to those places when I was on the drink. The place was a trap for fools.

We were having a good time until these black guys started putting shit on us. I couldn't understand them. There were two of us: we were both over six foot and weighed 16 and 19 stone, yet they picked us out. Maybe we were looking for trouble—it's a distinct possibility.

We didn't have to wait long. The black guys started to throw punches at us—we managed to belt a few of them before we left. As we walked out of the place there, in front of us, was the biggest team of black guys you ever saw.

They were waiting for us.

We were about to give it our best shot when the police

arrived. They told us to leave while we could. As we tried to leave, one of the black guys threw a king hit at me. He missed, but I didn't. Down he went like a bag of shit.

Fuck, I cut my hand on his teeth.

The police grabbed the guy and said to us: 'Fuck off you two, now.' I went home to bed. The next day I woke up in agony. My hand was up like a balloon. Debra drove me to the hospital where the nurse told me it was poison! They fixed me up and I went home.

A few days later Kenny invited Debra and I to lunch at Prunier's restaurant in Woollahra. We met at the bar and had a few drinks. We were talking when all of a sudden he asked me about Chapman.

'How long since you've seen Chapo, mate?'

I told him the truth. 'I haven't even heard from him since we got out on bail.'

'Well, stay away from him, Ned. [*Two police*] are going to pinch him soon.'

On the way home from lunch I told Debra what Kenny had said. We discussed it and decided I had to warn Chapo, so I rang him and we met. I explained what Kenny had said.

'Fuck them all, they aren't that smart,' said Chapo. 'Let them pinch me.'

Well, I tried. I couldn't perform miracles and put brains into empty spaces. If he wasn't worried then why should I be?

Two weeks later I heard that Chapo was arrested for two bank robberies. He got bail again, Christ only knows how.

I met Kenny again and he said: 'I want you to meet someone. Meet me at the Lord Dudley Hotel [*in Woollahra*] at five this arvo.'

I turned up on time. Kenny was there with Murray Riley. Kenny introduced me to Murray who, after one drink, handed me a bag. It was an ordinary bag, taped up with sticky tape.

'That's yours. There is $30,000 there and it's all yours.'

I took the parcel.

'Thanks, Murray.'

I was ecstatic. This would pay off the police over the armed robbery charge—and then I would be out of the shit.

'You did well. There will be more work and much more

money for you next time round.' He then moved off to chat with someone else.

Kenny was thinking like me.

'You can get [*a policeman*] paid off now. And you will still have a bit left to keep you going until the next go.'

Kenny told me he had arranged for me to meet [*the policeman for the pay-off*] at 9am the next day outside the main entrance to the Showground. I was not excited about the meeting.

'Listen mate, can't you fix him up for me?'

'Not really, mate. [*The policeman*] wants to talk to you about something. He's sweet.' I told Kenny that the copper may have been sweet for him, but I wasn't sure about anyone else.

The next day, Kenny and I went to meet [*the policeman*] in Moore Park. There was only one car near the entrance so we pulled up alongside it. [*The policeman*] was there, sitting with the door open and his legs outside the door.

I left my car and walked over. He seemed friendly enough. We exchanged greetings and I assured him I had the money. He got to his feet and looked around, taking his time.

'All right, Neddy, put it on the front seat.'

I did as I was told.

He stood there for a few minutes talking shit, then hit me with a bombshell.

'That was a very silly thing that you did warning Chapman.'

I nearly had a stroke when he said that.

'Chapman talks on phones. Don't make the same mistake again. Remember what I'm telling you.'

There was no way I would make that mistake again.

He then explained the reason he wanted to see me: what would happen to me on the robbery charges. What he said that afternoon turned out to be right.

First, I was taken back to court. My bail was reduced from $10,000 to $2000 and I no longer had to report to the police station.

It wasn't long before the hearing was put on at Central Court. The magistrate threw out the armed robbery and attempted murder charges—all except the gun that the cops loaded me with. On the gun charge he sent me for trial. On the robbery, Chapman and his wife were both committed for trial.

As I left court a very happy man, Roger Rogerson came over to me.

'Neddy, come and see me when things quieten down. We'll see what can be done about the gun charge.'

As he walked away he told me to keep in touch. I celebrated that night. I was the luckiest person alive. I had beaten the armed hold-up charges. All I had to do now was get over the gun.

[*Smith says he paid $10,000 to Detective Sergeant Roger Rogerson for the gun charge to be 'fixed'; this involved police changing their evidence and supporting a concocted story that Smith did not know about the gun; that the weapon was in fact owned by Smith's father-in-law, who, dying of cancer, bought it to commit suicide with. The jury, to the surprise of Smith and police, didn't believe the story and Smith was convicted. He appealed and the conviction was later quashed.*]

6
Double Bay Days

[By early 1977] The Double Bay mob ... began to dominate the heroin traffic, and the Sydney drug subculture became progressively more violent.

Dr Alfred W McCoy *Drug Traffic, Narcotics and Organised Crime in Australia* 1980

I was going up the ladder at last, up the ladder of success. Everything was going right for me. The money was rolling in. I had left the pub job—no need for that any more. It seemed as though I couldn't put a foot wrong, whatever I did.

I saw Kenny every day and Double Bay became my regular hangout. I met lots of people, people I never knew existed. I was meeting doctors, lawyers and all sorts of businessmen. All my life I had been mixing with the wrong sort of people. No more.

At The Oak Hotel I met a nice guy called Neville Biber. (Years earlier, Biber had been stood over by Kevin Gore and Johnny Regan—until Regan used Biber's warehouse to kill Gore.) Biber was a huge punter. He was also a big earner—he went through millions of dollars. The General introduced us one day. 'Neville has a problem that I think you may be able to help him with.'

Neville explained: he had been stabbed by a friend of his in front of his wife and kids. He was keen to have something done about it soon. Was I interested in doing something for him? (Is the Pope Catholic?) But I wanted to know the circumstances before committing myself.

It turned out that Neville was working with a guy called Greg. Neville asked Greg if he wanted to earn $5000. It was an insurance job and Neville needed a hand doing it. Greg never once asked Neville how much he was getting—he just accepted the $5000 that was offered. The job was done and Greg got the $5000 as promised. Later, he heard that Neville got $50,000 for the job.

He blew up and stabbed Neville in his own house in front of his wife and two kids.

Greg was technically in the wrong. He should have asked how much the job was worth before he accepted the money. I knew Greg, so it was not easy for me to accept the job. I agreed to go and see him and have something done for Neville. I checked on Greg and found out he was running an SP in the Cross, so I went to see him. I was not sure what I was going to do. I'd known Greg for a few years, but he was not what I would call a friend.

We talked for a while. Greg admitted being in the wrong, but then he started to argue with me. That's one thing I can't see any sense in—arguing. That was what finally made up my mind.

Greg continued to argue, so I just blanked out and gave it to him. He ended up in hospital with several stab wounds to the ribcage and punctured lungs. When he came out of hospital he left Sydney for a while.

Next time I saw Neville he was very happy to see me, in fact he was all over me. He took me to lunch and told me how pleased he was. He wanted to know the details, but that's not my go.

After lunch he gave me a few thousand dollars and asked me if I was interested in working for him full-time.

I remember thinking to myself that I might be out of my league with this guy. He had made and lost millions. Too smart for me.

'I'll think about it, mate. Let's have a drink.'

After lunch we all went to The Oak for a quiet drink. The General was there as usual. After Neville had a quiet word, The General came over and said: 'Listen, Ned, you have kicked a goal. Neville likes you and wants you to work with him. He is a genius, mate. Believe me, you won't regret it.'

The General filled me in on the benefits.

'It won't be hard work, mate. All you have to do is look after him.'

Neville came back to the bar: 'Well, mate, what do you say? Are you in with me?'

I looked at him for a while.

'Well, buddy?'

'OK, Neville. I'm in.'

From that night on for the next 10 years I never needed anything nor did I ever look back. Neville Biber and I remained good friends until the day he died, never once doing the wrong thing by me. He was into almost everything, but he refused to become involved in drug dealing. He also wouldn't be involved in slinging police. He hated them. 'Let the arseholes get out and earn their own money,' he used to say.

Before long Neville had me on a $500 weekly retainer. On top of that I had several other things going with Kenny [*heroin dealing among other ventures*] and I was making money collecting for bookies. Things never got boring.

By this time [*early 1977*] I was living at Sans Souci in a rented house, driving my first Mercedes Benz, drinking every day at Double Bay, eating in the best restaurants and wearing the best clothes.

Another Double Bay drinker that I remained friends with for many years was Tony Eustace. [*Eustace, a big heroin dealer, was a victim of the so-called Sydney 'Gang Wars'. There is more on Eustace and his murder, pages 181–2.*] Tony used to hold court at Eliza's restaurant. It was like his office: he had the corner reserved for his business only.

Every Sunday Tony had lunch at his home, lunches that became famous. I was a regular guest. Others to attend Tony's famous Sunday lunches were [*Smith names three policemen*], all of them suspended over some form of corruption or other. Tony had a lot of police sweet. He helped me out of a few problems using his connections within the police force. These lunches sometimes went into the early hours of the next morning, no one cared.

Over the next eight years, Tony and I did a lot of business together such as SP bookmaking—and we were both heavily involved in selling heroin.

Tony had expensive tastes, and so did I. He was a big spender with the ladies. The media gave him the name 'Spaghetti Tony'. Christ only knows where they got that one from. He was a Pom and his friends called him 'Champagne Tony'. The media will do anything to sell papers.

I met Murray Riley again at the Coachman Restaurant in Redfern. I was invited there for lunch. [*Murray Riley, also known as Murray Stewart, is now in his late 60s. He won a gold medal at the 1950 Commonwealth Games in Auckland in the double sculls. His partner was Merv Wood, later NSW police commissioner. Riley resigned from the police force in 1962 after serving almost 20 years. He became involved with a poker machine company, then with Sydney's Double Bay crowd, a loose criminal group that included Neddy Smith. Riley was arrested in 1978 over his involvement in the importation of 1.5 tonnes of hashish into Australia. He was later jailed over a traveller's cheque fraud (described below). Also active in other drugs scams through the 1980s, Riley was, at the time of going to press, on the run from a British jail, where he had been serving a five-year term for plotting to defraud British Aerospace of £50 million.*]

During lunch Murray asked me: 'Do you know anyone who is interested in handling a million-dollar parcel of American Express traveller's cheques? Also some Thomas Cooks?'

(Murray was convicted over this scam: I am not telling on him.)

He then produced a book of these cheques and handed them to me. 'Take these as a sample so you can show the people. If they are interested, get back to me.'

After lunch I got straight on to it. I found two people who took quite a bundle of the cheques—and I made a small piece of change out of the deal. But there were still a lot left and Murray wanted to get rid of them.

I decided to see a friend of mine, a shoplifter who had toured the world several times, thieving his way around. If anyone knew what to do with these cheques, he would.

When I showed him a sample, he was very keen to get his hands on more of the cheques. The only condition he made was that he be given the first go with them. He didn't want to bump into anyone else while he was doing them.

Murray gave me the cheques that the shoplifter requested on the nod. Murray's price for them was half the ticket, or half the face value (a big ask).

I found out later how my friend did it. He got a team of guys and girls that he knew and had worked with before.

They headed for Hong Kong and Singapore to cash the cheques. First they had to get false passports for the whole team—and that was right up Neville's alley. So I put them together and they agreed on a price for the passports.

The scam in Hong Kong went well. They got rid of a lot of the cheques by buying jewellery and through money-changers. They brought the jewellery back here to sell and made a decent drink. Murray got his money—but he still had a lot of cheques left.

He asked: 'How did your friend do it?' I opened my big mouth and told him. I also told him that it nearly came undone and that was why my mate cut his stay short.

Murray hired a similar team and set off to Hong Kong. He said he had the go off the police in Hong Kong to do it over the weekend and get out before the banks opened on the Monday.

As expected, something went wrong. One of the guys he sent got greedy and spent too much in each shop. They got suspicious and the word went out like wildfire all over the shopping district of Hong Kong.

Murray was fortunate enough to be there watching the scam go down. He grabbed the gear that the guy had already purchased and got it back to Australia OK.

Apparently the guy decided to buy a very expensive watch—at the hotel where he was staying. Stupidity! He came undone, was arrested and refused bail. Murray was able, through his police contacts, to bail the guy; as soon as he was bailed, Murray had him shipped out of the colony on a merchant ship.

They set the guy up in New Zealand. He was given money and everything he needed, and told to stay there. Under no circumstances was he to try and contact his wife or anyone else in Australia. What did the guy do but ring his wife. And naturally police traced the call. The silly bugger was arrested and brought back to Australia. Again Murray pulled some strings and the guy got bail. Later he was committed for trial—but the case never got to trial as Murray did something and it was no-billed [*when a charge is dropped by the prosecution before it gets to trial*].

One Thursday night I took my wife to the new Chequers in town for dinner and a show. She enjoyed it. For the first time since we'd been together we had it good—it was a great feeling to wake up and not have to worry about where the rent was coming from or how we were going to be able to afford this or that. Life was good to us and we were enjoying it.

That night, after dinner and the show, the mug came out in me. I told Debra that we were going to call into a disco for a nightcap. She didn't want to go to any of the discos that I frequented, but I finally convinced her to go to this filthy rotten Hazy Land disco. Had I been sober I would never have taken her to such a low dump. I was stupid to go anywhere near that shithouse. She was reluctant to even go in when she saw it.

Before we went inside I got an axe out of the boot of my car and secreted it under my jacket. I was about two parts under the weather when we went in. As we reached the top of the stairs—I had a mate with me as well—the bouncers saw us and nearly had a baby. One got the manager—it was the same guy that Abo had stabbed. He'd since been promoted. He came over.

'Hello, Ned.'

I just couldn't resist the temptation to have a go at him. 'Have you still got that gun in your pocket?'

He wasn't one bit impressed.

'Look, Ned, it is very quiet here tonight.'

'Just how I like it,' I said.

I walked over to the bar to get a drink. It looked like the manager was telling the truth—it was quiet. I looked around and guess who I spotted sitting in a large group? The black guys, all together in one big happy bunch.

Debra saw where I was looking and immediately tried to get me out of there as quickly as possible. The black guys had seen me and were pointing my way. That did it. It had been long enough. I should have done something about it long ago.

I told Debra to go outside and wait in the car. She wouldn't go. Debra wasn't silly. She knew what was going to happen. 'Please leave now, with me. You have just gotten out of trouble. Think of me and the kids.'

But there was no telling me when I'd had a few drinks.

I was psyched up. There was no stopping me. These guys would wish they had never heard of me. I walked over to their table and, as I got near, one said to me: 'Hi bud, who's the good sort?'

That did it. Out came the axe and I started to tear into them, lashing out recklessly, not caring who got it. As long as the axe found flesh, I was happy. As I attacked, they were trying to escape from me. I just kept on attacking. The guy with me was also attacking them with whatever he could get his hands on at that time.

I came to my senses and started to worry about my wife.

I saw her standing near the top of the stairs waiting to try and get down and out of the joint. She had a look of terror on her face—she had never seen this side of me. I went over and grabbed her arm: 'Get out of here, now.'

She was screaming: 'How can I?'

She pointed to this black guy crawling back up the stairs where my mate had knocked him. She was frightened to pass him. I soon fixed that. As he reached the top of the stairs I gave him a backhander across the head with the axe. That fixed it, and my wife got out of the place as quick as her little legs would carry her.

We decided that the time had come for us to take our leave. Down the stairs we went and we managed to leave the area without any problems.

As I drove home, Debra was crying all the way. She kept saying: 'You're insane, Ned. I cannot believe that you are the same person that I have children to.' I wasn't very talkative. We managed to pick our kids up from the babysitter and off to bed I went.

The following morning I was up bright and early. I turned on the radio hoping that there wouldn't be anything about my stupidity on the news. There wasn't.

I tried to sweeten Debra up, but I had no luck.

'You're off your head,' she kept saying.

I decided to sell my grey Mercedes in case any of those guys saw it and told the police what car I was driving. (It wasn't registered in my name.) I took Debra and the kids along the Princes Highway looking for cars. I pulled up at a car yard where I saw a nice XJ6 Jaguar, about a 1974 model. I traded the Benz in, made up the balance in cash, and drove home in the new Jaguar. That didn't go in my name either.

Debra was still blueing about the fight.

'I will never, ever go to another disco with you as long as I live. And I don't ever want to see that side of you again.'

About a week had passed. I was at the Sheaf Hotel with Neville Biber, having a quiet day, when in walked these two low cops that I knew. [*Smith names the two police. For legal reasons their names have been edited out. For ease of reading we will call them Adam and Ben.*] I had done a few small things with them in the past. I didn't trust either of them or like them much. They came straight towards us.

Neville blew up: 'Go and annoy a child molester or something.' (Neville refused to pay police: 'Let the dogs earn their own like we do'.)

Adam was the spokesman. 'Neddy, can I see you outside, on your own?'

'No, you fucking can't,' said Biber.

I told Neville to be quiet. I walked outside with the two cops. Out in the beer garden we got a beer and sat down at a table.

Adam began: 'Neddy, you know why I am here, don't you?'

'No, I'm not certain I do. You tell me.'

'It's concerning the axe attack on several Aboriginal men at Hazy Land last Thursday night.'

I refused to say anything and let them continue talking.

'We get a regular drink [*a cash payment*] from there, you know that. We don't want shitmen like you causing problems for us.'

Ben started shouting: 'Who the fuck do you think you are, cunt?' (Nice guy to have around.)

Adam went on: 'This isn't the first time you've attacked people up there.'

Tough guy Ben was still raving on about nothing in particular.

I'd been there 10 minutes when my solicitor at the time, Frank Lawrence, walked over to us.

'Are you OK?'

'Sure.'

Adam said: 'Who are you?'

I told him: 'This is my lawyer.'

'Do you think that you require a lawyer?'

I told Frank to go inside. 'I'll be OK.'

By this time I knew they were not going to pinch me. They would have already done it if they intended to.

'Look fellows, what is it you want from me?'

Ben started to get up and leave: 'Fuck you, cunt.' (A real well-mannered guy, wasn't he?)

Adam looked around before telling me they wanted $10,000.

'No way!' I said. 'You'll have to settle for $4000. That's all I have. Take it or leave it.'

Adam finally said they would accept it. I saw Neville to borrow the money from him. At first he wouldn't give it to me.

'You're not paying those fools.'

After I explained what I was in bother over, he gave me the money: 'Pay the fools before they change their minds.'

Adam and Ben took the money and told me I was never to go anywhere near Hazy Land again. They did me a favor barring me.

Thank Christ for corruption. I couldn't have survived without it, and nor could the majority of crims that earned their living the hard way. That night I got home and told Debra what had transpired.

'Serves you right,' she said. 'Now maybe you'll stay away from low places like that.'

7
Educating Neddy

'Stick with me lad, and together we'll go a long way.'

Bill Sinclair

By 1977, I was making even bigger money, and things only got better when Bill Sinclair came into my life.

I first saw Bill at the Lord Dudley Hotel in Woollahra. He was arguing with Kenny and Murray Riley over money. I walked over and Murray introduced us. Apparently Kenny had short-changed Murray and Bill by about $40,000 each. (Wow! There had to be plenty more where that came from—I sensed an opening for a smart lad.)

By this time I had quite a few connections, some stolen from Kenny and Murray, others I got myself. I had always harbored thoughts of breaking away from Kenny and Murray and making a go of it on my own. It went without saying, Kenny wasn't to be trusted. Plus I could see the writing on the wall as plain as I could see my nose. Kenny and Murray wanted the world, they were always talking in telephone numbers.

We used to call Murray 'The Prince of Promises'. He used to come up with a new scam at least once a day. Maybe— and I mean maybe—one out of every hundred came to anything. In those days it was a rare treat if one came off, the reason being that he used to come up with the idea, then leave all the planning and work to Kenny. Moreover, Kenny was into snorting coke and his brain wasn't functioning properly.

Kenny and Murray left the pub, still blueing about the money. I stayed and talked to Bill. We seemed to get along all right, so Bill suggested we should meet again without the other two knowing.

Bill was obviously well connected. He had plenty of money, he had style and class, he seemed to know what life was all about. I thought: here is another opening for a smart lad—take it!

Bill puzzled me a bit at first. I kept wondering why he wanted to mix with criminals like me. He had everything that he could possibly want out of life, so why do it?

Before long, we teamed up and attempted to give Kenny and Murray a wide berth.

Bill was, as I thought, very well connected. He had people more or less working for him in most countries around the world. He was also friendly with several members of the New South Wales Parliament. Bill sort of took me under his wing. He wanted to, as he put it, educate me to the finer things in life. 'Stick with me, lad, and together we will go a long way,' was his favourite line with me.

It was about a fortnight after I teamed up with Bill that six of us—the guys from Double Bay—decided to see *Rocky*, a new movie that was receiving plenty of publicity. It starred Sylvester Stallone as a tough, street-smart boxer on his way up. Everyone was raving about it. We went to the afternoon session. It was a Monday, I know, because it was settling day. The movie turned out to be a top show; it had everyone hyped up. I think it was the music that did it. I know the music got my adrenalin pumping.

After the movie we all retired to The Oak for a few quiet ones. Everyone was in a good mood and having a good time. A few guys went on to the Golden Sheaf; I stayed a while longer for the settling at 6pm. Neville Biber stayed with me. Settling out of the way, we went to the Sheaf to catch up with the others.

When I arrived, everyone was yahooing and having a good time—so I joined them.

The place was starting to pack out—Monday was always a big night at the Sheaf. We always congregated in the corner near the juke box and they kept playing the theme from *Rocky*. Now and then we got a little out of hand playing up, but we never bothered anyone else. We always kept it among our own group.

Kenny was there with his girl. He was out of his head on

coke and the drink wasn't helping any. The boys started to play up a bit, still continuously playing the *Rocky* theme. This friend of mine, a television journalist named Grant, decided to hop up on to the bar and then dive off into my arms. I was supposed to catch him. The only thing was that he forgot to tell me. I was standing watching Grant, not knowing what he was about to do, when all of a sudden he dived off the bar straight at me. I tried to catch him but had no luck. We both ended up on the floor, but not before we managed to knock over a few guys' drinks.

It was all done in good fun, so we got up from the floor laughing and went over to the three guys that lost their drinks and offered to buy them a new round. We were in the wrong, so we thought: 'Why not buy them a drink?'

The three guys were only average-sized guys, but they had huge mouths. Straight off they started to abuse me. 'You fool,' one of them said. I tried to tell them we were only having a bit of fun, but no matter what I said they wouldn't have a bar of it.

The theme from *Rocky* was playing in the background and these guys were getting aggressive. Maybe it was the music, I don't know. Anyway, one of them decided to take a swing at me. Silly move.

I was all hyped up with the drink and the music. I was also as fit as a Mallee bull at that time. He missed but I didn't. The first guy went down and out. I didn't give the second one a chance, I hit him flush on the jaw before he could make up his mind what to do. Down went number two for the count. The third one backed out of range so I chased him a few steps and stepped into him as well. He wanted no part of it. Bad luck, he was with the other two so down, but not out, went number three.

The manager, Peter Ryan, came over.

'Ned, I saw that. You weren't to blame. If you had been I would have barred you for life.' Then he escorted the three guys out of the pub.

That shook a few people up, so they drifted off. Not us.

We all went upstairs to Julie's Bar where it was a 12 o'clock finish. Kenny started to play up. Standing at the bar was this guy and he wasn't one bit impressed with Kenny. He called Kenny a loudmouth.

'Who is he, Ken?' I asked.

'That's [*we will just call him Joe Bloggs*]. He's a karate champion, just won some sort of world title.'

We continued to drink. Bloggs and Kenny were glaring at each other. I could see that it was a special to be on any minute. The guy told Kenny to get outside. Them's fighting words. Well, out they went to the landing at the top of the stairs. Kenny was shooting off his mouth instead of cutting straight into the guy. Big mistake. The guy put Kenny on his arse with a single blow. I never saw the punch—it was too quick. Then this guy turned to face me. He was probably going to ask me if I wanted to do anything about it. No way, Bud. I don't give starts. Before he got a word out, I hit him flush on the jaw with a left hook. He went down, but not quite out.

There was no way I was going to let this bloke get off the floor. No way. I kicked him in the head a few times and, just to make sure that he wasn't getting up, I ripped the red phone off the wall and smashed it over his head a few times. Full of money, it weighed a ton.

While I was bashing Bloggs about the head, the girl who ran the bar, Julie, tried to drag him out of harm's way. Well, I was not having any of that. I took hold his legs and started to kick him in the balls. There was no way I was going to even consider letting this guy off the floor. I was not silly! That put a scare into all those drinking there, so they left and the place was closed for the night. I went home to sleep it off.

[*Two days later Smith was arrested and charged with assault occasioning actual bodily harm. According to Smith, when Bill Sinclair discovered that Neddy was under arrest he contacted a senior policeman to ensure Smith was granted bail. He was. Smith was released with a $2000 surety. His bail conditions included not being allowed in Sydney's eastern suburbs under any circumstances. Hours after being released, Sinclair told Smith that he would see a very high-ranking policeman to see what could be done about Ned's 'problem'.*]

Bill Sinclair and I became very good friends over the next two years. We made a lot of money together and I was fortunate enough to travel overseas with him and meet many influential people.

Over the first few months, Bill rang me every morning

and I usually met him in town. We would have a bite of
lunch somewhere and discuss some business deal or other
that he had taken on. He was forever introducing me to
people he thought I should know—people that 'had something to offer', as he used to say.

In the two years I travelled with Bill I learned so many
things. They may sound silly to some of you, but to me, the
things I learned were invaluable. Bill taught me how to order
wines at restaurants without making a fool of myself, like
so many people do. He taught me how to conduct myself
in company. It all sounds silly, I know, but to me, a boy
straight out of the slums, it was something else. Just the fact
that he took the time to show that sort of interest was
enough for me.

We saw very little of Kenny and Murray. We were all
doing our own thing and going a thousand times better. And
the money was coming in faster than ever before.

I had the job of looking after the money that we made,
splitting it up equally and then sharing it out among those
who had earned it—in other words paying wages to people
that worked with us or for us.

Bill's favorite place was the Tattersall's Club in Pitt Street
in the city. He knew everyone there and would introduce
me to them. He had me wearing suits all the time, day and
night. I would usually take Bill's share of the money to him
at the Tatts, and sometimes it was a large amount. One
morning he asked me to drop the money off at his home
and then drive him into town.

I explained about my reporting conditions—that I couldn't
enter the eastern suburbs. He blew up.

'Meet me at Waverley police station at 11am sharp. Wear
a nice conservative suit.'

I arrived on time and Bill was waiting. He was wearing
a grey silk suit, and looked great. 'Come on, lad, we have
to see some people about this ridiculous ban on you.'

He walked me into the police station and straight into
the detectives' office. I had no idea what he was up to or
who we were supposed to be seeing. We walked in and sat
down with [*Smith names two policemen*]. Bill explained that
he needed me to enter the eastern suburbs and accompany
him on business trips, so I could look after his interests.
They agreed that the ban would be lifted and that I could

travel as I pleased. We took them both to lunch to show our appreciation. Not surprisingly, I paid. Bill must have had a snake in his kick because he never once paid a bill in the two years I spent with him.

At lunch, Bill had another surprise for me. He had fixed it up with [*one of the policeman*] for me to beat the assault charge for the princely sum of $12,000. Great.

[*When the case came to court, two key witnesses against Smith were not called to give evidence. The case was then dismissed by the magistrate due to a lack of evidence.*]

At the beginning of 1977, Debra's grandmother passed away. She was a lovely old lady and she idolised Debra and our kids. She left Debra some money, so we decided to start house-hunting. I was going well and we could afford the monthly repayments on a loan, so we started looking around for a little home to call our own.

After much looking we decided on a small house at Sydenham, a southern suburb. It was a great little three-bedroom house, just what we wanted. Debra arranged to pay the deposit. We put the house in both our names, only because we intended to get married soon. It was Debra's money that bought the house. I arranged the finance, a loan of $17,000 from a building society in Leichhardt. The full price of the house was $27,000. [*Although it is hard to estimate, and Smith is coy about his earnings, it is probable that by the end of 1977 and through 1978 Smith was earning more each week than the total cost of his first house.*]

We had two beautiful children and our own home. We were very happy and content. I had never expected to get this far in life. I had expected to go back to the nick. Things were definitely looking up for the kid from the slums of Redfern.

I was established in the SP business. I had several in hotels all over the city, but my main SP was done over the phone with cash punters. Bill provided me with lots of big cash punters who helped build up the business. Tony Eustace was also involved in the SP business and I used to lay off any bets that I couldn't handle with him. I was also selling a lot of heroin. My wife knew nothing about this side of my life and, right up until very recently indeed, she had no idea that I was involved with heroin. She was always of the opinion that I was only involved in SP betting.

The money was coming in too fast and in such large amounts that I had problems finding places to put it. I couldn't bank too much without raising suspicion at the bank—the same applied to building societies. Every two weeks I divided the money, giving Bill his and paying the others. Then I had to hide mine somewhere. I used to hide it at friends' places and in the safes of several pubs I drank at. But it wasn't easy. I can just read the minds of some of the smarties out there: 'I'd soon know what to do with it if I had it!' I just bet you would, too.

At the time, my main concern was to *make* money; I didn't give enough time to working out what to do with it once I had it. I lost a huge amount of my money because I didn't know what to do with it. Corrupt police finished up with a lot of it. Bill kept telling me that he would help me invest it, but he was always too bloody busy with sheilas overseas to put his mind to it.

How much is enough? I asked myself that question time and time again. I would settle on a figure that I was going to stop at, then go past it and tell myself: 'Just one more go.' It was always the same. I remember one day, a bit later, lying in bed and thinking to myself: 'How much would make me throw the towel in on crime?' After thinking for hours I decided that if I could get maybe $100,000 in one lump sum, on top of what I already had, then I would quit. (That was a lot of money in those days. It's nothing today.) I was making much more than that as it was, but I had never received one large payment. My first big earn passed that figure by a long way. But I kept going.

One morning, as I was giving Bill a lift into town, he suggested that it was time I made my first trip overseas with him. 'Would you like to mix a little business with some pleasure and come to Hong Kong with me?' I jumped at the chance. I had hardly been out of Sydney before. Here was the chance of a lifetime right in front of me! I told him I would go.

Bill had a travel agency called Wings Travel. He put me down with his company as one of the directors and arranged for me to travel first class for nearly nothing, just because I was attached to his company. The same concessions applied to hotels, too. I got a 70 per cent discount wherever I stayed.

After Bill made all the arrangements for me, he went

himself, early. His wife and daughter were already over there waiting for him. I had to meet him there the following week. When I flew out I had no problems at all. I travelled first class everywhere I went and also got the very best treatment at the hotels I stayed at.

My first trip out of Australia had to be on a false passport as I was still on parole and not supposed to leave the country. As it turned out, the precautions I took were unnecessary as no one noticed that I was gone. I thought that I had better play it safe and flew out from Melbourne. That was silly because the plane I took stopped over in Sydney anyway. I had expected all sorts of complications leaving the country but there were none.

This was my first time on a plane and I was terrified. For the whole trip to Singapore I never left my seat or undid my seat belt. I was too scared to even eat in case I wanted to go to the toilet. I suspect that the air hostess noticed, as she talked to me all the time, trying to calm me down.

Since that first flight I have travelled extensively, but I haven't been able to overcome my fear of flying. I am still terrified. I believe the reason is simply because I have no control over the plane—and I don't understand enough about flying.

I made an overnight stop in Singapore. When I got off the plane I was lost, with no idea what to do. I was standing there, looking like a spare dick on a honeymoon, when I heard my 'name' over the intercom: 'Mr Douglas Richmond, please come to the information desk.'

Over I went to the desk marked Information. They informed me that a reservation had been made and a car was waiting to drive me to the hotel. (Bill had anticipated my stupidity and arranged everything.) I spent the night in a five-star hotel and, the following morning, went back to the airport to continue my journey.

I arrived at Hong Kong at 4pm. Customs took advantage of my lack of knowledge about how to fill out the entry permits, and made me repeat the procedure several times before allowing me through. This time I knew what to do. I headed straight to the information desk to see if there were any messages. Instead, Bill was there waiting for me. 'Hello, Douglas,' he said.

He escorted me to a white Rolls Royce that was waiting

to take us to the hotel. On arrival at the Hong Kong Hilton we were greeted by Philip Paxton, the hotel manager. Again I got the royal treatment. If Bill was trying to impress me, then he was doing a great job. Bill told me to relax before changing for dinner at 8pm. 'Wear a nice suit, lad, we are eating with Philip.'

I spent a very active two weeks in Hong Kong with Bill and his family. There was never a dull moment. My days were taken up with meeting all sorts of people. At night, we usually went to a new restaurant and finished at some club or other. I was having a ball. I was invited to Bill's friends' homes for dinner. I met judges, prosecutors, police heads, the lot. Bill knew everyone who was worth knowing. All the time I was waiting for Bill to tell me the real reason for bringing me to Hong Kong. It never happened.

After two weeks, Bill told me that we were off to Manila. 'Better get your bags packed, lad, we're off tomorrow.' When we left, Philip Paxton said there would be no bill for our stay.

As we flew to Manila, Bill filled me in on the city and the lifestyle. He kept telling me about the women there, and how easy it was to get them. I was not really interested at that moment—I had the worry of being on a plane 30,000 feet up in the air.

When we arrived, we were met by a general or something similar. He took us to a Mercedes and had us driven to the Sheraton Hotel in Manila. Once more we were met by the manager—Arthur Lopez was another friend of Bill's. It was the same procedure as Hong Kong, five-star treatment. But there was one distinct difference here: the hotel had guards armed with machine guns on every floor. It was straight out of the movies. It was New Year's Eve, 1977.

Bill was in a hurry to show me the town, or so he said. It was boiling hot so we put on casual gear and went to look around. First stop was a small bar called the Yellow Brick Road. In we went. Said Bill: 'I know the mama san here, lad, it's sweet.' By now it was late in the afternoon and the place was packed with girls. I had never seen so many girls on their own before. Bill was making the rounds, kissing and hugging all of them like old friends, acting like he was 18 when he was over 60. Shit! We ended up staying in that bar all night because a curfew had been imposed.

Being there for the night we made ourselves comfortable. A good time was had by all.

The stay at Manila turned out to be very little like Hong Kong. I met plenty of people here, too, but they were different types. People like Tony Moynihan, or Lord Moynihan as he was called by the media, who was wanted by the law in most western countries for some crime or other. [*Lord Anthony Patrick Andrew Cairnes Berkeley Moynihan of Leeds, a British peer, made the Philippines his home in the 1960s and stayed there until his death in November 1991. He was suspected of drug trafficking and involvement in organised prostitution rackets.*] He couldn't leave Manila without the risk of being taken back to England to face charges. He was friendly with President Marcos and his wife—they were in business together. One night when I was having dinner with Marcos the Australian Federal Police managed to get a photo of us all having a mad time.

There were several Australians living permanently in Manila. Most owned bars and were content with their lot—so they stayed. Money could buy you anything at all. You could have someone killed for practically nothing. After a week of fucking and drinking, Bill said: 'We are off again, lad.' This time Bill was taking me to the drug capital of the world—Bangkok. It was then and there I knew Bill would come to the reason for bringing me.

We caught an early flight and arrived in a matter of hours. This time there was no car to meet us. We took a cab to the Dusit Thani Hotel, right in the centre of Bangkok. Bill did not have any clout in Bangkok. I noticed him slipping one of the guards a few quid—and we ended up with the best suite in the hotel.

Bangkok frightened me. There were armed guards everywhere you looked; you could see there was plenty of tension everywhere. This was to be the first of many trips I made to Bangkok. I didn't mind the place except for the poverty. It could even be called exciting because of the danger, I suppose. I met so many different people there, from all walks of life. I met the Triads through Bill, but I later found out that they didn't trust him too much.

Also I met Warren Fellows for the first time. [*A former Sydney hairdresser, Fellows had links to the Bangkok-based Thai-Chinese suppliers of heroin and could arrange for huge amounts of the drug to be supplied. He was also a heroin user.*] Bill made sure that Warren and I didn't get on too well that trip. He kept us apart for obvious reasons. I never knew that Warren was into the gear; he didn't look like a junkie.

I was really pleased to be home in my own country. It is without doubt the best country in the world. (It may not be run very well or have the best government, but it is still the best country in the world.) I was so happy to be home with my wife and kids; the house in Sydenham was ready to move into and all I had to do was to have the security installed. I had it fixed straight away as I felt safer with plenty of security. That way I wouldn't get any unexpected surprises from unwanted guests.

I was at it all day, every day—no rest for the wicked. Bill did sweet fuck-all when it came to the business side. But I preferred it that way. I liked to do things my own way with no interference.

Business was booming, I had plenty of connections now, I didn't have to go looking for them any more—they came to me. I got to know Warren better and we ended up quite good friends. He was a mad punter and I let him bet with me. (I wasn't doing him any favors.) Warren had an interesting background: he had travelled all over the world on many occasions and knew his way around. He was married and had a little boy. We used to go out socially all the time. Little did I know that his wife was a heroin addict. A man must have walked round with his eyes shut not to have known. His wife, Janet, used to always be wanting to leave early and her hands were bandaged up all the time. Heroin addiction never occurred to me as far as she went—I just didn't think of it.

I first met Dave Kelleher in Parramatta Jail while I was completing my 12-year sentence. We weren't friends then. One Friday night in 1977 we met at a nightclub called the Cooperidge at Camperdown. Dave was there with his mate, [*who we will call*] Randy Tofani. Dave was a big, young, fit guy who wasn't frightned to get out and earn his own. He didn't rely on anyone else to get his money for him. That's why we got on so well.

We soon became good friends. We shared the same

Thank Christ for corruption – without it, I would have been staring at granite walls at this stage, instead of wearing gold jewellery and silk shirts to Murray Riley's wedding, and rolling in money.

Left: Me aged seven or eight, with that awful old bat, my grandmother, hovering around behind me.

Below: At the beach at Etalong *from left:* me, Mum and brother Patty, brother Edwin, sister Maria and the old bat.

Above: The 1B class of George Street Primary School. I'm second from the left, top row.

Left: I'm not going to bullshit anybody that I became a criminal because I had an awful childhood, but it wasn't easy. Mum visiting me at Mittagong Boys' Home. That Home was the safest, most secure, most humane place I knew.

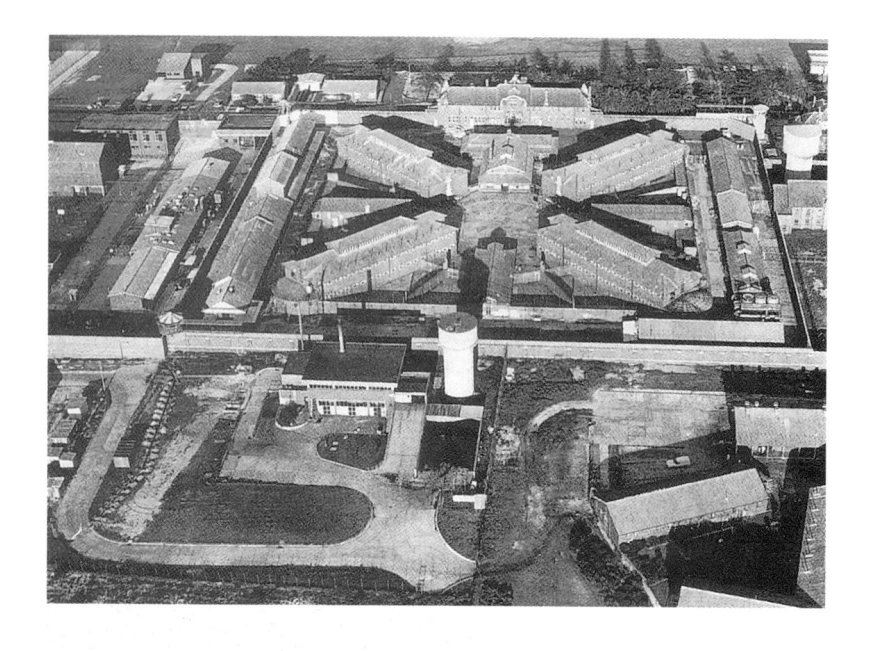

Top: Long Bay, home sweet home.
Above: Grafton. Part of the workshop block. Intractables even *worked* behind bars.

The best deal I ever did took place on 7 February 1980 at Long Bay Remand Centre. I married Debra Joy Bell. The late Neville Biber was the best man.

Below: A night out at Les Girls.
From Left: Debra, me, Bob (Chappo) Chapman and his de facto wife Sue. Chappo and wife Gail were my accomplices in the Fielder's Bakery job, a botch from start to finish.

I had a son, Anthony Kelly, from a previous relationship. We're pictured together at the Remand Centre, Long Bay Jail, when I was awaiting sentencing on the murder charge.

Family visit, Long Bay Remand Centre. *From left:* Me, Jaime and Daniel, Debra and Darrin.

Graham (Abo) Henry and me relaxing at his place down the coast. Tough, reliable, he's a good bloke to have around. Like me he's overly fond of a fight when he's been drinking and we got ourselves into some damn silly stinks that drained our time and money in fixing and bribes.

Murray Riley and me. We called him the 'Prince of Promises' as he had a new money making scheme every hour. But I liked him and still do. Ex NSW policeman Commonwealth Games rower, drug dealer, conman, Murray Stewart, as he has called himself of late, was last heard of as missing from a British jail where he had been sentenced to five years for an attempt to defraud British Aerospace Corporation of 50 million pounds.

Above: left: Roger Rogerson in the days when he was a rising star in the force.

Above top: Warren Lanfranchi. I set him up in business, he was making $10,000 a week but the money wasn't coming in fast enough for Warren

Above: Dave Kelleher and I were arrested for conspiring to supply heroin but were acquitted when the evidence went missing.

Left: Sally-Anne Huckstepp was a prostitute, a junkie, a federal and NSW police informer and Warren Lanfranchi's lover. She secretly taped her conversations with police.

interests: women, money and good clothes. What more could you want? We worked together for a long time and had many good times. Dave and I bought E-type Jaguars together. Dave had a convertible and I got a hard top. We weren't half posers in them. We drove everywhere just to pose. Dave, unlike me, came from a wealthy family so he knew how to handle his money and didn't like to waste it. He was a very smart boy in a lot of ways. His only real problem was his huge oversized ego. He had the biggest ego of any man I knew.

There was an article about Dave and me in *Playboy* and the author called Dave a 'blond God'. He must have been camp or something to write that. Anyway, Dave started calling himself 'the blond God'. After reading what that particular journalist said about us, I was never to believe another thing I read anywhere. There was so much crap that if my name hadn't been there in the article for me to see, I would never have guessed that he was talking about me.

I went overseas with Dave and had the best time of my life. He had travelled a lot before and knew his way around.

Another friend who had just come out of jail was Billy McLain, who'd run the SP for me at Parramatta Jail when I began working at the jail's clinic. He had served seven years for murder. Billy was a close friend of mine from childhood and I put him to work on the SP collecting the money from all the books.

While I was in jail a couple of years later facing drug charges, Billy came to my home every week and, even though she didn't need money, he would give Debra $300 every week without fail. (What he didn't know was that Debra used to give the money back to his girl.) He would spend his whole weekend taking my wife and kids out everywhere they wanted to go. Nothing was too much trouble for him. I loved the guy.

Billy was also the most violent man I knew. He was quiet, but when he was put out he was a lunatic. He was, as he described himself, a soldier not a thinker. He had no false illusions about his ability. It's a pity that there aren't a few more that know their capabilities better. I tried my best to leg him up into the business, but he wanted to do his own thing and just be with his girl and their child. I finally got him to work the SP for me, collecting all the cash on the weekend. He used to get his girl to drive him around collecting because he couldn't drive himself.

When I was eventually released from the nick, Billy came to see me: 'Mate, I have had enough of this life. If you don't need me I will split.' He went to live in a caravan with his girl and kid until he shot himself.

While I associated with Bill Sinclair I didn't get into one bit of trouble. He made sure that I was kept too busy to get into any bother. I continued doing what I was doing [*dealing in heroin, running an SP bookmaking operation and debt collecting*].

Bill asked me to go overseas again, this time straight to Bangkok. It was business again, so I went, but I wasn't too happy about it as I was fully aware of what was going on and I realised just how dangerous it could get.

We bought into a television program called *The Magic Wok*, a Chinese cooking show. Bill got the manager of the Hilton, Philip Paxton, to be the cook on the show as he was really a chef by trade. It ended up making it very big all over the world, but we made nothing out of it as we got out of it before it hit the big time. There were lots of perks that went with the program though, such as free first class travel anywhere in the world from Singapore Airlines, because they sponsored the show. The Hilton Hotel sponsored us too, which meant free accommodation.

Bill used to come up with dozens of legitimate business propositions, which was why I couldn't work out why he wanted to be involved in dope. I once asked him why he wanted to get involved with the shit and the low people that were involved with it. 'Money, lad. Plenty of black money,' he replied.

Another time we were in Hong Kong doing something or other when Bill told me that he had seen Murray Riley there that day. Old Bill was very cagey and I guessed that he was up to something with that team again, so I decided to watch him closely.

At breakfast one morning Bill came out with this scam. 'Lad, I have an interesting deal to discuss with you.' All we had to do was to put up $100,000 for Murray and we would get a one-third share of a shipload of Thai Buddha sticks [*marijuana flower heads wound around sticks*] that Murray already had on their way to Australia.

'No, thank you, Bill.'

Bill was adamant. He wanted a share, right or wrong.

I asked him who else knew about the scam.

'Only Kenny,' he said. That meant that [*Kenny's police contact*] knew, so half of Sydney would know, too. No thanks! We argued for hours. Finally, I talked him out of the idea. Lucky I did, as the lot were arrested over the scam. Kenny gave them all up; he even gave Murray up to save his own skin.

My last visit to Bangkok was with Dave Kelleher. We wanted to do some shopping in Hong Kong and decided to stop off in Bangkok on the way and take Bill some more money. Bill had asked me to get some cash to him because he was intent on purchasing a bar there. Bill had remarried in Bangkok— he was already married in Australia, but that didn't seem to bother him.

He rang me and asked for $100,000 so that he could buy the Texan Bar. It was a very profitable bar, right in the guts of Patpong Road, worth more than $100,000 any day. Bill had made up his mind that he was going to stay in Bangkok for good. He had bought a home unit and married a Thai woman. He was going to settle permanently.

I wanted Bill to return to Australia. He had several business ventures still here and without him we would lose money. Bill and I were arguing all the time. He would ring me from Bangkok every day. I was forced to change my phone number as he would ring drunk and say stupid things on the phone. When he got excited he would just say the first thing that came into his mind—I had to be careful.

I knew his son, Greg. He was a real gentleman and we got on well whenever we met. He used to run around Double Bay when he lived in Sydney. He went through university, then became a half-owner in a popular Brisbane restaurant.

I went to Surfers Paradise with Dave Kelleher, and while we were there we went to his restaurant regularly. During our stay, Greg took us out shooting. Greg was a gun buff like me. He had a really top collection of handguns and fully automatic weapons for us to try out. We had a ball. While there, I approached Greg about his father. He didn't know about Bill being married again. As far as he knew, his mother and his father were still married.

I explained to Greg that his father was planning to make

Bangkok his permanent home. Greg was upset about that. I could see Bill getting into a lot of trouble if he stayed in Bangkok much longer. He used to get loaded and shoot his mouth off to anyone that would listen. I asked Greg to go to Bangkok and have a talk to his dad: 'Try to persuade him to come back to Australia, mate.'

Soon afterwards, Dave and I flew to Bangkok, only intending to stay a short time; we wanted to go to Hong Kong. It turned out to be a much shorter stay than planned. We arrived late in the afternoon and booked into the Dusit Thani Hotel. I rang Bill and told him to come and see me. I had his $100,000 and didn't fancy hanging on to it.

Bill promptly arrived to collect his money. With him was his new bride. Straight away I took an instant dislike to her—greed was written all over her face, and she had a very slutty look about her.

For a pleasant change, Bill was polite. He asked me what I thought of his new bride. I kept my thoughts to myself. Dave had the connecting room to mine. I told Bill that I wanted to talk to him alone. He complained at first, but I told him he could trust whoever he liked with his freedom, but not with mine. He told his wife to go and wait in Dave's room. With her out of the way I gave Bill the $100,000 that I had brought for him.

'Bill, you are too dangerous, talking on the phone all the time. Pull up or I will have to drop off you for good.'

He started to rant and rave. I just ignored him completely. I still had a huge amount of his cash in Australia. I blew up and told him that our business relationship was over; I had had enough of his shit.

'What do you want me to do with the balance of the money I am holding for you?' I asked. He could see that I was serious and that he had gone too far this time.

'Come on, lad, we've been through a lot together. Let's cool down and discuss it sensibly.' But I had made my decision and I refused to change my mind. Bill invited Dave and I to meet him for lunch the following day at the Texan Bar.

We opened the door to Dave's room and caught Bill's new wife trying to get Dave into the cot. Well, Bill and her got into it hammer and tongs, nothing barred. It was real funny to watch them. I finally quietened them down and got them out of the hotel and into a cab. With them out of the way we decided to visit the Texan Bar for a look around. There were plenty of girls there when we arrived. We had a few drinks and then in walked Bill, drunker than ten men. Bill was all over me like a rash, talking shit till he couldn't talk. I just humored him till he went. Dave and I stayed on and had a real ball.

The next day we arrived at the Texan Bar as arranged. Bill took us shopping; he knew the best places and by now he spoke the language fluently, which came in handy when it came to bargaining.

We agreed to meet at the bar for lunch. When we got there, Bill was drinking with another Australian guy. He called Dave and I over to meet the guy and introduced him to us: 'This is Frank Davies, he is with the Australian consulate. He is a good friend of mine.' We shook hands and had one or two drinks.

We didn't have a lot to say to Bill's new friend. Dave must have had the same thoughts about him as I did; we were looking at each other all the time. Bill was full of brandy and talking too much shit for my liking.

'You are like my own son, Ned. You have the shits with me at the moment, but you will get over it.'

He called Frank over to us, then dropped a bombshell. In front of Frank he said: 'Ned, Frank is going to come in with us. He has agreed to smuggle heroin into Australia in the diplomatic pouch.' Dave and I nearly had a heart attack right there and then.

'You fucking old fool,' I start yelling at him. 'Fuck you, cunt, you're insane.'

Dave and I started to walk out of the bar.

'I want no part of that shit, Bill. You can have it all to yourself.'

Frank came over to talk to me. 'Listen, Ned, I am interested in having a chat with you about a few things. Can we talk?'

This guy had to be insane, too.

I told Frank that I had to call into the jewellery shop to pick up some gear that I had purchased. 'I'll be back in an hour, Frank. Sober Bill up and I will be back and I'll see you then. Then we will straighten out this mess.'

'Sure,' said Frank. He was sure he had us hooked.

Dave and I walked towards the shops and, as soon as we were out of Frank's sight, we caught a cab straight to the airport. We left our clothing behind and all. We were lucky that we had our passports with us. Straight on to a jet and we were on our way to Hong Kong, leaving Bill with his new friend.

On our arrival in Hong Kong, I phoned Bill and told him to pay our hotel bill and send our clothes to Australia.

'Bill, you fool. That Frank is a federal cop, stupid.'

Bill went off his head over the phone. 'You're mad Ned, I know Frank well.'

Bill sent our clothing back to Australia for us. But I was right. Frank, it turned out, was indeed a federal cop.

I had been in Hong Kong only two days when I got a message to ring home. I called Debra and she told me to ring Roger Rogerson urgently. I rang Roger and he said that my gun charge was due for mention the next day. 'What do you want me to do?'

'Don't worry about it, mate, I will fix it for you.'

I thought about it for some time, then decided to fly back. I couldn't take the chance of them putting a warrant out for me for failing to appear. I caught a Qantas flight back to Australia and arrived home just in time to go to court. I rang Roger to let him know I was back.

'I'll meet you for a cup of coffee before we go to court,' I said.

'Don't worry about it as I have already arranged for the matter to be put off until the next sittings. Get some rest and get hold of me tomorrow.'

I spent a very nice day at home with my family. Later the same day I rang [*Smith names a Sydney detective*]. I wanted to speak to him about Bill. I knew that they were friends and that he could talk to him. I met [*the detective*] at the pub. I tried to explain to him what sort of bother Bill was headed for mixing with people like Frank Davies. He understood and promised to talk to Bill before the end of the week.

I sent my half-brother Edwin over to Bangkok three times with money for Bill. When he came back the final time he told me that Bill was bagging me to the Triads and also to Warren. The Triads had no trust in Bill anyway, so I had no problems there. Warren was the only person that the Triads would discuss business with. Any time that Bill tried to discuss business with them, they politely changed the subject.

The Triads were very closely knit. It wasn't easy to get in their company. I tried unsuccessfully, many times. They always treated me great, but it was a no go when I talked any business. When Warren was arrested he gave one of the Triads up. The guy ended up beating the charges, but not before he spent over a year in jail.

About that same time, Murray Riley and his gang were all rounded up over the importation of millions of dollars worth of Thai Buddha sticks. The Australian Federal Police had had them under surveillance for the entire time they were doing the scam. Most of the gang was caught in the first swoop but not Murray and Kenny. They were lucky.

What happened was that they went to the ship with a truck and took off a load of the gear. They took it back to Sydney and sold it for $2 million without the rest of the gang knowing. They escaped the first swoop by robbing their friends. But they didn't stay out long. [*The policeman who Kenny worked for*] heard about it and told Kenny to hand himself up before they arrested him—that way he would get bail.

[*The police officer*] made a deal for Kenny to hand Murray up and he would get a light sentence when he eventually fronted court. Kenny told them where to pinch Murray, but Murray had been warned by the corrupt law clerk Brian Alexander. Alexander had a lot of cops sweet and one of them warned Murray. Murray didn't turn up for the meeting with Kenny—but they got Murray not too long after that.

Murray Riley's photograph was plastered all over the newspapers. He never had a chance of getting away. They eventually got him in Adelaide, and he was sentenced to 10 years for his part in masterminding the scam.

While Kenny was out on bail, he tried several times unsuccessfully to set me up for [*Smith names yet another Sydney detective*]. Kenny had got a deal: he would get only a short sentence if he set me up. However I was warned, and every time Kenny made a meeting with me, I dodged him. But the damage had been done: thanks to Kenny, police were now investigating me.

The BCI [*NSW Police bureau of crime intelligence*], run

by a policeman called Dunn, put me under 24-hour surveillance. I couldn't move an inch. I spotted them frequently following me. I took very little notice of them as I was assured that they would not load me [*plant evidence such as drugs*] by two friendly police.

[*One policeman*] told me that the Feds wanted Bill over the Buddha stick scam with Murray. He said: 'Tell Bill not to come back to Australia just yet, wait until I can arrange something for him. I can fix it, but not just yet.'

There was no way I was going to ring Bill, so instead I flew to Brisbane to see his son, Greg. I let Greg know all that [*the officer*] had told me concerning his father. Greg said he would fly to Bangkok and tell Bill face to face. Greg couldn't understand his father getting involved with Murray in such a stupid deal, especially when I had warned him. Bill kept on ringing me, but I wouldn't accept his calls. I couldn't be certain that Bill wouldn't say something stupid over the phone.

Bill ended up ringing [*a policeman*] and got him to ask me to contact him. I went to the GPO and rang Bill. I didn't talk for long.

'If you want to talk to me, Bill, then fly over to Hong Kong. I will ring you at 12 o'clock at a bar called Jimmy's Kitchen in Kowloon.' Bill knew the bar. He flew to Hong Kong and I rang him there. It turned into a shit fight between Bill and me. He said that I was suffering from paranoia and had to go to Bangkok and see him. I refused to be contacted by him again until I was told by my sources that it was safe to do so. Quite naturally, he wasn't too happy about that. He complained that he needed more money to complete negotiations over the bar and building expenses. Finally I agreed to send him the money he required within the week. I rang his son again and asked him to fly down to talk to me.

Greg arrived the next day. I told him I was in possession of a very large sum of his father's money. I told him about his father's suggestion that I send it to him in Bangkok. Greg was furious about the money and we decided to only send him half of it. I gave the other half to Greg to hang on to—I was bailing out of my partnership with Bill.

I got Paul Hayward [*a former star New South Wales rugby league player turned criminal*] to take the remainder of Bill's money to Bangkok. I paid Paul $30,000—out of Bill's money—for taking the cash across. Paul flew to Bangkok with Warren, who had come to see me, complaining that Bill had threatened him. Warren said he wanted to go to Bangkok to straighten things out with Bill: I told Warren that it was entirely up to him but, if he was going, he may as well go with Paul. So they flew out together.

Up until then I had been cruising along at a mad pace. I had everything imaginable, wanted for nothing. I owned my own home, drove a brand new Mercedes Benz, had a 35-foot cabin cruiser moored at Rose Bay. People had said I wouldn't reach 30. And here I was, the boy from the slums, sitting on top of the world. I had shown them all.

But it was a simple, silly thing that brought me undone—in this case Warren's stupidity. Without my knowledge, Warren rang and booked his and Paul's tickets to Bangkok using my phone, the fucking fool. I was aware police had been watching me and I knew that there were risks involved in the trade, but I had police looking after me so I wasn't really concerned.

But Warren's phone call was the break that the police watching me had been waiting for. Warren even used one of his false passports to book the tickets. Police immediately put Warren under 24-hour surveillance. They knew every move that Warren made from the time he left Australia.

8
The Bangkok Business

The Arthur Smith that Sinclair knew was a man associated with off-course, illegal bookmaking and illegal casinos. Rough and all that he was, he liked the fellow ... Sinclair had taken him on the trip through the East simply because he enjoyed his company.

> Kingdom of Illusions: the William Sinclair Story, 1982
> Richard Shears and Isobelle Gidley, a book containing
> Sinclair's views and recollections of events

[Smith's rise in the heroin trade was swift. From his introduction to drug dealing by Kenny in 1976, business boomed. At first, Smith handled heroin personally. But that didn't last long. He realised that to survive in the drug trade he needed to distance himself from the merchandise. By 1978, Smith was probably the biggest heroin dealer in Australia. It is believed that Smith received 15 kilograms of heroin about every six weeks from his suppliers: the drug importers. The 15 kilos would then be cut (diluted) to produce 45 pounds (20.4 kilograms), which would then be sold, in amounts no smaller than one pound—which then cost $30,000—to various drug dealers around the Double Bay area. This all came to a sudden end in October 1978.]

Five days after Warren Fellows used my phone to book his flights to Bangkok, all hell broke loose.

It started with a radio report, then the afternoon newspapers came out. The Sydney *Sun*'s front page headline screamed: LEAGUE STAR IN DRUG CHARGE.

[The story, on 12 October 1978, followed: 'Sydney Rugby League start Paul Hayward and two other Australians have been arrested and charged in Bangkok on drug charges involving an alleged $3 million (8.5 kilograms) of heroin. Thai law provides for death by firing squad for drug traffickers. The alternative is up to 40 years in a Thai jail. Hayward, and a Sydney travel consultant, Warren Edward

Fellows, were arrested by Thai narcotics agents in Bangkok as they prepared to leave their hotel. A third Australian, William Charles Sinclair, who operates a bar and travel agency in Bangkok, was arrested later . . .']

Early the next morning, several police rang me to tell me my home was under surveillance. They said I would more than likely be arrested. They refused to give any details over the phone; they'd taken a huge risk as it was, because they knew my phone was bugged.

I immediately got on the phone to find out what I could do. I knew my phone was off [*being bugged*], but there was no way I was leaving the protection of my fortress-like home. (There were strict rules about using telephones in my home. They stayed in force for the next 10 years, particularly for my children. I explained to them about bugged phones and always told them never to answer any questions about me or my whereabouts on the phone to anyone. They were very good with the phones and never spoke out of school.)

My Sydenham house had steel windows and doors, a 2.5-metre high brick wall, closed-circuit TV cameras and spotlights. I started ringing police I knew, trying to put something together to stop myself being loaded up or worse. All the cops I contacted told me I would not be loaded up by these police. 'Just act normally and you won't have any problems.' I did as I was told.

I am a compulsive gig [*someone who can't mind their own business*], so I went outside to see what I could see. I spotted a van with blacked-out windows across the street. I went to investigate and looked inside—there were two cops lying on the floor. I went back to the house smartly. Something big was going on here.

Visitors began arriving. First came Paul Hayward's wife; then Warren Fellows' wife arrived. They were both upset about their husbands being arrested. Billy McLain, who worked in my SP business, called in to see if I was OK. Other friends came, too—it was turning into quite a gathering. Things didn't look good so I phoned Edwin, my fool of a half-brother, and told him to see me straight away.

When he arrived I explained that I was going to be arrested over the Bangkok business. I advised him to remove any incriminating evidence from his house. I told him: 'Flush it down the toilet straight away.' I also gave him two guns and told him to dump them on his way home. Now the fool not only didn't dump the guns and the gear that he had, he hung them on his wall at home and put two pounds of pure heroin into the boot of his own car. Stupidity and greed got the better of him.

At about 11.30am, Tony Eustace [*friend, fellow heroin dealer and SP bookmaker*] phoned. 'Come and have some lunch, mate, I have that money I owe you.' I always enjoyed eating at the Four Seasons [*a restaurant in Redfern frequented by Eustace*], so I decided to go. Before leaving I called my solicitor and told him I might require his services later that day: 'Will you be available if I need you?'

'Certainly.' He said he would be waiting to hear from me.

Off I went to lunch with Tony. I owned a white Mercedes Benz, but not wanting to upset the police, I took an old car instead, just for appearances. As soon as I left home, I realised that I was being followed. Several hotted-up cars kept right behind me. I pulled up at a set of traffic lights and suddenly saw a man and woman get out of their car with guns in hand. That didn't make me happy at all, so I took off through the red light, with them hot in pursuit. It wasn't long before there were several cars after me. They soon cut me off and jumped out of their cars screaming, 'Get out of the car', 'Keep your hands where I can see them' and 'Spread your legs, now.'

I did as I was told. I tried to talk to them.

'What seems to be the problem here, officer?' The reply I got from New South Wales' finest was: 'Shut your fucking face, cunt.'

I was handcuffed and searched. The car was searched too. Nothing was found. I was then driven home, where my house was systematically searched for drugs. They found nothing at all. While this went on, several people who called to see us were taken into custody for no reason at all. That's our police for you, always looking after the public.

They wouldn't let me ring my solicitor. It turned 3 o'clock and my daughter Jaime needed to be picked up from nursery school, so police escorted my wife to pick her up. With Debra was a friend who also had to pick her children up from school. After she had met her children, police let her go. Before she left my house, I gave her my solicitor's number and asked her to ring him and ask for someone to help me straight away. This woman was terrified but did it for me, God love her.

Within an hour a lawyer arrived at my home. He was an ex-cop called Clive Sterne, who had become a barrister. The police made the mistake of thinking that he was still in the police force and let him in. Clive Sterne introduced himself to me and I immediately told him that neither my wife nor I had said a single word to any police officers.

By this time police had discovered some hidden money. One officer told me: 'You are being charged with being in possesion of $39,360 in cash believed to be stolen or from the proceeds of the sale of drugs, do you understand?' Debra and I both told him that we were guilty of no crime and had nothing further to say.

We were taken to the CIB, put into separate rooms and interviewed.

We were then taken to Central cells and kept separated until the following day. Roger Rogerson came to see us both early the next morning and arranged for us to see one another and fixed it so that Debra didn't have to go back in the cells. Debra was in a state of shock after her ordeal in those filthy cells.

The next morning at court, Debra got $4000 bail. Meanwhile I was refused bail and remanded to the Bay.

Before Debra was released, the cops grabbed her and put her back before the court and charged her with a further goods in custody of another $90,000-odd. Apparently police had searched my home again looking for more money but instead found a bank slip for a safety-deposit box in Debra's name. They got a warrant to open the box and then charged her with possessing $90,000-odd.

The media made a big thing out of my arrest, aided by crap that police furnished them with. Police said I was responsible for the three arrested in Bangkok, and claimed that I made them import the heroin.

Not long after my arrest, police searched my half-brother's house and discovered the two weapons I'd given him and several plastic bags containing heroin residue. Stupid Edwin had not listened to me when I told him to dump all the gear.

He was for it for sure, I thought. They would throw the book at him.

But somehow he avoided being arrested. I don't know

how he did it, because the fool was driving all over Sydney in a purple car with a boat on the back—and two pounds of pure heroin in the boot.

Police soon rounded him up and, after a search of his car, discovered the two pounds. The officer in charge of the case, Barry Dunn, was ecstatic. It was the single biggest find of the time. Edwin was taken back to police headquarters and set about making a dozen or more statements involving me in drugs. Most were pure lies.

Meanwhile, police went to Thailand to interview the Bangkok Trio. After they returned, I was visited in jail by a detective.

'Listen, Neddy, we have enough evidence to charge you and your wife with conspiracy to import heroin. Kelleher and [Greg] Sinclair will also be charged, but, for the right price, we might just leave Debra out of it. Can you afford to meet the bill?'

I was sick of their shit. 'Let's stop the games. You give me a price and I'll give you a yes or no.'

'$50,000. That covers Debra not being charged with anything.'

I agreed to pay. I didn't want Debra going through this shit. Then I got instructions where to deposit the $50,000.

'Get your wife to deliver the money to [Brian] Alexander's office tomorrow, OK?'

I rang Alexander from jail and warned him that he had better not fuck me around with this business.

'No sweat, buddy,' he said. 'It will be handled by me personally. You can believe me, mate. You haven't a worry in the world.'

I rang Debra and told her to deliver the money the next day to Alexander. It was a con to get my money, a straight-out con. Those dogs got me again.

[*About a week later, Smith, Debra, David Kelleher and Greg Sinclair (Bill Sinclair's son) were charged with consiracy to supply heroin. All except Neddy Smith were released on bail.*]

After I got back to jail I got in touch with that low-life, Brian Alexander. Before long he visited me. I said to him: 'Where is my $50,000, cunt?'

He took a few steps back. 'Calm down, it's all under control.'

I told him I wanted the money back or else I would have something done about it. He tried to con me again by saying that [*Smith names two police*] were looking after me. I told him to go fuck himself and to tell the others to do the same.

Alexander came to see me the following day. He said he had $25,000 to return to me, but that [*the two police*] were keeping the rest. He returned the $25,000 to my wife the next day.

[*Within days of being arrested in October 1978 over the Bangkok conspiracy, Smith's parole on the 1967 rape conviction was revoked. He now had to serve more than three years in unexpired time.*

Meanwhile, Smith was found guilty of goods in custody, the charge relating to the $39,360 found at his house. Said Smith: 'The money was confiscated but that didn't worry me too much as there was a lot more where that came from.'

When the heroin conspiracy charges came up for a committal hearing, they were dismissed against Debra and Greg Sinclair. Kelleher and Neddy Smith were sent to trial. For Neddy Smith, it all added up to more time behind bars.]

I spent 25 months in custody, mostly at the remand centre, even though I was effectively a sentenced prisoner.

I teamed up with Murray Riley and don't regret one second of the time that I spent in his company. He never tried to hide the fact that he was once a cop. A likeable rogue, as he liked to be called, Riley backed down to no one in jail and never walked away from anyone that had anything to say about him.

Murray had an enormous zest for life and a great sense of humor, and we had some funny times in jail.

We were at Central Court one day. In those days you could get a drink or a girl if you wanted one—if you had the money you could get anything at all. We had a few dollars so we decided to get a few dozen cans to liven the boredom up. We ended up blind drunk. The police put us in the wagon and sent us back to the Bay. When we arrived, we got out of the van only to be greeted by the governor, who was standing there to inspect the new prisoners.

Instead, he saw Murray and me blind drunk. One look at us and he said: 'What have you two been up to?' Murray walked over to him, kissed him on the cheek and started to dance with him. Then Murray started to sing (he was an awful singer). The governor had a good sense of humor and sent us to our cells to sleep it off. The next morning we were taken before the governor, who said: 'You're not a real good dancer Murray,' then burst out laughing. 'Get out of here, you clowns.' That was the end of that incident.

During my stay I had a much bigger cell than most others, with a private toilet to myself—a rare privilege, I might add. Other possessions I was allowed included a TV set, a radio, a fan and the biggest privilege of all: access to law books from the library.

I spent every spare moment reading law to try to get some sort of understanding of it. I don't profess to understand a lot of law, but I learnt enough to get me by.

While reading a law book one evening, I discovered what I thought was a loophole in the Parole Act. If I was correct, it meant I was not getting remissions that I was entitled to. I couldn't wait until daylight to ring [*Solicitor, Trevor*] Nyman. After ringing him, I awaited his visit, excited out of my skin.

As soon as he arrived I explained what I had found. At first he was not too enthusiastic, but after reading the precedent he agreed that the case was worth looking into.

'Chester Porter is the man you need for this one, he is the best.'

'Well, get him to have a look at it and let's see what he says.'

An anxious few days passed and Nyman got back to me.

'Porter says you have a certain winner here!'

'You fucking beauty!' I couldn't contain myself.

'Porter will undertake the case for you but he is very expensive.'

'Get him, regardless of the expense.'

Off went Nyman to engage Porter.

Porter was to tell me exactly how the case would go: 'Neddy, you will win the first case in front of one judge. The Crown will appeal, the Appeals Court will offer you a small amount of your remission back, then we go to the High Court and you're a free man. Can you afford that and are you willing to go to that much trouble?'

I certainly was.

Every single word Chester Porter told me came to pass. I took the prisons department to the High Court of Australia to force them to release me. The High Court ordered my immediate release with court costs (one for the baddies). As a result of the High Court decision, hundreds of other prisoners were released earlier than they normally would have been. One prisoner named Les Burr received eight years off his sentence after my decision and another called Pat James got seven years back.

I was granted bail on the charge of conspiracy to supply heroin and, after 25 months, I was finally back with my family. No one would ever take me away from them again. I swore to that. My wife had stuck to me through all the trouble and never complained once. She visited me every day and sat there with me for up to four hours each day. I can never repay her for her loyalty.

Edwin, my half-brother, told a lot of lies. He gave misleading evidence to the royal commission headed by Justice Woodward, who went on record saying that he believed it. The evidence Edwin gave was mostly crap, no one could believe a word of it. Not one of his allegations was ever substantiated or corroborated by a single person or fact.

A lot of people were caused a lot of trouble by his stupid lies. If he had told the truth he would have done all right. He got up in court on several occasions and accused me of everything from murder to smuggling drugs (though he was right about the smuggling bit).

My brother talked about alleged Mafia connections and hit men coming to my house to kill me. He claimed that I had millions of dollars at my home. He said I was the leader of an international drug syndicate. He also claimed that Greg Sinclair and I planned to kill Greg's father and take over this imaginary gang of drug smugglers. He said we put it off because someone in the Mafia told us to cool it. If it wasn't so serious it would have been funny.

He gave evidence of large amounts of heroin being imported into the country by myself and others, and the selling of large amounts of heroin. He tried to implicate people who had no involvement whatsoever. A lot of innocent people were put through hell, plus the expense of fronting the commission.

His best lie was to say that I told my mother I would kill her. My mother was in court to hear him and since that day she has never spoken to him.

All he did was to fuck my life effectively for two years and cost me a lot of money.

The media, too, helped make my life a misery with their untrue accounts of things I was supposed to have done.

This was my first experience of how our media worked. For example: one story that I have to clear up was about Dave Kelleher and myself. It was exaggerated out of all proportion.

Dave and I had been having a few drinks. Dave never used to drink a great deal. We ended up at a nightclub of sorts in Bondi. We were having a quiet drink by ourselves and Dave ordered some fondue. While we were eating, a team of Kiwis arrived and decided they were going to eat some of our food. One of them started to help himself, so Dave knocked him straight out. It was on for young and old, we were right into it. Dave and I just stood there knocking out fools everywhere. We barred no one. We must have knocked out about a dozen of them before the violence started. One of the guys tried to stab Dave with a fork. That was the end of being Mr Nice Guy. We started picking up anything we could get our hands on and we smashed everyone in sight over the head with it. Now the rumor went like this: we supposedly knocked out 30 men in one night. Even Ray Martin asked me about it when he interviewed me on TV. Just goes to show how shit gets exaggerated. There wouldn't be one person alive that could knock out 30 men, I don't care who he is.

Once I was released on bail, in October 1980, my main objective in life became beating the drug charge. I was desperate to beat it. It carried 10 years jail then. So I set out to discover the best way to go about achieving my goal. I left nothing to chance.

I got the very best lawyers that money could buy: Bruce Murphy QC, barrister Clive Sterne, and Trevor Nyman.

I sent a solicitor to Bangkok to see the 'Bangkok Trio'— Warren Fellows, Paul Hayward and Bill Sinclair. He managed to procure certain documents for me and also visit the three men. He got statements from them saying that I was not involved in the heroin importation. They said in their statements that [*a policeman*] had tried to get them to implicate me, but they wouldn't do it.

The solicitor also managed to obtain all of the evidence

concerning the arrests of the three in Bangkok, which gave me a good idea what the police had on me, if anything. It was apparent that money could get you anything in Bangkok—*anything*. These documents proved to be invaluable at my trial, I knew everything that the police had on me and what they could prove. Eventually, for a mere $4000, I was able to get my hands on the whole police brief [*details of the evidence to be used by the prosecution*]. That allowed me to know exactly what they had and what they were intending to produce in court.

That slimy law clerk Brian Alexander came to see me. He was acting for my brother and had a proposition for me. He wanted to sell me all the statements that Edwin had made about me, which he just happened to have in his possession.

'Are you interested in purchasing these papers?'

Corruption everywhere.

'Sure. Why not?'

I was learning fast. How does that song go? 'Money talks but it don't sing or dance and it don't walk.' Appropriate, eh?

I bought the material he had for sale and it came in very handy.

[*Brian Alexander was last seen on 22 December 1981. Days later his car was found at The Gap, a notorious suicide area at Watsons Bay, indicating that he had taken his own life. Alexander had financial problems at the time of his disappearance; he had also left his job after facing charges in a highly publicised court case over assisting the Mr Asia drug syndicate. Alexander was cleared of the charges, yet was then expected to be a witness before the Stewart Royal Commission and tell authorities about the activities of the Mr Asia syndicate.*

The suicide theory, however, was not accepted by Mr Justice Stewart, who noted that Alexander's friends and family said it would be out of character for Alexander to pursue a violent death: sleeping pills were more likely. Stewart noted that Alexander, whose body was never found, may also have been murdered, or may still be alive, having disappeared either voluntarily or under duress.

This is Neddy Smith's version of what happened to Alexander:]

At the time of the Woodward Royal Commission into drugs [*1977-79*] Alexander was running very hot collecting huge amounts of cash for the police and getting his share of it. He was the official bagman for [*three NSW police squads*].

A rumor got back to certain police that Alexander was talking to investigators from the [*Stewart Royal Commission (1981-83)*]. The rumor was that Alexander was going to be granted immunity from prosecution if he told all. Police discussed Alexander's future and decided to get rid of him before he implicated any of the police that he had done business for.

Alexander was invited for a drink with three police in the King's Head, a hotel situated next to his offices. He was last seen, very drunk, getting into a car with the three police. He hasn't been seen since.

Rumor has it that he was driven to the Darling Street wharf in Balmain, where he was picked up in a police boat. The boat went out through the heads then continued for about a mile or two offshore. I was told that Alexander was crying his eyes out as he fell off the back of the boat. He didn't float back to shore: with weights and an old stove tied around you, you don't wash back.

I got in touch with Roger Rogerson, who was serving in the hold-up squad. Through Roger I got in touch with [*Smith names a detective*]. I needed Roger to sort of guarantee me with [*the detective*]. Roger told him that I could be trusted 100 per cent. Over the years, my relationship with [*the detective*] turned into what I thought was a friendship—there was not a thing that he wouldn't do for me (admittedly he was well paid for it).

[*The detective*] told me that he and other police—meaning himself, [*Smith names two more police*]—for a price would take the two pounds of heroin that my half-brother was caught with from the exhibits safe, cut it maybe four times, and return the cut stuff to the safe for when I went up for trial. Sounded good to me. A price of $30,000 was agreed on. The dirty deed was done and the heroin tampered with. For $30,000 I'd hit the jackpot. I knew that without the heroin they would have a very weak case when it came to trial.

[*The detective*] advised me to get my lawyers to ask for

an independent analyst's report on the heroin before my trial started, which I did. This unusual request alerted police and they did another test. Bingo. Did they get a nice surprise when they received the result? The exhibit they were holding to produce at my trial had gone from 90 per cent pure heroin to less than 20 per cent pure.

At my trial in June 1981, the prosecution didn't mention anything about the missing heroin. Then my lawyers asked that an independent person check the heroin to make sure the police had the evidence they claimed they had.

The shit hit the fan.

The prosecutor and my lawyers went behind the scenes and discussed this new, startling development. It was decided that with my lying half-brother's evidence not being worth two bob, and now the heroin going missing, it may be best for both parties if the jury was instructed to go out and bring back a verdict of not guilty on all charges.

So Dave Kelleher and I were acquitted on all charges relating to any heroin. My half-brother Edwin, who had pleaded guilty to heroin charges, was sentenced to 10 years for his trouble. Right whack for him.

[*In 1981, the Bangkok Trio was convicted of heroin trafficking. Bill Sinclair was sentenced to 33 years and eight months jail, Warren Fellows to 33 years and eight months, and Paul Hayward to 20 years. In May 1982, a Thai appeals court overturned Sinclair's conviction and he was freed. Once back in Australia, Sinclair helped write* Kingdom of Illusions: the William Sinclair Story, *a detailed and passionate defence of his reputation and vehement protest against the charges that saw him spend three years and eight months in jail. Sinclair's acquittal was total, but an attempt to sue the newspaper publishers John Fairfax in 1986 failed: a Supreme Court jury found that John Fairfax had established that Sinclair was of 'such an unsavory character that no person of good standing should associate with him'. Fellows had his sentence cut by four months on appeal. Hayward did not appeal. In 1989, Hayward was released from jail and returned to Australia. Fellows followed in early 1990. In May 1992, Hayward died of a suspected drug overdose. At last report, Fellows was seriously ill with AIDS, contracted from drug use in a Thai jail.*]

9
The Green Light

Church people tend to be innocent in such matters, but working in East Sydney, you'd have to be Blind Freddie not to realise it [organised crime] was there. If you let this thing increase the ordinary citizen is in a dilemma—to whom can he turn if the gendarmerie is corrupt?

The Rev Bernard Judd, AO 1993

Debra Joy Bell and I were married on 7 February 1980 in the governor's office at Long Bay Jail. My best man was Neville Biber. I married Debra because I loved her. She was the best thing that had ever happened to me and I simply wanted to stay with her. We also had two children, Darrin and Jaime.

In October 1980, after winning my High Court case, I was released from jail. Debra had waited for me for two years. I had every intention of going straight after beating the drug charge. I thought I owed her that much.

I lasted maybe six months before the boredom got to me. I had a good time while it lasted, but inactivity got to me. I couldn't handle the quiet life any longer. I started looking up old acquaintances, among them Dave Kelleher. Dave had branched out on his own by this time, effectively having taken over the heroin business I'd been involved with when I was jailed in late 1978. We did the odd thing together, but mainly went our own ways. [*In 1983, Kelleher was arrested for the possession of heroin. He was acquitted, but only after having spent many months in prison on remand. In July 1985, in a joint NSW-Federal Police investigation, Kelleher was charged over the importation of three kilograms of heroin. He was found guilty and sentenced to life in jail.*]

Soon after my release, a young bloke who I'd met in Long Bay Jail in early 1980, Warren Lanfranchi, came to see me.

Lanfranchi had just been released himself and wanted to work for me, so I set him up in business. He was soon making in the vicinity of $10,000 every week. He loved it and never complained.

Warren and I were friends and business partners. He was a good kid, but he was born in the wrong time. He was more suited to the roaring twenties. Warren wanted everything he could get out of life. There was nothing wrong with that—his mistake was that he wanted it all too quickly. He didn't care how he got it, or who he had to hurt to get it.

One Saturday, Warren, Graham 'Abo' Henry and I were having a drink at the Broadway Hotel. It was Anzac Day and we were running the two-up there. [*There was a long-standing pub tradition of two-up on Anzac Day in Sydney being illegal, but tolerated. Playing the game on Anzac Day was finally legalised in 1989.*] All was well until Warren got into this stink with some guy. Warren flogged the guy badly. The next thing I knew, Warren was driving his motorbike through the pub. He ran over anyone that got in the way. Not to be outdone, Abo started bashing people with an aluminium baseball bat. He didn't care who he clobbered, either, he just lashed out regardless. Naturally, I was involved, too. I did my share of damage to the people and the pub itself. The fighting lasted about 20 minutes with Abo smashing everything in sight before the three of us left and went to the Forest Lodge Hotel in Glebe. We were only there a very short time when it was on again. It was a repeat of what had happened at the Broadway Hotel. The place was wrecked.

Those two little incidents were to cost us $12,000. Detective Sergeant John Openshaw, who I'd met before through Dave Kelleher, got in touch with me and said he wanted to see me. I met him at Eliza's restaurant in Double Bay.

'I have some bad news for you, Ned,' he greeted me. 'You are being fined for being stupid the other night. $12,000 should cover damages and look after us.' He also informed me that I was to attend a meeting with [*a senior policeman*] at a hotel in town called the King's Head. I was to meet him downstairs at 4 o'clock the following day.

I turned up for the meet on time. The cop was polite, but strict and confident. 'Neddy, you are never to set foot inside the Broadway Hotel again. I am seeing you like this because you are well-liked by many senior officers. Don't let me down. I am showing you the respect I think you have earned, so do me the same and respect my wishes.' I assured him that I would indeed respect his wishes, and I did. He kept his word to me and I to him. We had a few drinks, talked shit, then went our separate ways.

Warren worked well until, unknown to me, he teamed up with Sallie-Anne Huckstepp, a prostitute and federal police informer. I had never met Sallie-Anne Huckstepp in my life until I saw her at Warren's inquest. Warren never let me know that he was living with a junkie; he knew I would have told him to get rid of her.

One day Warren came to see me. He was very concerned about a cop. The cop's name just happened to be Roger Rogerson! He told me that Roger wanted to arrest him over ripping off a drug dealer. Warren asked me if I would contact Roger on his behalf and see if something could be done.

I told Warren that Roger was a very dangerous man. 'Don't fuck with him.' He continued to ask me to contact Roger on his behalf. 'OK mate, but don't fuck him about or it will fall back on me.'

Warren never told me that he was under suspicion for the attempted murder of a motorbike cop. Apparently he had tried to shoot a young cop while attempting to rob a bank. I rang Roger and made arrangements to meet him about Warren. I thought the reason for the meeting was to arrange for the heat to be lifted from Warren, because he had been ripping off drug dealers, nothing else. Roger, like Warren, didn't tell me about the attempted shooting. Warren was a very willing young bloke, maybe too willing for everyone's health. That's why he had to go, I believe.

I was with Warren on 27 June 1981 when he was shot dead in a laneway called Dangar Place, off Abercrombie Street in Chippendale, while attempting to bribe Rogerson. I was the person that took Warren to this fatal meeting. There was an inquest and both sides threw plenty of shit at one another. I was right in the middle of it all.

I could do nothing to bring Warren back to life, so I did the best thing I could. I know Warren's family suffered deeply, but I cannot do anything about it. Rogerson was commended for bravery and exonerated from any wrongdoing. There has been a lot of controversy over the shooting of Warren Lanfranchi by Rogerson. Well, don't expect me to enlighten you further. I told my story to the coroner when I appeared in court.

[*Smith's evidence supported Rogerson's contention that Lanfranchi had pulled a gun and threatened the policeman. Smith was the only non-police witness to the shooting. The jury at the inquest found that Rogerson shot Lanfranchi twice 'while endeavoring to make an arrest'. They could not agree that the action was 'in self-defence'. There were many matters relating to the killing that remained unresolved, yet despite calls from Lanfranchi's family for an inquiry into the shooting and subsequent police investigation, the State Government let the matter drop.*]

I knew my life would never be the same after Warren Lanfranchi was gunned down. For months after his death, I wouldn't leave my house. It was nothing to do with my being afraid of anyone. People bled the same way I did. I was afraid of no one at all. I just felt inside myself that I had betrayed everything I was brought up to believe in. I was ashamed of what had happened to Warren, ashamed because I had gotten up in the witness box for a cop. And not just any cop, but the most hated cop in Australia, Roger Rogerson.

I had no one I could discuss it with—not that I had much to say. One day I had the best name among the crims, and the very next I'm being bagged behind my back over helping the most hated cop in the force. No one ever spoke out loud what they were thinking, but I could feel it when I entered a room, and when I left it was like they were relieved to get rid of me.

[*Smith names two police*] came to see me after the inquest. [*One of the police*] thanked me for 'doing the right thing by Roger', as he put it. He was very friendly towards me.

'Neddy, you are not a fool,' he said. 'We have spoken among ourselves about your future. It's clear to us that you are always going to be involved in crime in some way or other, so we decided for helping Roger we are going to give you a Green Light. Do you have any idea what I am saying to you?'

I knew what he was on about, but I hadn't expected this, especially not from him.

'Yes, I know what a Green Light is. But I refuse to tell on anyone.'

'Has anyone asked you to?' he said. 'Just accept it and if you ever hit a blue, get whoever has you to call either me, [*a detective*] or Roger straight away.'

That day was to bring enormous changes to my life. I underwent what might be called a transformation. Roger and the team that were involved in the Lanfranchi killing all took me to lunch at the restaurant of a friend of Roger's. This was to be the first of hundreds of social outings with police and even with their families and friends. I was even invited to their homes.

Soon after Warren's inquest, I decided to have a holiday and take my wife away for a rest. When I got back I noticed changes in the way police treated me. It was uncanny. Police that hated me, and police that did not know I existed, were going out of their way to talk to me and offer me assistance. Nothing would ever be the same, I felt; and it wasn't.

I often asked myself: 'Why me?' I haven't come up with the right answer yet.

I couldn't do a thing wrong. No matter what I did I was never arrested. My friendship with Roger proved beyond any doubt that he was a real force to be reckoned with within the police.

There have been many articles and a few books written about Rogerson. A lot of people have taken it upon themselves to give what they consider a fair and unbiased opinion of him. I have known Rogerson for some 16 years and, after reading almost all the profiles of him, I have to say that not one of them covers both sides of the man. It seems that few people knew the side of him that I knew—and if they did, they were too scared to write about it.

Rogerson was and is a man of his word. If you were fortunate enough to be given his word then you could put your life on him keeping it, no matter what may happen. I believed Roger would rather go to jail than break his word to anyone. He was a very dedicated cop who loved his work and he was ambitious beyond belief. Nothing was allowed to stand in his way.

Agreed, he killed men in the line of duty, was very vicious and wouldn't hesitate to lock you up and flog you badly—with the help of other police, of course. Rogerson had the reputation of being feared all over New South Wales by all of the so-called underworld. He earned that reputation while wearing a badge. But Roger was not a physical person as far as actually giving you an even chance. He preferred to have the odds on his side all the time.

Don't get me wrong—Roger would kill you as soon as look at you, but he didn't have the monopoly on killing people or violence. People tend to forget that he is human just like you and me. He bleeds the same way and, believe it or not, he eats, talks and walks the same as we do. When he wore that badge, however, he was a man with a mission—and that mission was to make life as hard for criminals and as easy for Roger as he could. And that is what he did.

I've already described my first meeting with Rogerson in 1976, after the Fielders bakery disaster with Chapo. I must admit that at the time I was frightened by him, not so much by the man but by the power he seemed to have over the other police around him. When he spoke they jumped—all of them.

As I got to know the man and not the cop, we became friends and I grew to respect him as a man of his word. He treated me as an equal and we became very close, despite what the media have written. They only know what he wanted them to know about him.

Roger was a good friend and a bad enemy. He was loyal, as long as it didn't involve any discomfort to him. I trusted him more than most would, but I always kept my guard up at all times. I never underestimated him for a second. He was a man who could turn on you in a flash. Our friendship was really one of convenience. He used me to suit his own purposes—I paid Roger and his police friends millions of dollars over the years—and I used him to get what I wanted and needed. Also, he kept me out of jail for 15 years. Never once in our friendship did he ask me to inform on anyone, never. Only one policeman ever asked me for information—that was [*Smith names the officer*] and I belted him on the chin. I realise that Roger can never tell the truth now because he said I was an informer under oath and to admit to the truth now would fuck his credibility completely. But that *is* the truth. I was never his, or anyone else's, informer.

Shortly after Warren's inquest, Roger and I started going to lunch at Dimitri's Bar and Bistro, a restaurant in Surry Hills.

We sometimes went to lunch two or three times a week. There would always be other detectives with us as Roger introduced me around his friends and contacts in the force.

I met dozens of police, not all of them detectives. Some were high up in the uniform ranks. There were a select few that we dined with regularly. After a few months of these lunches and sometimes dinners—when Roger was satisfied, I suppose, that I had been accepted by the other police—he decided it was time I met his family.

One day I was meeting Roger at a hotel when he said: 'Hop in mate, I've got to make a pit-stop at home for a few seconds. Come with me, I want you to meet my wife, Joy.'

I was surprised, but I got in and went to meet Joy for the first time. When we got there he introduced me to his wife as a friend of his. We exchanged greetings and, after a short while, Roger drove me back to pick up my car.

That was my first meeting with any of the cops' wives or families.

Joy was a very nice quiet woman. Later on, when Debra met her, she liked her, too. They got on well together, as my wife did with all of the cops' wives that she met socially over the next decade.

My next meeting with Roger's family was a few weeks later. I was having a few quiet drinks at the Lord Nelson Hotel at the Rocks when he rang me there. (Roger knew where to find me 24 hours a day; we had arranged it that way in case either one of us needed the other in a hurry.)

I got on the phone: 'Hello mate, what's up?'

He laughed. 'Nothing mate. How long are you going to be there?'

I wasn't going anywhere. 'I'll be here most of the night.'

'Look mate, I'm in the area with my wife and two daughters. Why don't I drop in for a quick drink and you can meet the daughters.'

I was surprised again. 'Great, Roger, I'll see you when you get here.'

About an hour later, Roger and his family arrived at the hotel. Roger got one drink for himself then he introduced his two daughters to me. They were very nice girls, polite and well spoken. They didn't drink and Joy was driving, so she didn't drink either.

They only stayed for 20 minutes, then said goodbye and

left. After that, I met a lot of the cops' families and went out socially with all of them to restaurants and clubs. This went on right up until Roger and Joy split up and he moved in with another woman.

I was on top of the world at this time. I wondered to myself: how many criminals have there ever been that had been accepted into the circle of close cops like I had? None, I'll bet. I had to be the only one ever.

Here I was, the first and probably the only criminal ever to be socially accepted into the inner circle of Roger Rogerson. I had no idea what the cops told their wives about me—who I was or what I did for a living. It was never discussed. After several social outings, I discovered that these cops were only ordinary people just like me, no different. They acted the same way I did, especially when they dropped the facade of being a cop and acted normal. I always enjoyed myself in their company, in fact some of the best times I've ever had in my life were with Roger.

Debra never liked Roger, and she still doesn't. They spoke to one another, but that's as far as their friendship went.

I was well liked by the majority of the police because of my friendship with Roger. They would all go out of their way to speak to me if they saw me anywhere on the street, or out and about.

From the day I was given the Green Light in 1981, I was not once charged—until the Federal Police forced the state police to arrest me on 31 October 1987 for murder. If I was required for questioning or anything, I was contacted by phone and politely asked would I mind attending the police station. I was always told to bring a solicitor with me.

The main reason I was given the Green Light was because of the assistance I gave to Roger when I got up for him at the inquest into Warren Lanfranchi's death. When you come to look at what I did, it's understandable that they treated me so well. By giving Roger my support and helping clear him of allegations that he had murdered Lanfranchi, I had burnt my bridges with much of the criminal element: many crims disliked what I'd done and started to give me a wide berth.

As it turned out, I did myself a big favor by getting myself cut off from the so-called criminals. Most of them were too stupid to get out of their own way. And, as I was to find out, they weren't the real criminals at all. The police ran all the worthwhile crime in New South Wales, not the crims. You had to get the OK from the police before you could do any reasonably large crime, otherwise you were soon put out of the picture without much fuss at all. You either went missing, or, the most popular way was to load you up and get you put away for 10 or 15 years.

My success depended entirely on the connections that I met through The Dodger.

10
With A Little Help From My Friends

'Do you have the money we agreed on?'
Rex Jackson, Minister for Corrective Services

[A *detective*] and I got up to many shifty moves.

Over the next few years we ripped off many drug dealers and even got up to the odd armed robbery or two. Sometimes he would get me to pose as a drug squad cop. He would give me his badge, tell me who the target was and I would do the rest.

I used to get different guys to help me, but it was mostly Abo [*Graham Henry*] that I took with me on these excursions. Sometimes we rented cars similar to police cars. Now and then we used real police cars.

On one occasion I took Abo with me on a rip-off organised by [*the detective*]. It was a house occupied by a team of bikies who were selling gear [*heroin*]. He told us where to look for the gear—and that the house was bugged. We watched it to make sure no one was home, then went in. Abo got in through the roof so as not to set the alarm off. Once inside, he fixed the alarm and let [*the detective*] and I inside. Once in, we went to work looking for the stash. Abo discovered the safe upstairs—we had to get a friend of ours to open it—and much to our surprise it contained $100,000 in cash. We soon confiscated that. There was also a pound of pure heroin in the safe. Abo took charge of that: he cut it, sold it, then the money was whacked up equally.

We went out to lunch together to celebrate our good fortune. Abo did a few more with [*the detective*] and I over the next two years. This was Abo's very first experience with having police protection while you worked. He had no trouble getting used to it.

He commented to [*the detective*] while we were celebrating: 'How long has this rort been going on? Where have I been hiding all these years?'

On another occasion, the same team did another rip-off. This time we went in posing as cops to rip off people [*the detective*] had been keeping under surveillance for a long time. Abo didn't have a suit, so I had to take him out and buy one. Abo loved the idea of impersonating a cop. I think he was a frustrated cop at times. Abo desperately wanted to be a cop, he wanted the shoulder holster and the whole bit. He was enjoying it too much.

[*The detective*] drove us in his police car to a house at Campsie, I think it was. Once there, Abo kicked in the front door and we went in. Abo was carrying on like a real cop: 'Get down on the floor, move it, now,' he shouted. He went straight upstairs while [*the detective*] and I put the people up against the wall and searched them. [*The detective*] was questioning them, one was a girl. Abo came down the stairs smiling, carrying on like the movies—he was doing the tough guy-nice guy act all on his own. [*The detective*] and I were in stitches laughing at Abo, who was having a ball. Anyway we got an earn out of the rip-off. Not a lot or anywhere near as much as we had been led to believe was there. We ended up with $60,000 cash and Abo found a pound of hash also.

[*The detective*] wasn't satisfied, so he pinched one of the guys and ended stamping him for $50,000 before he let him go. He was getting out of hand, time to slow down. I started to drop off [*the detective*] then. He was going too far with some of the guys that he was ripping off.

At one stage Abo fell foul of the undercover squad. He was set up by the police over on the north side of Sydney while trying to unload heroin to a cop. Abo had met this guy at a hotel and the guy wanted to purchase a pound of heroin. Abo came straight in and he made a meet with the guy for the following day. Abo turned up for the arranged meeting with the heroin in his car, still with no idea that the guy was a cop.

He parked his car outside the pub and left the heroin in the car. Then he went into the hotel to do the deal. While discussing the money, Abo told the guy if he tried any funny business, he would kill him.

Apparently they took Abo seriously, because when Abo went to the car to get the heroin for the guy, a garbage truck casually pulled up in front of Abo's car and started to back up towards where Abo was sitting in his car. Abo got a little bit suspicious at the way the would-be garbos were acting so, as he sat there, he looked around to see if anyone else was taking any notice of him. All of a sudden, at some given signal, one of the men posing as a garbo reached into the back of the truck and came up with a pump-action shotgun. He aimed straight at Abo's head and let one go at him.

Luckily, Abo sensed that there was something wrong and ducked just as the guy fired. He was very lucky—he only got some pellets in the shoulder and a few in the face.

The police were quick to converge on the car. One cop threw a handgun into the car, and it landed on the seat beside Abo. It was unnecessary, as he already had one on the seat beside him anyway.

Abo was charged with trying to sell the heroin to an undercover cop and the two guns. He had a low court hearing and got committed for trial.

The charge he faced carried 15 years at that time. Enter [*the detective*] again. Here is where he came in very handy. [*Smith describes a series of events that have been removed for legal reasons.*]

Abo pleaded guilty and received seven years with 18 months on the bottom—an 18-month non-parole period for a pound of heroin. Everyone was happy with the result. (It goes without saying that Abo was a very relieved man that day.)

That wasn't to be the end of Abo's good fortune, either. That improved one Monday when I was having lunch with Neville Biber at Pruniers. We were on the way to do some settling at The Oak later that day, and had called in for a bite to eat, when Rex Jackson [*then Minister for Corrective Services in the Wran-led New South Wales Labor Government*] and a few of his friends walked in. They stayed for lunch also. After lunch, I was sitting at the bar talking to Neville about racehorses when Rex and his team came over for a few after-lunch drinks.

I never knew Rex then, but Neville did. Neville introduced

us and we sat discussing racing. Rex told me that he had done his cash at the Saturday meeting—'he did his arse' as he put it. I knew about shifty Rex and his early-release scheme, but then everyone knew about it, it was not a well-kept secret. I just happened to drop Abo's name and told Rex that he was in the nick and was having problems keeping his family together. Rex came straight in. He asked me would my friend be interested in an early release?

'He certainly would be. Can anything be done to help him?'

Rex knew of me as my name was always coming up in Parliament over some shit or other. [*Smith's name was raised a number of times in the New South Wales Parliament in relation to drug trafficking and police corruption.*] He also knew about my association with Roger. He let me know all of this over a few cool ones. We discussed getting Abo released early. Rex said that it was not a problem if the necessary money could be found to cover his bill. The sum we eventually agreed on was $10,000—and it had to be cash up front. He added: 'As soon as possible.' I told Rex that I was willing to put the money up for Abo to be released. We made arrangements to meet the next day at Parliament House at 10.30am.

I arrived the next day on time. I asked this guy on the door to locate Rex for me—I explained that I had an appointment. The guy took my name and left. A short time later he returned with Rex. Rex directed me to a little sort of office off to the left of the main entrance. Once we were inside he locked the door. He didn't waste any time.

'Do you have the money we agreed on?'

I opened the briefcase I was carrying and gave him the money. He must not have trusted me because he counted every dollar of it. Then he put it away in his pockets and explained how the release would take place.

'First, I have to send Abo to Silverwater Jail for a short period of time to make it look good. He will get home-release nearly straight away, I will fix that myself. Then, after being there a short time, you must get his wife to apply to have Abo released on licence. That way I can cover any inquiry that might surface over him being released early.'

Rex stuck to his word and Abo was released earlier than he would have been under normal circumstances. Abo was the last person to be released under Rex Jackson's release scheme. (Rex Jackson wasn't the only politician I paid money to. The names of some of the others may surprise you. For now, I won't reveal them publicly. The ICAC knows who they are. One case was in 1981, after I'd just sold 2000 pounds of marijuana—it took three weeks to get rid of the gear—for Robert Trimbole [*a well-known Italian crime figure*], when there was a deal done with a politican so Trimbole could get out of the country. [*Trimbole fled Australia on his own passport. He died in May 1987 while on the run in Spain.*])

A few problems resulted from my visit to see Rex at Parliament House. It seems that I was spotted while I was paying Rex a visit. John Dowd and John Hatton [*two anti-corruption MPs*] put a blue on in the house over my association with Rex. They accused me of being involved in the early release scheme. It hit the bloody headlines in all of the papers.

A few days later, Roger got in touch. He said that [*a group of politicians*] wanted me to do them a small favor. Would I write to Jackson, via my solicitor Val Bellamy, complaining about the lies that Dowd and Hatton had said about myself and Jackson?

I did as they asked and I got my solicitor, Val Bellamy, to compose a nice letter denying any involvement with Jackson. It worked, because a week after my letter was received Roger got back to me again, wanting me to do yet another turn for the same people.

This time the politicians told him to let me know that I could pick my own QC to handle my case and that they would grant me legal aid for the entire cost of the excercise if I would take on Dowd and Hatton and sue the pair of them. It did not matter if I won or not, as long as I gave them plenty of adverse publicity.

I prepared to do it for them. I was thinking ahead—maybe they could one day do me a favor in return. But it wasn't to be. Rex came undone over the early release scheme and he hit the nick. Abo still got out, even though Rex had bitten the dust.

[*Rex Jackson was jailed for seven and a half years in September 1987 after being convicted of accepting bribes in return for the early release of prisoners. He was released in*

November 1990 *after accumulating points for good behavior.*]

One day I was drinking at the Star Hotel in Alexandria when [*the same detective as mentioned earlier in this chapter*] arrived. I had the SP book at the Star and never had a moment's trouble in the hotel. The owners, Joe and Zeena, were great, down-to-earth people. [*The detective*] knew Joe well—in fact a lot of police got to know Joe because I often met them at the Star. Every different squad that had me under surveillance sat off the Star at some time or other. The Australian Federal Police had a room straight across the road from the hotel on top of a garage. They used to watch us and, I suppose, wonder what we were up to. I never let on that I knew they were there because it suited my purposes—I was one-up on them by knowing that they were there.

[*The detective*] got a drink and explained that he had an insurance job he wanted me to do.

'Are you interested in doing an armed robbery in town? It's a sweet go,' he said.

'Tell me more about it,' I said.

'Well,' he said, 'It's worth just over a million in diamonds. The job has to look like the real thing. There will be independent witnesses present that won't have a clue what's going down. It is to be done as the guy leaves his office in Clarence Street in the city.'

I asked a few questions. 'Any cash involved?'

'None at all.'

'Listen, I have no one capable of taking such a large amount of diamonds in one go. You will have to unload them.'

He agreed. 'OK, we already have one person interested in them.'

[*The detective*] wanted to know who would do the robbery with me. I told him it was not necessary for him to know at this stage. We discussed the way the robbery would be done for about 20 minutes.

'What sort of help will we be getting?' I asked.

'The very best that money can buy.' He was laughing at his own joke. He gave me the address and the details I needed so I could have a good look at the scene.

The following day at 6pm I went to Clarence Street to

look at the layout. It was about the same time of day that we would be doing it and I wanted to see what the traffic was like. It was bloody bedlam. Traffic was packed up all along the street waiting to get on to the Harbour Bridge. There was no way we would be able to park anywhere near the robbery site. That was a problem, but one we could overcome with a bit of thought.

I rang [*the detective*] and told him there was a minor problem. We met at the Star Hotel again.

'I have a plan that needs your approval before I can say yes or no,' I said.

'What is the plan?'

I was laughing to myself. 'How do you feel about parking the police car nearby and picking us up after the robbery? We won't come anywhere near you if there looks like being a problem.' (This wouldn't be the last time that he arranged similar things for me).

'I will have to make a few inquiries and get back to you on that.'

The next day I saw a friend who I knew was into armed robs. I mentioned that I had a sweet go, but didn't tell him that it was with the police—not yet, anyway.

'Count me in,' he said. 'Just give me 12 hours' notice in case I have anything else on at that time. It will give me time to make other arrangements.'

That out of the way, I went to see [*the detective*] again at the Star to hear his answer to my question about picking us up in the police car. The Feds must have been going out of their minds wondering what [*the detective*] and I were up to with all the meetings.

'Not a problem,' he said. 'We talked it over and we agree that is the best way out of the area.'

I'm thinking quickly: 'Who is the *we*?'

He burst out laughing. '[*Another policeman is named*] is my present partner on this one, no sweat, mate.'

I didn't like [*the second policeman*] one bit. I wanted to know how many people were involved in this caper. [*The detective*] explained: 'It's like this, Ned. We pool all the money and there is a whack-up at the end of each month. We share it all equally around.' He told me that the proceeds of the robbery would be split equally between my partner and I, and the [*police*]. He had no idea how much the

With A Little Help From My Friends

whack-up would be—he didn't know how much we could sell the diamonds for.

He continued: 'We have to go to Double Bay to meet [*the second policeman*] and the guy you are going to rob.' We drove to Double Bay in a police car. [*The second policeman*] was there with two men. The men gave me the details I needed to do the job. The diamonds had not arrived in Sydney—they were on their way from Israel and expected any day. [*An employee of the diamond company*] gave me a direct line to his office so that I could ring to find out when the diamonds arrived.

Every day I rang to see if there was any news. Just when I was about to give the job a miss, the guy said it was a go.

The bloke that I was doing the robbery with wasn't real keen about the idea of the police picking us up afterwards—but he went ahead with it.

We rushed around to get ready. We planned to ambush the diamond couriers as they emerged from a building in Clarence Street in the city. We couldn't wear masks because we had to stand at a bus stop waiting for the guys to come out of the building with the diamonds. There were heaps of people waiting to catch buses. Some looked at us strangely—but maybe I was getting paranoid. We waited for what seemed like hours. Several times I checked to make sure that [*the two police*] were waiting in the spot I had chosen for them while we did the robbery.

Waiting and more waiting.

At last three men walked into the arcade, one carrying the briefcase. They looked around and started chatting. It appeared they suspected nothing. We crossed the street and came up on them from behind and hit them hard and fast. They had no warning, no chance to do a thing. My mate grabbed the briefcase while I pushed the other two up against a glass window. We both had guns pointed at them. The one with the case started to yell: 'There is nothing but my paperwork in the case.' The other two took advantage of the noise and grabbed at my mate. That was a bad mistake on their part. They were immediately bashed to the ground, where they lay bleeding.

We had the case and no more than two or three minutes had passed. It seemed like hours. We walked away briskly—we didn't run as we had already attracted enough looks from passers-by. As we got to the arcade we slowed right down and looked around to see if anyone was following. There was no one, so we made our way quickly to where [*the two police*] were waiting. We reached the car, our guns still in our hands. As we got into the back seat of the police car, [*the policeman*] said: 'Put those guns into the case right away.' We did so and we drove away, heading over the bridge. They dropped us outside the North Sydney police station. I threw the case and the two guns in the boot of the police car. [*The detective*] said: 'We have to hurry back over the other side to be first on the scene so that if any problems arise we can take care of it.' They went back to the city—and we caught a cab to the Star Hotel to celebrate with a few cold beers.

The following day we saw [*the two police*]. Said [*the detective*]: 'You haven't got anything to concern yourself about. The blokes you robbed are all right, just a few bruises and cuts, but they'll get over it.' But there was a small problem—they couldn't get rid of the diamonds straight away. Could I do anything about it?

'I doubt it,' I said, 'but leave them with me and I will make a few inquiries with some guys I know in Melbourne. I may have a bit of luck there.'

He went to the boot of his car and got out the case and the two guns and handed them to me. I placed them in the boot of my Mercedes and asked: 'Is all the gear there in the case?' I knew what [*the detective*] was like, not to mention [*the policeman*]. They would rob their own mother for two dollars.

'Check the bag yourself, mate,' he said. 'It's all there.'

That was a funny thing to say as we had never opened the bag. How would we know what was there? He assured me all the gear was there. He also told me the insurance money was being handled by the [*police*]. I had no luck selling the diamonds. There were plenty of buyers, but no one had the ready cash. To my surprise, [*the detective*] told me their luck had changed and a bloke was willing to take the lot off our hands for slightly less than anticipated.

They got rid of the diamonds OK, but I still believe [*the two police*] short-changed us in the whack-up. We never saw any of the insurance money as the employee who organised the raid went overseas with our share—and a hell of a lot of other people's money.

[*The two police*] came to see me about a month later, wanting me to do a payroll robbery. No way, I told them. They didn't like my refusal, but I couldn't give a fuck one way or another. They didn't give up there. They conned my partner into doing it and he just lashed on them cold [*didn't pay police their share of the proceeds*]. So they charged him with the armed robbery. He was also charged over a big heroin bust. [*The detective*] came to see me and got me to weigh in $10,000 for my mate to beat the armed robbery charge. I paid the money and they kept their word—the charge was no-billed. I deliberately avoided doing anything further with [*the policeman*]. He was not to be trusted because he was bucking for promotion.

11
Mixed Fortunes

'Twenty thousand dollars, or you both hit the nick.'
        Policeman to Smith and an associate

[In 1981 the Smith family moved to Kiama, a coastal town about 70 kilometres south of Sydney. For Neddy Smith, domestic life had never been better. In June 1981, Debra gave birth to their third child, Daniel—coming after Darrin and Jaime—making Neddy Smith 'the proudest man alive'.

But the move to the coast was temporary. The family returned to Sydney and lived at Blakehurst. Work beckoned. Smith needed to oversee his heroin dealership and SP bookmaking business—and enjoy himself. With Graham 'Abo' Henry serving his jail term on heroin charges, yet to benefit from Rex Jackson's early release scheme, Smith began working with a series of new partners. This produced mixed fortunes.]

I was a partner in Neville Biber's business, but I had to keep my mouth shut and my head out of it. His company, Harry S. Baggs, was the biggest wholesale business to ever hit this country. It had outlets in all states and was getting bigger every day.

Harry S. Baggs dealt in everything from sunglasses to fridges. There was nothing Neville didn't have for sale at some stage and he could do no wrong as far as Harry S. Baggs was concerned. He had advertiser John Singleton handling the publicity for him. The adverts appeared on TV and on radio personality John Laws' program. Neville was at his peak. Finally he had kicked a goal. After all this time he had made it legally.

[*Neville Biber had a colorful background, but few criminal convictions. For illegally copying cassette tapes, he was fined $300. In the television advertisements for Harry S. Baggs, Biber appeared unshaven and shifty-looking, and referred to the possibility that the warehouse goods had come off the back of a truck. The commercial ended with Biber fleeing with the till money to the noise of approaching sirens.*]

Neville's success meant that I, too, had kicked a goal, even if I could not come out publicly and announce it like Neville did. I used to avoid going near the warehouses and offices too much as I didn't want to bring any attention to the place. I collected a good wage every week and as part of the deal I had a Mercedes Benz supplied for my use.

Well, the shit was soon to hit the fan.

Neville was just beginning to negotiate selling franchises to the Harry S. Baggs name. Money was flowing in at an enormous rate. I continued to stay away from the business. I was too hot and I didn't want to bring any heat on it.

The federal and state police got tired of not being able to catch me or make any charges stick. They could see the way Harry S. Baggs was going and they knew that I was involved in it, so they spread the word to the media that I was involved and that the company was involved in drugs and used to launder drug money.

[*The news broke on 7 April 1982, only two days after questions were raised in Parliament about Smith's relationship with Minister for Corrective Services, Rex Jackson. Questions were again asked in the New South Wales Parliament, this time about links between Smith, drug trafficking and Harry S. Baggs. The links stemmed from investigations into the Bangkok heroin importations by the Woodward Royal Commission which named Smith as a major heroin dealer, and a man named James Richard White as a criminal and professional shoplifter. White also happened to be one of the directors of Harry S. Baggs. To further reinforce the connection, Neville Biber, in rejecting allegations that he was involved in drug dealing, acknowledged the following day that he was a good friend of Smith; they drank together regularly. The final piece of 'evidence' linking the company to 'criminal activity' was the revelation that Smith had driven a car owned by a Harry S. Baggs subsidiary on the day he took Warren Lanfranchi to his fatal meeting with Detective Sergeant Roger Rogerson.*]

Neville was accused of being involved in importing drugs into Australia. The media loved it and they spread it across every front page for weeks. Neville was a bit of a rouge, certainly. But to my knowledge he was *never* involved in drugs.

The end result, however, was that the public, not wanting to be linked with anything to do with drugs, dropped off buying stock from the warehouses. The business went into a decline and all our plans to go straight went sour. Both Laws and Singleton went on national TV proclaiming their innocence. As soon as the media mentioned Neville's alleged involvement in drugs, these two well-known personalities dropped Neville like a hot potato.

In all fairness to John Laws, I must say that he was never involved in drugs with Neville or myself. It was a rumor started by the police because of John Laws doing the publicity for Harry S. Baggs, nothing more. The media crucify many people and have ruined many an honest man. As for Singleton's involvement in the drug scene with Neville and I, well, I don't like Singleton one bit and I would like to say that he was involved in the drug scene with me, but he wasn't. Both men were wrongly accused by the police and victimised by the media.

The police and the media dealt the company a death blow. We were gone for good, ruined beyond repair.

For many years Neville had been involved with Jimmy White, who was a partner in Harry S. Baggs. Jimmy was a shifty guy who systematically robbed the company for years without Neville finding out. Jimmy White deserved full marks. He was the only one to finish with any money out of the business. He left the country under a cloud, wanted by the police on a number of charges. I would like to have a little chat with Jimmy White myself one day.

Neville tried to hang on to the company. He thought that the bad times were certain to pass. He was wrong. He moved the company from his offices in Redfern to a much smaller place in Glebe, on Parramatta Road. It wasn't to be. The pace was too fast and the pressure got to him.

One afternoon, nine months after the allegations were first raised in Parliament, while working at his office desk, Neville died of a massive heart attack, brought on no doubt by the pressure and stress of losing his life's work. It had been the first honest thing he had accomplished.

Neville was not involved in any drug business with me at any time. I don't believe that he ever had any involvement with any form of drugs at all. He was a good friend.

One day I was drinking at the Quarrymans Hotel at Pyrmont when Danny Chubb walked in. [*Chubb was one of Australia's biggest heroin importers and distributors in the early 1980s. He initially imported two kilograms at a time; within months, Chubb, with a partner, was bringing in consignments of up to 50 kilograms. From 1981 until his murder in November 1984, Chubb was Neddy Smith's principal source of heroin. It is estimated that Smith purchased about three kilograms every 10 days, which was then sold in Sydney and Melbourne.*]

Chubb walked over: 'Can I speak to you for a few minutes, Ned?'

'Sure, what's on your mind?'

We walked over to a quiet place and sat down.

'Ned,' he said, 'You know that I have got [*a police officer*] sweet, don't you?'

'Yes, I'm well aware of that. Why?'

'[*The officer*] has passed on to me some very important information that you need to know about.'

He had me interested, that was for sure. 'Let's hear it and we'll see.'

He said: 'This is the message exactly as [*the officer*] told it to me, OK?'

'Go on.'

'Don't meet the Chinese guy on Thursday. Stay away from Judy and stop talking on her phone. If you meet the Chinese guy you'll be pinched.'

I said: 'That's not for me, Danny.'

'I know that, Ned, but [*the officer*] said that you would know who it was meant for.'

I told him that I wasn't too sure that I did.

'Well, I will help jog your memory a bit, OK? The message is for Randy Tofani [*pseudonym of a Sydney criminal with a conviction for conspiring to import heroin*]. He is supposed to meet two Chinese guys on Thursday night to collect two kilos of heroin. [*Two police*] are just waiting to pinch him. His phone is off and they are ready to pounce on the lot of them.'

We discussed it some more and Chubb told me that the bill was going to be a big one for that information.

'Okay, I will get the drink [*the payment for the information*] to you tomorrow at the same time here.'

Chubb left and, within a matter of minutes, The General walked in. He had exactly the same message for me to pass on to Tofani. This time it cost $2000.

Things looked like they were hotting up. Time to warn Tofani. It took me two hours to drive to Kiama where he lived with his wife and young son. I related Chubb's and The General's messages. He appeared to know exactly what they meant. He thanked me and said that he would not go near the Chinese at the motel. He gave me $8000 to whack up between the two cops that had passed on the warning to him.

The money had been well earned, or so I thought, anyway.

The next morning Tofani's partner, also a close friend of mine, came to see me. I told him what I told Tofani the previous night. He knew exactly what it was all about. He didn't volunteer any information to me, so I didn't ask.

The next day I drove to Sydney to fix up Chubb and The General with the money to pay the cops. I didn't want to keep them waiting. When I met Chubb and The General, I split the $8000 equally between them. The General nearly had a fit. He gave me $2000 back. 'Don't spoil them,' he said.

Chubb wasn't so kind. He snaffled the remaining $6000. I finished the business with those two and then I went to the Lord Nelson and finished up on the drink. I stayed until the pub shut, then I drove home to Kiama (don't ask me how I managed that). I was no sooner in the front door than the phone rang. At that time of the morning, I knew it was not going to be good news.

I picked up the phone expecting the worst—and I wasn't disappointed. It was Randy Tofani's partner, who I'll call Charlie.

'Ned, Randy's pinched!'

'What the fuck for? Surely he didn't keep that meeting with the Chows?'

'Yes, he did, mate. They caught him in a cab with two pounds of heroin.'

I couldn't believe that he was silly enough to do something so stupid. It got worse.

Charlie said: 'Can you come up to Sydney and pick me up please, mate? I have a hostage and I will kill her if they try anything with me.'

I couldn't think straight. Things were rushing through my mind.

'Just don't do anything silly, mate. I will be there as soon as I can, OK.'

I woke Debra and told her I was heading back to Sydney because there was a problem. I was about to close the front door behind me when the phone rang again. I thought it was Charlie again. I picked up the phone and said: 'Yes mate, I'm just leaving.'

At the other end was someone else. 'Hello Ned, it's Roger here.' That was unexpected.

'What's the matter, mate?'

'Listen carefully, Ned. You have to get in touch with Charlie. Can you manage to get hold of him straight away?'

I told Roger that I should be able to.

'Why? What's the matter?'

'Listen to me mate. Charlie has taken this bloke's wife hostage over a dope deal. He took her as security in case something went wrong. [*A policeman*] and the rest of the taskforce know that Charlie has her. Now, if Charlie lets her go unharmed, he will be looked after. If he hurts her in any way, then he is off tap. It's up to you to pull him up before it's too late.'

'I'll give it my best shot, Roger, but I can't promise anything.'

'Try hard, mate. And when you have her safe then ring me at the office.'

Trouble just seemed to follow me wherever I went. I drove straight to where I'd arranged to meet Charlie. When I arrived I could see he was very nervous. He had a death grip on this woman that was with him. She was terrified. They got into my car, with Charlie tightly hanging on to her.

'Listen to me, Charlie,' I said. 'They know you are holding the girl hostage somewhere. Now you have to think carefully about what you are doing. No sense in going off half-cocked. I want you to let me take the girl to Roger. You will have to trust me.'

Charlie said he would do as I suggested, as long as I promised that there would be no shifty business on Roger's part.

He gave me the girl—she was terrified and crying—then I dropped Charlie at a cab stand and told him where to go and to wait for me. Then I rang Roger and told him I had the girl with me.

'She is very shaken up, Roger.'

'That's OK mate, just bring her straight to me, now.'

I drove to meet Roger—and there were cops everywhere.

'What the hell are you up to, mate? You never said anything about all this.'

'Calm down, Ned, you've done well. It is all right, don't panic.'

Police came over to my car and took the girl. An ambulance took her to hospital.

Roger hopped into my car: 'Drive away from here, go somewhere we can talk.'

I was as anxious as Roger was to get away from the area and drove quickly out of there. On the way Roger told me that Charlie had raped the woman and done all sorts of foul things to her.

Then he said: 'But she is safe now. We should be able to work something out for Charlie.'

We talked about what had gone down. Roger told me that he wanted to talk to Charlie. I pulled up at a public phone and rang Charlie.

'Mate, The Dodger wants to speak to you. The girl is safe.' Charlie agreed to speak to Roger on the phone. I put him on then walked away.

A short while later, Roger called me back and I again spoke to Charlie.

'Listen Ned, will you bring Roger over here to see me now?'

I didn't drive Roger directly to see Charlie as I was still a little toey over the Lanfranchi affair. I told Roger not to make this another Dangar Place [*the laneway in which Warren Lanfranchi was gunned down by Rogerson in con-*

troversial circumstances]. Once was plenty for me. I didn't want a repeat performance.

Meanwhile, Roger filled me in on how Tofani was caught. The taskforce had been on to Tofani and Charlie for ages. They had dozens of taped conversations of them talking on the phone and they just sat back and waited for them to make their next move. They watched the two Chinese guys and let Tofani trap himself, which dopey Tofani did. His greed got him caught.

The taskforce had watched Charlie take the guy's wife hostage, but had not counted on losing him, which they somehow did while they arrested Tofani. While Charlie took off with the hostage, Tofani did the business with the Chows and managed to get himself caught. The rest is history. Tofani went to jail for a long time. While in jail he went on protection and named Charlie as trying to kill him in the cell one night. There was something very wrong inside Tofanis's head.

Roger and I got to the meeting with Charlie. Roger and Charlie talked for about an hour and came to an agreement. Charlie was to meet another policeman the next evening at a restaurant.

Again I was concerned. I told Roger: 'Let's get one thing perfectly clear before I become involved in this. I am not going to be party to another Dangar Place, no fucking way!'

Roger had a warped sense of humor. He laughed: 'Just be dead on time.' Very fucking funny. Roger was in hysterics laughing at his own joke.

I drove Roger back to the city to pick up his car. 'Look mate, no more funny business, OK?'

'Look mate, you have my word on it. Isn't that enough?' It was. Roger did a lot of low things during our friendship, but he never once broke his word to me.

The next day at 7 o'clock we arrived for the meeting. Although I believed what Roger had said, I was still very careful. I looked all over the place. Charlie wasn't worried. He was armed up and ready to go.

We went into the restaurant. [*A copper*] was sitting at a table with Con [*the restaurant's owner*] and Roger. [*The copper*] hadn't changed since I last met him, he still had a snarl on his face. We sat down and Con left the table so we could talk business. [*The copper*] and Charlie were glaring at each other across the table. It was plain to see that they didn't like each other.

Roger calmed everyone down. 'Listen to what I am saying. [*The copper*] here is not real keen to do any business over this matter. The only reason that he has agreed is because they have decided to empty him [*throw him*] out of the taskforce. He is filthy on them and wants to even up with them.'

[*The copper*] said they had a video of Charlie, Randy Tofani and me picking up a shipment of heroin from Judy's house at Hurlstone Park. The video and all the police running sheets [*chronological reports of the police operation*] were for sale for $20,000 cash. It was not negotiable, he said. '$20,000, or you both hit the nick with Randy.'

Roger told me the video existed and so did the running sheets. Charlie and I moved away on our own to talk. We decided to pay the $20,000 to the arsehole rather than take the chance that he wasn't telling us the truth.

Back to the table we went. 'OK, we will pay the $20,000, but we want the originals of the video.'

'No problem,' he said. 'But you two listen to me. This doesn't make us friends or anything like it. If I can pinch you pair again for any little thing then you are off, get me?'

Charlie yelled: 'Go and fuck yourself.'

'You can do your best, cunt, because I'll be doing mine.'

I thought that [*the copper*] and Charlie were going to attack each other. Roger pulled it up in time: 'Listen, all of you. I am responsible for this meeting. I gave my word. Let's keep the conversation restricted to the business at hand, OK?'

We made a meet for the next day to pay the money. I was not meeting at any closed-in places, I wanted it out in the open. We agreed on Centennial Park, where there were always plenty of people about. The meeting was due to take place at 9 o'clock the next morning. I got there at 5am just so I could observe anything out of the ordinary. Nothing happened so we waited. Right on 9am, a police car pulled up exactly where we were to meet them.

We were both apprehensive about the meeting and made sure that we were both armed up in case of any shifty business.

I was driving a green Mercedes and Roger recognised it

as I pulled up alongside him. Roger was driving and [*the copper, in the passenger seat*] wound down the window. I passed the money over to him, he in turn passed over the video and the running sheets to me.

As they drove away, [*the copper*] said: 'Make sure that you burn them after you've satisfied yourself that they are the originals.'

They went one way and we went the other. After giving the video and the running sheets a good check we burned them and went our own ways.

I kept in touch with Charlie, who was doing well on his own. One day Danny Chubb turned up with more news—all bad. This time, however, it was Charlie that had the problem. Apparently the same team of cops that arrested studid Randy Tofani had rented a place across the street from Charlie. He had been under surveillance for several months—the cops were ready to pinch him any day now. The message went like this: 'Tell Charlie not to drive to Sydney to meet the Chinese fellow. They are just waiting for him to go to Sydney. As soon as he does, they are going to grab the whole team.'

I asked Chubb whether anything could be done for him.

'Look Ned, you are sweet. You know that, but they don't like the company you have been keeping lately.'

'How much is that tit-bit of information going to cost, mate?'

We agreed on a figure of $5000 and I arranged to pay him the money the next day.

I then had to warn Charlie without coming undone myself. I went to a public phone and called him. As soon as he answered, I said: 'Charlie. You know who this is. Don't say a word just listen to me.' I told him what Chubb had said. I also reminded him about his stupid mate not taking the advice when he had the chance. 'Don't leave the house, mate.'

Charlie assured me that he would not leave the house. The fucking fool then did exactly the same as Tofani had! He went straight to meet the Chinese and got buckled [*arrested*] for his trouble. He was charged with importing heroin and got 15 years for it. My curiosity got the better of me, so I went to visit him at the Bay after he was refused bail. I had to know why he had ignored my warning and gone to meet the Chinese. When I asked he just shook his head. 'I don't know why I went there, mate, I just don't know.'

I'll never know why people pay the police for information and then ignore it.

A few days after Charlie was arrested, Roger came to see me. 'You did a silly thing, mate. The Feds are not pleased with you getting on the phone and then opening your big mouth about them being ready to arrest him.'

Fuck! I was getting caught all the time, especially when I was wasting my time. What was the sense in sticking my neck out?

But that wasn't the end of the story. The Chinese guy who was arrested with Charlie was going to turn Crown evidence against him. One day I was sitting at home when Val Bellamy, my solicitor, rang me. He said that Charlie's girlfriend, Jenny [*Jennifer Lewis*], had been arrested for killing the Chinese guy. I couldn't believe it. But there was more.

'You are required to attend the CIB for questioning over the murder, too.' Not again. I went in and met Val and Roger to find out what I could do. Before I had a chance to say anything, Roger said: 'Before you blow up, I had a talk to the cop that is handling the murder investigation and you have nothing to concern yourself about. It's just a formality. You did receive a mention, but it is sweet. Calm down. I will take care of it myself, stop worrying.'

Roger explained what happened. 'Apparently, two young constables spotted Jenny acting silly and tried to pull her up for questioning. She bolts and they chase her and catch her. When they look in the car they find this gun and blood everywhere. Jenny refused to say anything so they made a thorough search of the area and find a shallow grave with this Chow in it.'

We discussed who the likely killer was. I couldn't work out anyone likely to be involved in such a sloppy go.

Roger said: 'You will more than likely have to go in for a formal interview, but you don't have to worry about a thing.'

Then he spoke to Val Bellamy: 'Val, you might like to give them a ring now to make a day you're available to go in with Ned and get things sorted out.'

Roger gave Val the detective-in-charge's name and phone number at the homicide squad. Val got straight on the phone and arranged for me to go in with him the next day. I went in with Val for the interview and it was just as Roger said it would be—a formality, nothing more.

A few days later I received a phone call from Val telling me Jenny had hanged herself at Mulawa Jail. Jenny couldn't handle life very well. Charlie used to send her batty. Getting pinched for murder was the last straw.

Harvey Jones was a frustrated gangster if ever there was one. He always carried a gun and he often fired shots into the roof of the different discos that he went to. Harvey desperately wanted to be known as a tough guy, Christ only knows why. He worked on Parramatta Road as a used car salesman, and from what I heard he was classed as the best one there. He should have stuck to selling cars.

I first met him one night at the Star Disco at Bondi. He was trying to impress me at every opportunity. I was having a drink with Dave Kelleher when Harvey pulled out this huge gun, a .44 magnum or something similar. Anyway, he was flashing this gun around, letting people see what he was doing. Every now and then he would look at me, smiling. I thought he was camp.

I finished my drink and was trying to catch the barman's eye to get another. Harvey saw me waiting. Well, he jumped the bar, gun in hand, grabbed the barman by the shirt, pointed the gun at his head and said: 'Can't you see that Neddy wants some service?' The poor fool of a barman shat. He had no idea what was going on. Nor did I. That was my introduction to Harvey Jones.

I got friendly with Harvey and would go out with him now and then. The nights always ended in a stink, with me having to do the fighting. He couldn't hold his hands up. Harvey was forever pulling his gun out and shooting at something. I can't remember just how many times I had to stick my neck out to fix the blue up for him.

When I first met Harvey he was fronting court over a gold bullion robbery. Funnily enough, Roger just happened to have him pinched on the robbery and, you guessed it, Harvey wanted me to approach Roger for him to see if he would talk business.

I didn't mind doing him a favor, but I was concerned that

he would open his big mouth about it and then I would be in the shit. I kept putting him off, saying Roger was too busy to see him. I eventually got around to seeing Roger, without telling Harvey. When I put it to Roger, he couldn't stop laughing.

'He is a fool, Ned. Are you sure that you're not getting mixed up with fools?' We discussed it for a few minutes. 'He is a fool, Ned, but a fool and his money are easily parted. A fool's money spends the same as the next guy's. If you want to do the business yourself without bringing anyone else into it, then it's a go.' I thought about it for a week, then decided to help Harvey—just this once.

When I told him that I had spoken to Roger and that it was sweet, the fool tried to kiss me, he was so happy. I later had my doubts about his sexual preferences.

One night I went out with my wife and a few friends to the Coachman Restaurant in Redfern, and Harvey tagged along. After dinner, we all went to the bar for a few dozen drinks. My wife used to have a glass of wine; other than that she didn't drink. Harvey was his usual self, trying to impress everyone, shouting Moet & Chandon for one and all. I gave Roger a ring at Darlinghurst police station. [*In July 1982, Rogerson transferred from the armed hold-up squad to the detectives office at inner-city Darlinghurst.*] He was on night shift. I explained where I was and who I was with. Roger said he would pop in for a drink and a chat. He did just that—and brought a team of young cops that he was training.

I didn't tell Harvey that Roger was coming. I wanted to give him a surprise. Well, surprise is not the word to use: Harvey went the color of bad shit when Roger and this team of young detectives walked in.

I winked at Roger and he played the part well. He knew exactly what to do. He walked over to me and shook my hand. I introduced Harvey to Roger. 'Harvey, this is Roger Rogerson.' Harvey stood there shaking, he was in a state of shock. (Roger had that effect on some people.) Harvey finally found his voice: 'It is my pleasure, Sergeant Rogerson.' He shook Roger's hand. I thought he was going to hug him or something. Roger looked at Harvey real seriously and said: 'You can call me Roger, but only for tonight.'

Then we all burst out laughing. I was in hysterics. Harvey

was so relieved that he ordered a dozen bottles of Moet & Chandon. It cost him in the vicinity of $2000. Harvey didn't care, he had met the famous Roger Rogerson. We drank at the Coachman until after 4am. The young cops with Roger couldn't believe it. They didn't know what to think. Roger loved every minute of it, he loved an audience. Roger never saw Harvey again after that night. Unfortunately, I did.

Harvey Jones owned a brothel, Aunt Lucy's, at Homebush—that was his claim to fame. I was approached by John Openshaw who had a buyer, Louie Bayer, for the brothel. I saw Harvey but he had no interest in selling, so I told Openshaw the news. There were several attempts to get hold of Harvey's brothel, but he hung on to it—until he went missing.

Harvey was becoming a pest. He thought that owning a brothel and carrying a gun made him a gangster. Someone had led him astray when he was young. He continued his silly pastime of shooting up discos and nightclubs. I don't know what he got out of doing it.

I must have fixed up three or four shooting blues for Harvey. They weren't anything real serious, just shooting at the ceilings in discos. He refused to pull up. No matter how hard I tried to educate him, he wouldn't listen. Maybe it was my fault. He knew that I could fix the blue up for him, so he kept right on doing it.

It was becoming a regular event; every other morning he would ring me with some problem or another. There were times when he would arrive at my home unexpectedly, crying at my front door. 'Help me please, mate, I'm in trouble, help me.'

I always fell into helping the poor fool.

One Saturday morning I was about to drive to the pubs to give the guys their banks to stand up with for the betting that day when the phone rang. It was Ron Daly. He was raging, blowing right up.

'Calm down,' I said. 'What's up?'

'You tell that lanky big cunt that he's off when I get my hands on him.'

'Slow down and tell me what he's done.'

'You can't help the cunt this time, he's gone too far.'

After I calmed Daly down, I found out that Harvey had been up to his old tricks again. The fucking idiot had shot up Shelia's Disco in Daly's territory, North Sydney.

From what Ron Daly told me, Harvey and a guy known as Bob the Basher went to the disco and started to play up. The bouncers tried to eject Harvey, so he let two shots go into the ceiling. The fool had to pick Daly's turf to do it in. I could understand why he was so mad. Ron Daly liked a quiet turf and rode roughshod over it, like an old-time marshal or something. I promised to see Harvey personally.

Before I could get out of the front door, the phone rang again. It was Harvey. 'Hello mate. I'm in deep shit, I need your help.'

'You fucking fool, what do you think you are doing to me? Have you any idea who is looking for you?'

Harvey started his crying routine again. 'Help me, please mate.'

'Fuck you, shithead, you are off tap this time. I can't pull the man up.'

'I know mate. Ron Daly has already been over to see my mum and she is frightened to death. He told my mum that this time I am off.'

I abused him for all of 10 minutes. 'What else did you expect, stupid?'

'I'll pay anything, mate, just talk to him for me, please.'

Money was the magic word, especially with Ron Daly. I told Harvey to ring me at the Star Hotel in an hour. Then I rang Daly back and said I needed to see him straight away.

'OK, meet me at the coffee shop across the road from the station in 30 minutes.'

I arrived on time and Ron was waiting, furious. He cut straight into me. 'Fools will get you into trouble. Why do you persist in helping the cunt of a thing?'

I calmed him down a little and explained that Harvey wanted to give him a large piece of change. That soothed the temper.

'I'll do business with you for that cunt just this one last time. It will cost him every cent he has. Tell that lanky heap of shit that if I ever see him again it will be the last time that anybody sees him.'

I told him I would get in contact when I knew how much Harvey had in cash. Then I headed for the Star and rang stupid. 'Listen to me, you fuck, I have fixed it this time. It's

Mixed Fortunes

the very last time I am going to do it for you. This is going to cost you the earth.'

Harvey was crying again. 'Thank you, mate, I love you, mate. How much do I need for the man?'

'How much cash can you rake up today? It has to be today before he changes his mind.'

'I have about $30,000 in ready cash here with me now. Will that do?'

Before I could answer he went on: 'If that's not enough, I will get more.'

'Hang in there,' I said. 'I'll ring and check.'

I rang Daly and mentioned $30,000. 'Is that enough to calm you down?'

He replied: 'Take every fucking penny the cunt has and tell him what I said. I never want to see him again.'

I gave Harvey the news and arranged to meet him a day or so later so I could collect the money for Daly. When the day of the meeting arrived he didn't turn up. I was howling on him for keeping me waiting. After a few hours I started to worry so I rang his mother at home. She was concerned too.

'Isn't he with you, Ned?'

'He was supposed to meet me but he hasn't turned up. I have people waiting to do things for him. They won't wait forever.'

She knew what I was talking about. Harvey told me that he told his mother all his business. I asked her to make sure that as soon as she heard from him, he should ring me at my home. Daly was blueing on me. I told him Harvey hadn't turned up.

About a week later there was still no Harvey. His mother kept ringing me, crying. 'Can you possibly come to see me please, Ned? I am too old to travel myself.' I went to her house and took my wife to see if she could do something to help. Harvey's mother was very upset.

'Harvey is a good boy, Ned. He would not make me worry like this. There is something very wrong.'

I thought so too, but I didn't want to upset her any more, so I kept my big mouth shut. We stayed for a few hours trying to offer her some comfort then left, promising to keep in touch.

Two weeks went by and Roger rang me: 'Well mate, it's on once again.'

'Give me a clue what you're on about, mate.'

'You, my friend, are required to attend the police station at your convenience for questioning about your part in the disappearance of one Harvey Jones.' He was laughing. He was a joke a minute. 'Come on, mate, what have you done with the body?'

'Pull up, Roger. Someone will think you're serious.'

'You are to ring a friend of ours called [*a detective*] at homicide now.'

I'd had enough of being called in for questioning every time some fool went missing or was murdered. 'I'm not going into the homicide squad any more. Fuck them.'

'I told you he is our friend. Just ring the guy for me.'

I rang [*the detective*] at the homicide squad rooms. 'This is Ned Smith here. I believe that you want to talk to me.'

'Yes, mate. Just a formality for you. Pop in one day when you're in town with nothing to do.'

'I am not coming in to be put on show any more.'

'No need to get upset. I will meet you wherever you like.'

I met him at the Fosters Hotel in the city. This was my first meeting with him, but I knew he was on side with Roger, so I was sweet.

[*The detective*] showed me a statement by Bob the Basher, who said he saw Harvey meet me outside the Star and walk in. He saw me walk out an hour later, but had not seen Harvey since. The Basher said Harvey had a large sum of money on him to give to me. I read this load of shit and handed the statement back to [*the detective*]. 'Am I going to need a lawyer for this? It is all shit.'

He said: 'There's no problem about this, mate. Roger has vouched for you. Just pop in when you can and I will get you to sign a formal denial of the allegation. That's all that will come of it, OK?' I thanked him and left. I never got around to signing anything related to Harvey Jones. I made friends with [*the detective*] though. He was always joking about Harvey going missing.

I put Alan Dillon to work for me. He had just finished doing a life sentence for armed robbery and murder. I knew him from the nick. He was penniless when they let him out. I had Roger check him out first, then gave him some work.

Alan was a top guy. He was always there when I needed him, and he never once let me down.

One day we were drinking at the Lansdowne Hotel on Broadway. It was Barry McCann's hotel [*McCann was a major Sydney heroin dealer who was shot dead in December 1987.*] McCann owned the Lansdowne Hotel, but it was registered in his father's name because McCann was unable to get a liquor licence with his record.

There were lots of people there when we arrived. McCann always had the place full of bouncers; he would have no less than six bouncers there at a time. This particular night they were all there, including Terry Ball (a real nutter), Roy Thurgar (a very good boxer) and that old Saturday [*would-be*] gangster Billy Stevens. They were just a few of McCann's gang.

We were having a drink on our own, minding our own business when Alan started to freak out.

'What are those fools staring at us all the time for?' he asked.

'Don't go getting all paranoid on me, Al.'

As if they had planned it, some fool decided to have a go at us over some shit incident or other. That was mistake number one for them. I knocked out McCann's eldest son—he was only young then, just past 20. Then one of the bouncers said something, so he got it too. We decided to go. As we were leaving five or six of the bouncers decided to have the last say. Mistake number two. They followed us out to my car, still mumbling away to no one in particular, just trying to build their courage up a bit.

They thought they had frightened us, but they were in for a big shock. I grabbed an aluminium baseball bat from my car that I kept for just such occasions, then started bashing into the lot of them. They couldn't get away from me quick enough. While I was bashing into them, Alan grabbed a .38 revolver from the car and, at gunpoint, lined some of the bouncers up against the wall. While they were lined up, I attacked them with the baseball bat, flogging them until they dropped. It was a silly thing to do and completely unnecessary at the time. But they wanted to play tough guy, so we accommodated them.

Maybe two weeks went by. I was drinking at the Quarrymans Hotel in Pyrmont. Alan wasn't with me this night—I was with a mate of mine, Jimmy Traynor. I was driving a red Mercedes sports car—easy to spot. They must have seen my car because as I left the hotel with Jimmy Traynor, I saw a car parked on the footpath with three guys sitting in it and the engine revving.

As I walked around to the driver's door of my Mercedes, the car on the footpath took off with a screech of tyres. It came straight at us, a gun barrel pointing out the rear window at me. It happened so quick I didn't have time to think. I tried to get my car door open so I could get a gun from under the seat, but I fumbled getting the key into the door lock. Jimmy was standing at the other side of my car waiting to get in. Four shots rang out. I let my natural instinct take over. I know that I got out of the way very quickly, as no shots hit me.

One hit the wall near my head and one other hit the pub window, some feet above me. Jimmy wasn't so lucky. He copped two blasts from the shotgun, one in the chest and the other in the shoulder and left arm. I ran into the hotel to grab another gun that I had there for this type of emergency. By the time I got back outside, they were gone. Jimmy was lying in the gutter bleeding badly.

Tex was with us, he was shitting himself. [*Tex was a drinking partner of Neddy's. A bosun in the merchant navy, Neddy described Tex as: 'A big guy. He was as strong as a bull and fought real well. He never trained one day in his life but he used to knock blokes out with no trouble at all.'*] It was the first time Tex had been involved in anything like this. Tex rang an ambulance for Jimmy. I tried to get hold of Roger, but he wasn't available. Instead, I rang John Openshaw at home. I told him what had happened and he told me to ring the police and report it straight away to cover myself. I did so, then rang Val Bellamy at home and got him to come over in case things got out of hand with the police.

It was lucky I rang Val because dozens of police arrived as soon as they discovered who I was. They tried to blame me for the shooting! As they talked to Val, Openshaw arrived on the scene. He spoke to the trump in charge and fixed everything up. I went to the hospital.

Jimmy was shot up pretty bad. He would live, but had about 60 pellets in his body. Some of the muscle was torn away from his side and a little muscle was gone from his arm. He was lucky that the would-be killers didn't have enough sense or knowledge to load the shotgun with the double Os. Had they done that, he would have been off tap [*dead*].

Over the next couple of days I tried to find out who attempted to kill me. I never gave it a moment's thought that McCann could have been responsible for it. I just didn't believe that he had it in him.

Roger advised me to sit tight: 'Sit back and just wait and keep your ears open. It won't take long for some big mouth to let it out. Then you make your move.' It was good, sound advice, so I did just that. It was as Roger had predicted, they couldn't keep their big mouths shut. It *was* McCann's gang that had let go at me and hit the wrong guy. Rumors were spreading like wildfire. McCann's gang were going around armed up all the time—they were jumping at their own shadows.

Silly old Billy Stevens carried a sawn-off shotgun down the leg of his trousers. Christ only knows how he expected to get it out in a hurry if I did appear. People were stirring things up and they kept ringing the hotel, telling them that I was out the front in my car with a gun. Well, silly old Stevo tried to get the shotgun out and ended up shooting himself in the foot. The old fool lost two toes. (I have run into Stevens in jail since then. He makes sure that everyone is told that the shotty was not meant for me.)

McCann and I had a feud for a short time. It ended up dying out, nothing ever came of it. And the answer is No, I did not kill him. McCann was shot and killed by someone during the 'Gang Wars', but it was definitely not me.

It was a Sunday, a day of rest. Tex and I were having a quiet drink at the Lord Nelson Hotel at the Rocks. It was catering for a lot of tourists at the time, so the place was crowded. About 4pm a crowd of blokes walked in and they looked like they were looking for trouble. I kept an eye on them, just out of curiosity. Can't be too careful.

I recognised one of the guys as Tony Brizzi, an ex-painter and docker from Melbourne. We acknowledged each other with a nod and later, when I went to the toilet, I stopped and chatted with him for a minute or two. Then I went back to Tex and we continued to drink. Towards evening, Tex began to get a bit niggly and started picking arguments with everyone. On two occasions he walked deliberately past Tony Brizzi, staring at him. When he came back after the second time, he told me that Brizzi was flashing a gun.

'Don't let it bother you, mate, just ignore him.'

A few drinks later, Tex was getting worse. He was glaring at Brizzi and I could see trouble brewing. Tex could really fight, but when real violence came into it, he shat himself. I warned him to be careful: 'He won't hesitate to let go at you, Tex, so make sure that you get in first if you are going to take him on.'

Tex was all revved up. He went past Brizzi again, snarling. I decided to go over and calm the blue down. Just as I got close they started to exchange words. Brizzi wasn't going to fight Tex: I knew this, but Tex didn't. Just as I reached them—and before I had a chance to say a word—Brizzi pulled a gun and started to point it at Tex. I moved in close to Brizzi and hit him flush on the chin before he had the chance to fire. Down he went, but he managed to pull me off balance with him so down I went on top of him.

There was a small table between us so I had trouble doing anything but holding his hand with the gun in it. He tried to point the gun in my direction. I called to Alan Dillon, who'd been drinking with us: 'Hand me your gun.' Alan handed me his gun and I shoved it straight into Brizzi's mouth, breaking his teeth. Brizzi couldn't talk—his mouth was full—but I could see by his eyes and the expression on his face that he didn't want to go on with it any further.

There were people going everywhere. I couldn't shoot the guy unless he tried to shoot me, in which case I could have rightly claimed self-defence against any murder charge. Instead I flogged him and took his gun.

Tex had been frozen solid. I said: 'What happened to you, cunt? Why didn't you try to grab his gun while I was on top of him?'

Tex was in a state of shock, he had nearly been shot. At least it sobered him up. Brizzi left the pub but returned an hour later. I thought it was a back-up, so Alan and I grabbed our guns and waited to see which way things went. Brizzi was all for calling it quits—he just wanted his gun back. I emptied it and handed it back to him.

Two days later—in an unrelated incident—Brizzi shot a

friend of Tex's five times in the chest and left him to die on the kitchen floor. Then he calmly took the wife of the bloke he had just shot to bed. Brizzi ended up being jailed over the shooting. It didn't take long for the story to get exaggerated and find its way to police. Roger heard it and asked what went down. I explained. Roger then told me that there was this cop named [*Smith names an officer*], a friend of [*a policeman*], who was making enquiries about me with a view to pinching me—it didn't matter what for, he just wanted to make a name for himself.

I asked Roger what he thought would be the best way to approach [*the officer*]. 'Don't waste any time arguing with the fool, Ned. He is going to confront you tomorrow at the Lord Nelson Hotel with a team of his cronies. He will try to get you to blow up and then he will pinch you.'

'What's his go, mate? Is he any good?'

'No, the man's a fool, but don't wait until he loads you. Get in first.'

I told Roger that I would take his advice.

'Listen Ned, you can't afford to let this clown get over you. Get to the pub tomorrow and have Val [*Bellamy, solicitor*] with you. Front him up-front, don't take a backward step from him. He will shit himself. Whatever you do, don't let him tumble you and attack him.'

Next day, Val, Tex and I went to the Lord Nelson to wait for the fool to arrive. I was only there long enough for one drink when in walked this huge team of cops dressed in shirts and slacks. They had their coats and ties off, ready for action. They had two beers before [*the officer*] got up the courage to front me. He didn't know who Val was. He came over, grinning back at his mates. He stared at me with his tough look and said: 'Are you Neddy Smith?'

As if he didn't know.

He goes on, as if I had answered him: 'I want to talk . . .'

That was as far as I let him get.

'If you have anything to say to me, then do it.' Val handed [*the officer*] his business card and informed him that unless he had a reason for harassing me, he had better leave or find himself in court. [*The officer*] was stunned. He didn't have a clue what to do. He picked up a coaster off the bar and made out he was writing something down. Val said: 'If that's anything about Mr Smith, you had better write it in your book because I don't think that coaster will look too good in court.'

The big goose had made a fool of himself in front of his mates. Out he stormed. He had the last word on his way out: 'I won't forget this, cunt.'

12
Back With Abo

partner *n* 1. a sharer or partaker; an associate. 2. *Law* one associated with another or others as a principal or a contributor of capital in a business or a joint venture

Macquarie Dictionary

Life was normal for a while. Business was booming, so in 1982 my wife and I decided that it was time we moved to the country for some of that peace and quiet everyone raves about. Debra's mother and sister lived at Warners Bay near Newcastle, so we went house-hunting there first. We found a nice little place so we bought it and moved up there. It certainly was peaceful, too bloody peaceful for me. The boredom soon got to me.

I used to catch a plane down to Sydney twice a week to take care of business with the SP. The dope [*heroin*] business was running itself. I had 10 guys working for me, so I only had to call in once a week to collect any money that was outstanding. But I couldn't handle the flying. It frightened the crap out of me. I used to lose weight every time I got on the plane. So I switched to driving down, but that took three hours until much later, when they fixed the roads. My wife and kids loved living at Warners Bay, we had some really top times together. But I couldn't cop the quiet life.

I started going to Sydney for two and three days at a time and playing up on the drink again. The drink was getting to be a real problem for me, but I had no idea that I was becoming an alcoholic. I used to average at least 30 beers a day while I was drinking with Tex.

In 1980, I'd found myself developing the shakes on my right side, especially my right hand. I saw a series of doctors before I was diagnosed as having Parkinson's disease. I was devastated. I took to drinking to try to hide the effects of the shaking: I had always been a fitness freak and finding out I had this incurable disease shook me up pretty badly. After some time, I began to handle the situation better—but I continued to drink.

Debra and I were to live in the countryside for the next seven years, first at Warners Bay, then at Kotara, where we bought a six-bedroom house with a 44-foot pool, an eight-man indoor spa, full-size pool room and two lounge rooms. Needless to say I installed some serious security around both houses: closed-circuit TV, attack dogs, spotlights, an intercom and various alarms.

We never had any problems with the neighbours: apart from a hello, there was never much communication between us. But there was plenty of talk around Newcastle. When I was granted bail in 1988 there was a special meeting of Neighbourhood Watch called to let residents know that 'Neddy Smith is back in town'. Despite this, the kids never had problems at school and Debra never had any problems either.

I didn't enjoy the country life much. It had its good points: it kept me off the drink for four days every week; I got to see quite a bit of my family; and Debra and I got on much better than when we'd lived in Sydney.

Through boredom, I also got back into training, and felt much better for it. Every day I was at home I did two hours on the weights, without resting between sets. I also punched a heavy punching bag, just to keep my hand in. When I stayed in Sydney, I had a steam bath and swam a few laps every morning at the Coogee RSL.

I had kept in touch with Graham 'Abo' Henry while he was waiting for his early release from jail. His wife Leslie had come to visit us on weekends. Abo was due out soon–Rex [*Jackson*] had done as he promised. I went to Silverwater Jail on the day Abo was released and picked him up as he walked out the gate. I took him for lunch and we discussed what he intended to do. Abo wanted to work with me so I explained what I was into—everything. After lunch, Abo and I parted company. We planned to meet at the Coachman for dinner that night.

I waited at the Coachman for about two hours and was about to call it a night when the head waiter came over and told me I had a phone call. It had to be Abo. It was. He was at Redfern police station, arrested for DUI [*driving under the influence of alcohol, the charge that preceded the .08 and .05 laws*].

On his way to meet me, he'd been driving down Baptist Street, Redfern, not knowing that since his trip to the nick they had made Baptist Street one way—and it was the opposite way to the one he was going. The horse patrol pulled him up and hit him with DUI. I called over the head waiter, George.

'Listen mate, can I get one of your boys to go up to Redfern police station to bail my friend out?'

George looked after me no end. He was the best waiter in Australia. George sent one of his waiters up to bail Abo out. Abo finally arrived, we got on the drink and carried on a bit over dinner. After dinner, about 11pm, Abo wanted to box on again. I remembered the last time he wanted to box on. 'No way, buddy,' I said. 'I'm off to the motel for some sleep.'

Abo was pretty drunk by this time, so I called a cab for him. I put him in it and told the cab driver to take him home to Ryde. Apparently, about two blocks on, Abo woke up and redirected the driver to the Star disco at Bondi. It was a bad mistake on Abo's part as he was full of it and looking for trouble. He soon found it. The bouncer at the disco made some comment to Abo as he was going in. Abo knocked him out and left him lying in the street in front of the disco. Abo had been training every day for 18 months so he was one jump ahead of all the poor fools at the disco. Abo went upstairs and it took him about two minutes to find a head he knew from the nick. They got on the drink and Abo started singing with his new friend. The bouncer objected and told Abo to pull up. Abo told him to get fucked so the bouncer told Abo to get out the front.

Out they went. The bouncer must have expected a fair go because he started to take off his shirt. Abo, seeing an opening for a smart lad, king-hit the guy knocking him out. He then stood on his chest yelling out to anyone else that wanted to have a go. The police arrived and Abo was still standing on the bouncer's chest. They asked him to get off. Abo started to abuse them. They told him to hop in the police car. Abo wasn't having any of that. One of the cops was [*Smith names the officer*]. He was trying to calm Abo down, when Abo produced Roger's card that I had given him only hours earlier for just such an occasion as this. [*The policeman*] looked at the card. He then let Abo go, telling him to give Roger a ring the next day. Off they went and, thank Christ, Abo headed home too.

I found out about Abo's little escapade the next morning when I was woken by the phone. It was Abo. He said: 'Hello, mate . . .' Before he could add any more, his wife grabbed the phone and abused me for keeping him out on the drink when his family were waiting at home for him.

He got back on the phone.

'Nice one, Abo,' I said.

'Ned, I hit a hurdle after I left you last night. I had to produce Roger's card.'

I arranged to see him straight away. When he turned up he was looking pretty bad from the drink. 'What have you been up to, mate?' He dropped the bombshell right in my lap. He told me all about the episode at the Star disco and how he flashed Roger's card. 'You might ring Roger, mate,' Abo said.

I thought I'd better get in early, before the cops did, so I rang Roger.

'Hello Roger, what's doing?'

He started to laugh. 'Hello punchy, did you have a big night?' Shit, the cops had beaten me to it.

'I can explain all about it, mate. I gave Abo your card because he is working with me now.'

'No need to explain. Just slow him down if he is going to be working with you now.'

I was relieved that he wasn't blueing.

'When do I get to meet this Abo?' Roger said. 'How about he shouts us lunch today?'

I arranged to bring Abo to lunch at Dimitri's restaurant at Surry Hills at 1pm. While we waited for Roger to arrive I decided to give Abo a scare. I told him: 'Listen mate, Roger is howling on you for last night. You are in deep shit.' Abo then tried to talk me out of lunch—but no way was he getting off that lightly. Roger and [*another policeman*] walked in. Roger was grinning as he sat down.

'Is this Abo?' he said.

I played the game. 'Yes, this is the cunt that dropped your

name all over Sydney last night.' Abo didn't know what to say. He just sat there. After that we all burst out laughing and Abo relaxed.

Over lunch, Roger laid down the rules of working with me. He told Abo that he had checked him out and discovered that Abo was not too popular with many police. But that was not a problem, he said, as long as he behaved when he was working.

Abo moved his family up to Valentine, near Warners Bay where I was. I kept him close so I could get hold of him at a moment's notice when needed. Abo did well and it wasn't long before I made him a full partner with me. There was more than enough money for both of us and we did well for many years.

[*Smith is coy about the money he made, although it is obvious that the amounts were enormous. Amazingly, he had no bank account: everything was paid for in cash. Over the next few years Smith changed his car every few months, always paying cash. He owned 19 different cars—Mercedes, Rolls Royces, Porsches, Jaguars—and they were never registered in his name. Some weeks he spent $10,000 on clothes and shoes. At lunch, he would entertain half a dozen people (mostly police) two or three times a week. He almost always paid the bills, which were typically $1200 to $2000. Sometimes, especially in the mid to late 1980s, the lunch would continue on to a brothel, where Smith might spend another $6000 to entertain himself and some police. Smith also spent money on 'young ladies', 12 of whom were given new cars. He spent $750,000 on jewellery for himself. Huge sums of cash were stored in hotel safes, in friends' houses and in steel boxes that were stored in banks.*

Yet any money that was put aside for a rainy day—and with the 'live-now worry-later' mentality Smith adopted, it is questionable how much that was—appears to have been spent on legal fees. It seems the Smith family has little, if any, wealth today.]

Abo had been out of the nick for only three weeks or so when he decided it was time he bought himself a car. He bought a new Mercedes Benz. Three months later he bought a huge block of land and began building a big pink mansion on it. He knew how to live and he made the most of it while it lasted. But Abo still couldn't keep out of trouble.

I had a meeting with [*a policeman*] about doing another drug rip-off, this time on a drug dealer he had been watching for months. Anyway, I left Abo and another guy in the car to wait until I finished seeing [*the policeman*]. I was away for the best part of an hour. When I got back to the car, no Abo. I thought that he may have got sick of waiting and called into the pub for a quiet drink. I walked into the pub—still no Abo.

All of a sudden I got a tap on the arm. It was a young detective. He looked nervous.

'Yes,' I said. 'Can I do something for you, officer?'

He looked around before speaking: 'Ned, can I speak to you for a minute, please. It won't take long.'

'Sure you can. Is there something up?'

'Ned, we have a Graham Henry at [*a suburban*] police station. He has been arrested with an unlicensed pistol in his possession and it is stolen. He showed me Roger Rogerson's card and dropped your name too. Do you know the man?'

'Yes, I do know him. What can be done?'

The cop's name was [*Smith names the officer: we will call him the suburban policeman*]. We had a talk. I told him I would get Roger on the phone to square things up for Abo. I tried to ring Roger but remembered he was fronting court at The Entrance, about 60 kilometres north of Sydney, so I rang [*a detective*] instead. I was told he was sitting for an exam. 'Get him to come to the phone, it is very important.' He came to the phone and I explained what had happened. 'Put the young cop on the phone to me,' he said.

I put [*the suburban policeman*] on the phone to [*the detective*]. After a few minutes talking, [*the suburban policeman*] handed me the phone. I talked to [*the detective*] again and he assured me all was well.

[*The suburban policeman*] was full of remorse about Abo's arrest.

'I'm sorry that this hapened, Ned. I'll go back and let Abo go. He will be with you in 10 minutes.'

About 10 minutes passed and Abo walked in. I blew up: 'What the fuck happened?'

Abo explained: 'The cops were watching a flat in the street where we were parked and they noticed us sitting there acting suspiciously, so they pulled up and searched us.' Abo handed them the gun without them even searching him. They shat and arrested him. Then he did that trick of his and handed them Roger's card straight away, without even checking to see if they were sweet or not. The story ended with us paying [*the detective*] $10,000 to give to [*the suburban policeman*]. And they gave us back the gun.

Over a long period of time, Abo and I worked well together and I got to trust him. He was good to have around at times, if you could keep him off the rum. We made plenty of money together and had a lot of good times. We got into a lot of trouble too, but nothing that I couldn't fix up for a dollar.

I had the Green Light, so how could I go wrong?

Abo and I were getting hotter as time went on. We were frequently under surveillance by the Australian Federal Police and several task forces that had been especially formed to trap us. Their biggest problem lay in the fact that I was getting inside help and information. The federal and state police never had a chance. It wasn't a case of me working for the police, it was the other way round—they were working for me.

A classic example of this was the Pelair inquiry. [*Pelair was a small airline that was suspected by the Australian Federal Police of being involved in importing heroin via Papua New Guinea. The former New South Wales policeman Murray Riley, then-serving detectives Roger Rogerson and Bill Duff, Sydney solicitor John Aston—who used to employ Brian Alexander as a clerk—Graham 'Abo' Henry and Neddy Smith were among those investigated. The story became public in March 1985 when a Pelair plane, about to depart from PNG, was stopped for a drug search after a tip-off from Australian police. The search was aborted when the PNG Prime Minister Michael Somare appeared at the airport: he had just been lunching with Aston and another of the plane's passengers. The plane departed without being searched. Somare was forced to resign and an inquiry was held into his behavior. It cleared him of any impropriety.*

The Pelair story made further headlines when a jet owned by the company crashed into the sea off Botany Bay in October 1985. This crash appears to have been accidental and unrelated to the allegations of drug smuggling.

According to Smith, however, information from within the police taskforce saved him and many others from going to jail: one of the gang was tipped off that police were waiting for a plane carrying heroin to leave the ground. Once the plane took off, the police, waiting for the aircraft in PNG and Queensland, would swoop in Sydney and make numerous arrests.]

My job was to contact the right people and make sure the fucking jet didn't leave the country. I got hold of the person and cancelled the plane. The leak in the taskforce was discovered, and again we made headlines. The strange thing was that the Feds knew everything that was going on—the identities of the gang were also known—yet not one of us was ever arrested or even questioned about the conspiracy to import heroin into the country. Thanks to the cop who supplied us with the information, no arrests were made.

While I was making plenty of money and had pull in the force, then they worked for me. And they liked it, too. I paid much better wages than the police force did and for much less work. I could do anything I wanted without fear of being arrested.

At first, I didn't take full advantage of it, but I soon woke up to what I was wasting, and made up for the time missed.

Police used to waste time following me. All they had to do was pull me up and search the car and I would have been off. But not once in 15 years did they search me or my car.

We had 10 guys working full-time on the dope [*heroin*] and things were going great. Every Saturday we would all meet at the Star Hotel in Alexandria. Abo would give them a pound or half a pound each week and tell them that the heroin cost so much. The dealers had to pay him that amount back, and any profit on top was split down the middle. It worked well. If the Feds had got off their arses just once on a Saturday and walked into the Star, they could have caught us with anything.

We didn't hide in back lanes meeting people. We did everything out in the open where everyone could see us. We met cops in public places, we had no reason to hide what we were doing. Who was going to pinch us? Except maybe the Feds if they got lucky and fluked us.

The Feds were definitely the best when it came to tailing

us. They had unlimited cash and equipment, and bought the very best in electronic gear.

But we had the answer. We had [*a policeman*] giving us all sorts of gear. I once spent $60,000 in one go on high-tech anti-surveillance gear. I bought bug detectors, leg detectors (you wear them on your leg and they let you know if someone is wearing a hidden tape-recorder), shotgun microphones, hand-held scanners (plus he gave us all the frequencies we needed, including supposedly secret channels), telephone scramblers—all sorts of things. We never used most of it, but I kept buying gear through the 1980s, just to stay ahead.

The Feds would think nothing of putting eight or more cars on you for weeks on end, whether they got a result or not. It didn't matter to them. I had many a game of follow-the-leader over the 15-odd years that they were on and off my tail. Sometimes I would spot them, but the majority of times I just knew they were there following me. It was a feeling I had developed over many years.

The dog squad [*New South Wales surveillance police, named 'dogs' because they follow people around*] were good at their job, too. I knew most of the dogs. I used to drink with them and I had a few friends in the squad that didn't hesitate to tell me if the dogs were on to me or any of my guys.

I was sweet with dozens of top cops. I met different police all the time and they all came in handy at some time or other. I even had cops coming to me looking for jobs. Some ex-cops did work for us.

Roger was a leading light in the New South Wales police force and I was his mate. Naturally, there were a few stray cops that didn't like him, but they all respected him, and that's all that mattered. I met so many important connections through my friendship with The Dodger that I couldn't keep track of them all. It was a case of horses for courses. Someone for every little thing that may one day need fixing. They all came in handy at some time in my career. I fixed everything from drink driving charges to murder blues. Nothing too big or too small.

Tex used to put on huge barbecues on the weekends at his home over the north side. Everyone used to attend these turnouts: top cops, magistrates, prosecutors, lawyers and, of course, dozens of crims. Many charges were fixed at Tex's place at these turnouts. No one cared who was who: they just took you at face value. You wouldn't be there if you weren't sweet. The barbecues began in around 1980 and continued through to around 1988. I didn't know that certain police had been dubbed members of the 'Barbecue Set' until recently, when I first heard that expression.

Tex's house was often under surveillance: we were aware of that, but it didn't worry us one bit. Danny Chubb was a regular at the turnouts. He was under surveillance over suspicion of importing drugs. He was sweet as he had [*a senior policeman*] on side, one of the most powerful jacks in the force.

The public believes that groups such as the Mafia and Triads run crime. They are wrong. Nothing goes down without the permission of the New South Wales police first OKing it.

13
Blood on the Streets

'If the money is there, Flannery will kill. And he doesn't care who.'

> Sydney crime figure George Freeman,
> to a National Crime Authority hearing, 1987

Danny Chubb rang me at home with a message—a guy from Melbourne was running around Sydney trying to drum up business; he was offering to kill me for $50,000. Not much, I thought. I reckoned I was worth more. The hitman's name was Christopher Dale Flannery. He was trying to establish himself in Sydney as a professional killer and standover man. He didn't know me or even know what I looked like. Money was the only reason he had for wanting to kill me.

The message came from none other than the great Dr Nick Paltos. [*Paltos, a Sydney doctor, pleaded guilty in 1986 to conspiring to import 7.2 tonnes of cannabis resin. He was sentenced to 20 years jail, with a 13-year minimum.*] Nick had told Danny Chubb to warn me—and I thank him for the warning he sent. When Danny told me, I grabbed Abo and we headed to Sydney. I wanted to get in touch with Roger and get in first, before Flannery got up the courage to get me. Abo knew where Flannery lived and what he looked like, so I was one jump up on him.

I met Roger and told him what Danny had passed on to me. Roger knew Flannery well—he was the one to get Flannery the start with George Freeman. Freeman was no dill, nor was Roger. They wanted Flannery where they could keep an eye on him and keep him under control. Roger advised me to let him handle it: if nothing worked out his way, then I could do it my way.

'Wait until I try to straighten this mess out, will you?'

Roger had never given me dud advice before, so I agreed to wait until he contacted Flannery and found out what the story was. Abo and I didn't sit around idle, though. We checked on Flannery's house so I knew where to find him. I saw several police and got every bit of information I could on Flannery. Then I waited to hear from Roger. He rang me later that day.

'Mate, we are meeting Chris at the Fosters Hotel tonight at 6pm. OK?'

According to Roger there had been a misunderstanding. I said that I would meet Roger and Flannery there, but I wasn't taking any chances. I got Abo to get there early so he could position himself in case Flannery had plans of his own. Abo staked himself close to the front entrance so he could see anyone entering without them seeing him. I was standing at the bar watching the other entrance when Roger and Chris walked in. Flannery was dressed in good slacks and an open-necked shirt. I could see that there was nowhere on his body to hide a gun. Roger brought him over to meet me and we shook hands. He seemed pleasant enough. I cut straight into him about his wanting to collect the $50,000 on me.

He said: 'Whoever told you that is lying.'

He wanted to know who gave me the message, but I wasn't silly enough to tell him. Roger, Abo, Flannery and I all ended up at the Lord Nelson Hotel blind drunk, but I still kept my guard up with Flannery. I had heard too much about him. It turned out that I was right not to trust Flannery, because the next day—after I had fronted him—he told Nick Paltos: 'That Neddy Smith fronted me with a cop, Rogerson, last night. He got Rogerson to pull me up. Lucky he did, because I was all ready to put him off.' I couldn't help myself. Next time I saw Flannery I related the conversation word for word. He didn't know what to say, except: 'I'll know not to open my mouth to *him* again.'

Chris Flannery was an evil person. He would kill anyone for a price, friends included. Roger got me to run around with Flannery for a short time to help out on a few minor things and I got to like the guy. Strange as it might seem, we got on pretty well together. If it had not been for the way his wife got him to act all the time, Chris could have been a nice guy, left to be himself.

About the same time I met Chris, the Australian Federal Police were stepping up their operation on Danny Chubb. Danny was heavily into importing both heroin and hashish in large quantities. Recently, he'd barely escaped arrest.

(Chubb also started bringing in handguns from the United States, then he brought in Kalashnikovs with the hash from Lebanon. Then he brought in machine pistols: Uzis and other makes. They were beautiful looking. The automatics cost $2000 and the pistols $1000. I used to buy as many as I could and had about 40 guns at one stage. I used to practice on a property at Woollongong: I'd go there once a month, or whenever I bought a new gun and wanted to try it out. Or sometimes we'd go downstairs in the cellar of the Iron Duke Hotel and let them off down there.

I always had a gun with me when I drank, one in the car, or where I could put my hands on one in seconds. Someone in my company always had one, there was one behind the bar, or the waiter carried one for me. I never got checked: I was unofficially allowed to carry a gun. There were times when I dropped a gun on the floor when I was drunk and a copper would pick it up and give it back to me.)

The Feds had four Chinese under observation at the Boulevard Hotel in the Cross. Danny was involved with them in a huge importation of heroin. The shipment had arrived and Danny was to take charge of the lot.

Danny offered me and Abo the first chance to sell it. The price was OK, so we agreed to take all the shipment off his hands. Danny brought me a kilo to test before we took the gear. The person who tested it for me said there was only one problem with the sample—it was pure chalk. I knew Danny wouldn't try any shifty business with me, so it had to be that the Feds were on to him and the Chinese. I immediately got hold of Danny and told him about the chalk being substituted for the heroin. I also told him to warn the Chinese. I don't know how Danny managed to get out of the hotel without being grabbed by the Feds, but he did. Danny got hold of his mate [*a policeman*] and told him what had gone down. According to Danny, [*the policeman*] told him that the Feds were watching the hotel, waiting to snaffle up the whole gang. He warned Danny to stay right away from the Chinese and the hotel.

It turned out the Feds had indeed made a complete swap

of the heroin at the airport when it first arrived. They had substituted chalk and let the Chinese carry on as though nothing had happened while they waited to gather up the entire gang all in one fell swoop. The Feds' operation was 90 per cent successful. They only missed out on Danny.

One Sunday Tex had one of his regular barbecues. Danny Chubb was there and acting a little strange; he was telling everyone about his good fortune. I talked some business and we arranged to meet a few days later. [*On Thursday 8 November 1984*] Abo and I drove up to Sydney and went to the Cook Hotel at the Rocks to meet Danny. It was an early opener, and while we waited for Danny we had a few beers. The publican gave me a letter from a guy in the nick. I often got mail at the pub as I wouldn't hand out my address to anyone.

Danny arrived and we had maybe two more beers, discussed our business, then stood on the footpath talking for a few minutes. Then I left with another person—Abo followed in his car—for the Star Hotel to fix up some business there. At the Star, Abo and I had just ordered a drink when I either got a phone call or I made one; I'm not clear on that point. Whichever it was, Tex was on the other end and he told me that Danny Chubb had just been shot and killed out the front of his mother's house by two masked gunmen. [*Chubb was shot dead about 11am.*] I thought Tex was having a lend of me. 'Sure mate, pull the other one too.' Tex insisted that he was not joking. 'I'm fucking serious, mate. Listen to the news and you will see that I'm not fucking around.' I went one better than that: I rang The Dodger.

'Hello mate,' I said. 'Have you heard anything about Danny Chubb getting shot and killed?'

'Yes mate, it's all over the radio. Police have just arrested a guy in a red Mercedes Benz seen driving away from the shooting.'

I had only just left Danny: I couldn't believe he was dead. He had no enemies I knew of. I found out later that the guy driving the red Mercedes was released. He had been drinking tea with Danny's mother at the exact moment Danny was gunned down.

According to the police report, two men had pulled up alongside Danny as he was just getting out of his car. One shot him four or five times with what police said was a .357 magnum revolver—the second man apparently put a shotgun to Danny's head and fired two shots into his face and throat. Whoever did it didn't muck around. They wanted him dead, that was for certain.

Before he was killed, Danny had been making untold millions. It had started to go to his head a bit and he was getting out of hand. He had once kept a very low profile; then he met this girl. Danny—who was the world's ugliest man—suddenly appeared out and about with this girl on his arm, flashing large sums of money all over the place. He was just asking for trouble.

Danny was involved with some very heavy police and a group of people that had imported container loads of cannabis from Lebanon and heroin from the Golden Triangle in Thailand. [*Chubb had driven a truck overland from Darwin to Sydney in February 1984. The truck carried part of a $40 million cannabis importation organised by Dr Nick Paltos.*] These people thought that Danny was telling people too much about their business. The Australian Federal Police were watching Danny and his associates and were getting close to arresting them. Danny had already had a close call when the Feds swapped the heroin for chalk. He had become too hot to handle—it was only a matter of time before he was caught. Danny Chubb's murder had nothing to do with the 'Gang Wars'. Danny Chubb was, I believe, murdered because he got out of hand.

Danny was supposed to have kept a little book with names of the people that he'd sold heroin to and the amounts they owed. It was also supposed to have the names of police on his payroll. If such a book existed, then it went missing, along with the huge fortune that he had amassed through his drug dealings. At the time of his death, Danny Chubb was owed more than $1 million by people who had taken kilos of heroin on the nod (the old pay-later scheme). Abo and I were doing a fair bit of business with Danny, but we always paid cash for ours. When Danny Chubb was murdered there were lot of relieved people in Sydney, relieved because they owed Danny big money from drug deals. And there were a few so-called friends that had borrowed large sums off him. They could all wipe the debts.

One person who owed Danny was Michael Sayers. Sayers

was gunned down outside his home three months later [*on 16 February 1985*] probably by the same people that killed Danny. Sayers was from Melbourne and, at the time of his death, he was facing drug charges. He was also involved in SP betting—he was a very big punter too. He often lost huge amounts but, like most punters, he won on the odd occasion too. Mick was a funny guy. He was friendly with Flannery—in fact I met him with Flannery just before he was shot down. Mick was on his way home after just having taken his girl out for a quiet dinner at one of the local restaurants. As he got out of his car to open the garage door, two men stepped out of the darkness and both shot him several times. Mick tried to run but both men followed him, shooting until he collapsed in a pool of his own blood. He was dead on arrival at the hospital. No one has ever been convicted of his murder. [*According to a report in the* Sydney Morning Herald *in May 1985, shortly before his death Sayers began moving into the lucrative Kings Cross drugs trade. Noted journalist Andrew Keenan: 'Sayers' greatest folly was that he appeared to think he was above paying anyone to stay in business. Unlike Melbourne, the system in Sydney is well established. Its rules and niceties are not mere formalities. They are what keeps it so stable by comparison with Melbourne's underworld.' In 1991 three men, Tom Domican, Kevin Theobold and a man we cannot name, were acquitted on charges of having murdered Sayers. In 1992 Coroner Greg Glass concluded that it appeared Sayers' murder was connected to his gambling activities. The coroner said it was not possible to determine who was responsible for the killing and recorded an open finding.*]

Chris Flannery and his wife had been at South Molle Island with me and Debra for the two weeks before Sayers' murder. Naturally, the police checked out our alibis and neither of us heard another thing about it. So, like so many other gangland murders, it remained unsolved and probably always will. Few gangland murders ever get solved. No one wants to solve them, they just say: 'Let them kill one another.' But what they don't realise is that the criminals are not always the ones who do the killing.

Barry McCann was the reason for the so-called 'Gang Wars'. A lot of people went missing and were shot down in the street and left to die—and there was no doubt that the victims all knew one another and were tied up in drugs or SP betting. But there was no evidence to say the murders were part of an organised gang war. Certainly, I believe Danny Chubb's murder was unrelated to the others; he was killed because he got out of hand.

McCann, however, certainly kicked things along. I knew McCann and had often seen him around, but there was no love lost between us. I never got into a conversation with him. He had too much money and got the idea that he was someone special. He set out to open a casino by himself without getting permission from the team that had been running the gambling for decades. He didn't want to pay the 'tax' that came with having permission to open a casino. Then he tried to go into slot machines without asking permission again. He was making heaps of money importing heroin into the country and had no reason to want more. He couldn't spend all that he had. Big money has the effect of turning some people into monsters, they seem to get delusions of grandeur or something. It goes to their heads.

Slot machines were a very big money-getter and, like everything else in Sydney, they were controlled by a group of men that ran most of the [*illegal*] gambling in New South Wales. It had been practically public knowledge for decades that Lennie McPherson and George Freeman had run gambling in New South Wales for many years. Now another gang wanted some of the cream off the top.

McCann and company started to put their own machines in different places, in hotels and shops. The machines that were already there were thrown out into the street. So McPherson sent a team of guys round to smash McCann's machines. Well, McPherson didn't get his way this time. The opposition wasn't going to back down that easily; there was too much money involved.

The opposition held a meeting. McCann was the man with all the money, so I presume he called the shots. At this meeting they discussed where the danger lay from the old-guard and came up with the name of Christopher Dale Flannery, or 'Rentakill' as the media named him. Flannery was a new addition to the old-guard's team. He was up from Melbourne and Rogerson had got him a start as Freeman's bodyguard. He was their biggest danger if there was going to be any trouble, so it was decided that he had to go.

On 27 January 1985, about 30 shots were sprayed from an Armalite rifle in an attempt to kill Chris Flannery as he stood outside his Arncliffe house with his wife and two children.

The police accused Tom Domican of trying to kill Flannery. Whoever it was, it was a very poor attempt. They should have gone bush and practised more as they never looked like hitting Flannery. They caused nothing more than splinters to fly everywhere and dozens of holes in his walls. If the attempt had been successful the first time round, then that would have been the end of it. But, by missing, they stirred up a hornet's nest.

The 'Gang Wars' had begun, and it was to involve lots of people, including many police.

Both sides had friendly police on side and each lot of police had their own blue with the police on the other side. The police were struggling for control of the organised crime that had been going for many years within the New South Wales force. So, for once, the police teamed up with the crooks and chose sides.

The day Flannery was shot at, I was home with my family. I always spent Sundays at home with them. I had not known Chris all that long. I had been out with him a few times and had been to his home once or twice. I was playing with my kids in the pool when my wife told me that Kathy Flannery was on the phone. I went in to talk to her.

'Hello, Kath, how are you?'

Straight away she began yelling into the phone. 'Chris has been shot and your dog mate Abo shot him. I saw him. He was in his blue Jaguar.'

'Listen Kath, this phone is bugged. You realise what you're saying?'

She kept on accusing Abo of having shot Chris. I tried to tell her that Abo couldn't have shot Chris, because Abo was up here at home too. I was in Warners Bay, and Abo lived only a few minutes drive up the road at Valentine. We were more than two hours' drive from Sydney.

'Put the dog on the phone if he is there with you.'

'He isn't here at my place, but I can get him here within 10 minutes if you like.'

'Yes. I want to speak to him. Get him to ring me at home from your place as soon as he gets there.'

I got in touch with Abo straight away and got him to come over to my home. When he got there I explained what Kathy Flannery had said.

'You better ring the woman and tell her that you had nothing to do with it.'

Abo rang her and abused her for accusing him of trying to kill Chris. They abused each other for 10 minutes before Abo told her to get fucked and hung up.

I went to see Chris the next day at his home. At the time, he didn't have a clue who had attempted to shoot him. He was blaming a group of guys from Melbourne and was all set to go down there and back-up on them. Before he had a chance to go to Melbourne, he received a call from a cop who had information for sale about who had tried to kill him. The cop had tapes of a conversation betwen two men discussing the near miss on Chris. He sold the tapes to Chris. They were supposed to be of a conversation between Barry McCann and Tom Domican.

The police were involved in the 'Gang Wars' up to their ears. Each gang had their own team of police doing what they could to help them win this silly bloody war before it got out of hand.

The police were prepared to do almost anything to protect their steady income. I was privy to a lot of conversations that took place between the gangs and the police. I attended meetings in restaurants with police and the two gang members that were behind the 'Gang Wars'. I took no part in any killings—I stayed right away from those.

Once the warfare started, Chris Flannery got totally out of hand. He was continually fighting with his own team, especially the cops that were assisting him.

Chris wanted to shoot people that were in no way involved in this fracas. One such incident involved a Sydney criminal we cannot name. [*The man, then in his mid-20s, was linked with McCann's faction. In 1991 he was acquitted on a charge of murdering Mick Sayers, who was shot dead six weeks before the man was himself wounded.*] He was leaving Domican's home in his car when Chris pulled alongside. Chris and two other guys then emptied their guns into the car, not caring who they hit. They shot him in the stomach once, wounding him seriously. He was rushed to hospital.

Chris fell out with [*a detective*] at a lunch we all attended at the Cross. They were discussing the 'Gang Wars' and how it was at a standstill. Everyone wanted Barry McCann out of the way, but McCann was presenting a problem: no one could find him. McCann was the money-man behind the opposition. It was believed that with McCann out of the way, things would return to normal. [*The detective*] was telling Chris what he should do and Chris blew up: 'Don't you fuckwits try and tell me how to do my job.' They were into it at the table. [*The detective*] opened his jacket revealing that he was armed. Chris pulled his gun out and said: 'You're not the only cunt that's got one.'

Another night he had a very bad blue with [*another policeman*] at the Lord Wolseley Hotel in Ultimo—they got right into it. Chris threatened to kill [*the policeman*] and guns were pulled by both of them.

There were many meetings between Flannery and certain police. In particular, they gave him information about Domican's movements. I was at one of these meetings between Chris and the police. Among those present were Bill Duff and four other cops. Flannery and I were the only civilians. [*One detective*] was getting impatient with Chris and the fact he had not got rid of Domican. He asked Chris what the problem was. Chris blew up, yelling at him: 'I will get rid of him when I am ready.'

They argued for 20 minutes before reaching an agreement. [*According to Smith, two police set Tom Domican up for an ambush, but Domican did not fall into the trap.*] Flannery and his mate Laurie Prendergast [*a Melbourne criminal who disappeared in mysterious circumstances in August 1985*] were sitting on a motorbike waiting for Tom. They had the bike running and Chris had a .357 magnum revolver ready in his hand. They spotted Domican and moved off. They made a pass to make sure it was him. Silly move, as Tom saw them straight away. They turned around for another run and Chris started shooting, missing with every shot. Tom grabbed a gun and started shooting back at the two escaping on the motor bike. He too missed.

Chris had fucked-up badly with his cowboy tactics and the fact that he had missed was the beginning of his demise. He lost any respect that he had had.

Some days later we were all at a meeting that became

pretty heated at times between Bill Duff and Flannery. Then Abo and Kathy Flannery had an argument: Abo hated her.

Bill Duff told Flannery that he had caused everyone a lot of problems by missing Domican. Chris went off his head at Billy, threatening to kill him. Chris was blaming everyone except himself. At one stage it looked like getting out of hand between them: both were throwing accusations at each other and guns were pulled. It was a madhouse.

Kathy Flannery stuck her head into the argument a few times, having a go at Abo: 'Just for curiosity's sake, how many people have you killed?'

Abo looked at her in amazement at first, then he said: 'If I had killed anyone you would be the last cunt I would tell.'

Kathy blew up: 'Apparently we're not on the same wavelength.'

'You're not wrong there.'

Chris started to go silly. He was chewing his beer glass and swallowing pieces of glass. I don't know what that was supposed to represent. He was yelling at everyone. Then came my turn for a bake.

'What about you, mate?' he said. 'How many have you killed? A dozen?'

'What is this, a game of twenty questions or what?'

'I have put plenty off, so I know what I'm doing.'

We got into an argument over what difference it made whether I had killed anyone or not.

'Get real, Chris. I haven't killed anyone, but if I had then I wouldn't have gotten caught for it. Haven't you been arrested every time you did one?'

He wasn't pleased with me at all, but I couldn't give a shit.

Chris and Kathy decided to leave. As they left, Kathy said to me: 'Are you coming with us or are you staying with these low jacks?'

'Listen Kathy,' I said. 'I'll run my own race and it would be a good idea if you ran yours.'

That wasn't the only time Chris threatened police and their families. The writing was definitely on the wall. Chris wasn't destined to grow much older. Next day I rang Roger and met him to discuss Chris and the way things were fucking up all around him.

'Listen Roger, I want nothing more to do with Flannery. He is out of control and he will get worse.'

Roger agreed with me but he asked me to just hang on for a few more days. 'It will all work itself out in the wash. Just hang in there.'

We both agreed that Chris was living on borrowed time. If the other team didn't get him, it was a certainty that the police would. A day later, Chris contacted me. He wanted to apologise for the way that he had behaved. I didn't say anything, just let him have his say. No way I was falling in with him again.

Tony Eustace was the next to die. Tony was a very nice guy—he was vicious, sure, but would rather do you a good turn than harm you. He was a good friend of Flannery's and had fallen out with a lot of people by taking Flannery's side. Tony supplied Flannery with money and weapons while the 'Gang Wars' raged, but the most important thing he supplied Flannery with was vital information. Tony was sweet with several high-ranking cops; they gave Tony all the information they could, and Tony passed it on to Flannery.

Tony was arrested over drugs, but he was killed before he could be tried on the charges. He was the owner of a restaurant at Double Bay, and involved in two others at the time of his death.

Tony and George Freeman didn't get along too well. Tony was bad-mouthing him all over town about something he'd done wrong. He bagged Freeman openly and George didn't take kindly to it. There was no doubt that Freeman was smart: he was well connected, too. George put a plan together to get rid of two birds with the one stone.

I attended a meeting at the place of a man [*whose name has been removed for legal reasons. He was named by a New South Wales District Court Judge in 1985 as 'a standover man closely associated with organised crime in Sydney'. The judge also said the man was 'believed to be an employee of Leonard Arthur McPherson'.*] Chris and McPherson were there to discuss progress in the war. Chris was in fine form. He never stopped bagging Freeman to McPherson. I couldn't believe that Chris was so gullible as to fall into that trap. McPherson just agreed with him about

Freeman: an old trick of their team. They con you into bagging them, then you end up missing or dead in the street somewhere. I listened but made no comment. Stupid. Chris was talking himself into a quick grave and I had no desire to join him.

At a later date Freeman told Chris that he would supply him with machineguns and all the money he needed—he even promised to set Domican up for him. In return he wanted Chris to kill Tony Eustace. He turned Chris's head with stories and lies about Tony. Now, Chris, being the low bastard that he was, decided to get back on side with George by doing him this favor. Chris fell straight into Freeman's trap. It made no difference that Tony was his friend, he didn't recognise friendship. He barred no one.

Chris rang Tony at his restaurant and arranged to meet him at Mascot. 'Bring $25,000 with you, mate. I have to leave town and have no ready cash.' Tony immediately got the money together and went to meet Chris in a side street at Mascot as planned. Tony gave Chris the money. He also warned Chris that there had been people from the opposition at his restaurant looking for him. Flannery thanked Tony for his help and said he would keep in touch. As Tony turned his back to walk away, Chris fired five bullets from a .45 automatic into his friend's back.

Who needs enemies with friends like Chris?

Tony died five hours after being shot. He refused to name Chris when questioned: he told the police to 'get fucked' when they asked who had shot him.

Chris was going off his head. He was going around threatening everyone including the cops that were helping him. He had to attend a meeting at the place of [*unnamed man, page 181*] again. He asked me: 'Will you come with me, mate, I don't trust them. There will be cops there from the other team. They want to try and settle things without any more trouble.'

'Chris, I don't want any part in any meetings. You are too anxious to get people involved in a mass war between us. There's no money in it for any of us. I see no sense in carrying on with it so no, I won't go with you.'

Kathy was there with him. She had to have her two bob's worth.

'You have no go in you! You're just like the others, no guts.'

We argued for a few minutes and I told her to go fuck herself. I found out later about what happened at the meeting.

Chris was his usual self. He got into an argument with [*a policeman*] and ended up threatening to kill [*the policeman*] and his whole family. Chris said to him: 'You're not a fucking koala bear. You can be killed just as easy as anyone else can.'

For some silly reason, Chris thought that he had a monopoly on violence and killing people. That wasn't the case, anyone can kill you—even a five-year-old can do it.

Everyone, including both teams of police, now wanted the 'Gang Wars' finished, before it got out of hand. Flannery wanted to carry on, regardless of what was said. Everyone, police included, decided that Chris was bad news, he was a threat to everyone, and no one was safe. Chris had proved this by the brutal murder of his friend, Tony Eustace. How could the police rely on or afford to trust anyone like that? They had no control over him.

The first thing I heard about Chris going missing was when his wife, Kathy, rang and asked me to call and see her. She was crying when she rang me. I arrived in the afternoon and she was visibly upset over something. She kept staring into my eyes, probably looking to see if I showed any sign of having known that Chris was missing. She hit me with it straight-out, she didn't pull any punches. 'Chris is dead. I know he is because he always rings me two or three times every hour to let me know that he is OK.'

She went on: 'He was on his way to meet George Freeman this morning. I rang George and he reckons that Chris never got there.'

I told her to slow down and tell me exactly what happened. She said Chris had left earlier that morning for Yowie Bay to see George about some guns.

Apparently, Chris had received a call on his pager telling him to 'Ring Mercedes'—the code for George Freeman. Chris went to a public phone and rang Freeman, who told him to come out to his Yowie Bay home: Freeman said he had machineguns, as well as information about the movements of Tom Domican and Barry McCann.

Chris told Kathy where he was going and went to get his car, a brand new Fairlane. Even though it was parked in a 24-hour security area, Chris checked it for suspect devices. It was clear, so he climbed in and tried to start the car. It wouldn't start—it had been tampered with. He walked back to his flat and rang Freeman, who told him to catch a cab.

Chris walked out to the front of the luxurious Connaught building opposite Hyde Park and waited for a taxi. No one seems to know exactly what happened after that, except that he did not arrive at Freeman's house that day, or anywhere else.

Kathy Flannery blamed George Freeman for killing Chris, but she had no idea. It was just like the time that she blamed Abo for shooting at Chris. She blamed the first person whose name came into her head.

Rumor has it that Chris was picked up by a policeman he knew well and trusted, who offered him a lift. The car went only a short way before it stopped at a set of traffic lights, where two ex-police climbed in. The car took off and Chris was then shot several times in the head and chest as the car drove along. But as I said, it's only a rumor.

Kathy was in a spin over Chris going missing. She blamed everyone. She was desperate for someone to back-up [*take revenge*] for Chris. I was there when she rang people in Melbourne asking them to come to Sydney to back-up for her. She tried to convince me that Abo had something to do with it and wanted me to set him up. I just humored her for a short time, then I left. I didn't bother to see her again.

I got in touch with Abo and got him to go to a motel and stay out of her sight until I could see Roger and fix this shit up. Bright and early the next morning, Abo and I went to meet Roger at Bankstown Airport.

We positioned ourselves in the middle of the tarmac so that we could see anyone that may have been watching us. Roger told me that there was nothing to concern myself about: 'Chris had to go, mate. He was becoming a danger to us all.'

I agreed wholeheartedly and I told him my views on the subject.

'George and that team are concerned that you may be thinking of backing-up for Chris. You're not that silly, are you, mate?'

I assured Roger that I had no reason or desire to back-up for Chris or anyone. Everything was all right. We could now get back to leading normal lives and making money once more.

About three weeks later, I was drinking at the Covent Garden Hotel in Chinatown when in walked [*a detective*]. He spotted me and a scowl appeared on his face. He was not too pleased to see me there. I went up, shook his hand and had a couple of drinks with him. He kept trying to steer the conversation in Chris's direction, but just couldn't get out what he wanted to say. I ended up asking him what was up; it broke the ice and he told me his problem.

'Neddy, you realise that Chris had to go, don't you? He was a danger to all of us.'

I nodded, waiting for him to go on.

'There are certain people worried that you might have something to say that could embarrass them and cause heavy problems for them. You are the only person left that knows anything about what's happened and you are the only civilian that was a witness to those meetings with Flannery.'

I could see now why he was worried about me.

'Stop worrying. I have nothing to say about anything that was discussed at any meetings.'

We got on the drink pretty heavily that night and [*the detective*] started to open up with me. 'Neddy, you are very sweet with the right people. You can go a long way if you keep your mouth shut about what's been happening.'

I just told him to cool down and stop worrying about me as I was not going to be a problem for anyone in the force. 'I just want to do my own thing and be left alone.'

Lennie McPherson proved to be one of the smartest men I have ever met. He had played all sides against the middle. He had kept sweet with Flannery, Domican and McCann as well—and all the time he was scheming to come out the winner. When Flannery went missing, Tom Domican paraded around town like a peacock, going to all of the places he knew Flannery frequented. It was a show of strength to let them know that Tom was still here—and Chris wasn't. McPherson and Freeman let Tom think that he was one of the boys. They took him out with them so that everyone would know that they were friends now. If anything were to happen to Tom, they would be in the clear.

It's an old trick and it always seems to work. Keep them sweet and they fall straight into the trap.

The next person to be murdered was Barry 'Sugar' Croft. Croft was one of McCann's gang. He used to sell heroin for McCann, operating out of a hotel in Alexandria. I never knew Croft. From all reports issued by the media and police, it doesn't appear that he was a victim of the 'Gang Wars', which finished months earlier. Flannery was dead and Domican was in jail. [*In 1986, Domican was sentenced to 14 years jail after being convicted of the attempted murder of Chris Flannery. He was later acquitted on appeal and was released from jail in May 1992 after almost six years inside.*]

So who was behind the death of 'Sugar' Croft? Apparently Croft received a phone call while he was drinking at the pub. No one seems to know who rang that night. The caller made arrangements to meet Croft and when Croft turned up, he was shot quite a few times in the head.

The only plausible thing that could have happened was that whoever the caller was, he must have followed Croft to the meet. [*On 6 August 1987, Croft, driving a Ford Fairlane, was at the corner of City Road and Myrtle Street, Chippendale, when a small blue sedan containing two men pulled alongside. Two shots were fired at Croft's car, one smashing the windscreen the second hitting him in the head.*] Croft didn't die instantly because after he was shot he continued to drive his car for 100 metres or more before crashing into a telegraph pole.

Rumors were everywhere and everyone was getting blamed for killing Croft. The real reason for Croft's death was revealed to me by a policeman I knew. He said that Croft, on bail over a big drug bust involving a few heavy drug dealers, was going to give evidence against the dealers at their trials. I know that there were a few very unhappy police when Croft was killed.

I was accused of murdering Croft, too. They always seemed to accuse me. I was accused of every murder that happened between 1975 and 1989. I wasn't interviewed over them all, but I was suspected of most of them. The media once again nominated me as having ordered Graham 'Abo' Henry to kill 'Sugar' Croft.

I know how the Australian dingo feels. Thank Christ the

dingo was around to wear the blue for Azaria Chamberlain or they would have tried to pin it on me.

[*On 27 December 1987, more than 18 months after Flannery disappeared and five months after his colleague Barry 'Sugar' Croft was gunned down, Barry McCann—the man Ned Smith blames for sparking the so-called 'Gang Wars'— was shot dead. By this time, McCann, 44, had moved away from illegal gambling and was concentrating on heroin importation and distribution. His inquest was told that McCann was the leader of a $162 million drug syndicate and that he was killed after a row about missing suitcases of heroin smuggled into Australia. He was shot down outside a toilet block in a Marrickville park. The killers certainly meant business: McCann's body was riddled with 38 bullets, including eight fired at point-blank range to form a circle on his head.*]

McCann was definitely not the easiest man to find when he didn't want to be found. During the 'Gang Wars' there was a price on his head of $200,000—someone wanted him out of the way. Everyone was out to collect it, including the police. Somehow he dodged them all. He changed cars every day and never slept in the same place two nights in a row. At one stage [*a policeman*] told Flannery where McCann could be found, but he had gone before Chris got there.

Then McCann made a fatal mistake. He trusted someone close to him—it had to be someone close to get him to meet him in a deserted park late at night. We all make mistakes sometimes, but his mistake proved to be fatal.

From being interviewed over murdering McCann and the media reports, I pieced together what supposedly happened. McCann went to meet some unknown person in this park to collect money he was owed. On arriving, he was shot dozens of times in the back and head, killing him instantly. Whoever did it made sure that he didn't survive by putting enough lead in him to sink a ship.

The headlines read ANOTHER GANGLAND MURDER, but I believe it was a falling-out over drug money. There was a lot of talk about McCann not whacking-up properly with his cronies and greed stepping in. It had to be someone close to him. That was the last thing that I heard about McCann's murder. I never even got called to front the inquest. [*A man was charged and acquitted of McCann's murder. He is now serving a 25-year sentence for conspiring to import about 80 kilograms of heroin, and is facing further drugs charges.*]

One murder I was accused of received huge media coverage. Even now, years later, it still gets attention. There is still a lot of speculation and guesswork as to who did it. Accusations have been levelled at many people, but the murder still remains unsolved. I refer to Sallie-Anne Huckstepp, police informer, prostitute, drug addict, supplier and despicable type. The media took up her cause and all but turned her into a saint. Why was she any different than any other person that sells drugs or their body for money? Sallie-Anne Huckstepp was, according to all reports, murdered by strangulation and an overdose of heroin and her body was found floating in the lake at Centennial Park one morning [*7 February 1986*]. I know nothing at all about how Sallie-Anne Huckstepp died, or who was responsible for her death.

When the news of Sallie-Anne Huckstepp's murder broke, there were a lot of happy people. Among those who celebrated were several police officers. But there was one police officer that was said to be in mourning over her death. He was a federal police officer who was having an affair with Sallie-Anne. She started out as his informer and ended up sleeping with him. Such a lovely girl our Sallie-Anne, she slept with one and all, barred no one either to sleep with or share the needle with. Then she would inform on them.

Roger Rogerson had to put in an appearance at the inquest in March 1987 into her death. Roger put on a show for the media. He accused Wendy Bacon [*a journalist who exposed numerous cases of police corruption in the 1980s*] of being responsible for Sallie's death. Also he said he believed that Wendy Bacon was having a lesbian affair with Sallie-Anne. [*Bacon denied the allegations.*] Some graffiti artist wrote on the wall outside the court 'Pig fingers Bacon'. That certainly seemed to suit the occasion. When the coroner's decision concerning Sallie-Anne Huckstepp was released, I was cleared of having any involvement with her death and, for a pleasant change, I didn't mind seeing the media report it.

What price am I of one day getting accused of murdering Harold Holt?

Another unsolved gang murder was Jackie Muller [*who was shot dead, aged 56, in the early morning of 7 June 1979*].

Muller was gunned down outside his home as he pulled into his driveway at Coogee. He never had a chance. Two men, one on each side, pumped bullets into his body. I don't know how many, but it was enough. Everyone knew that he was killed for his attempt on Freeman's life but they don't know the reason behind Muller trying to kill Freeman. Let me tell you why . . .

Freeman had a good friend. This guy had been friends with Freeman for years, going back to Freeman's shoplifting days: they'd often stolen together. Freeman's mate hit a hurdle and had to go to jail for a short time. He had a wife and kids so he asked his good friend Freeman to look after his family while he was away. Being the nice bloke George was, he accepted the responsibility and did a good job of looking after them—in fact he did too good a job. He ended up having an affair with the friend's wife and then he got her a job—in a brothel. A nice friend to have.

When the guy got out of jail he didn't have the guts to do anything to Freeman himself. He just shat himself. One day he called into a brothel for an empty and, by coincidence, his wife was working there. Yet he still he did nothing about it. Weak mongrel.

The woman in question was Muller's daughter. He took it very badly when he found out what had happened to his daughter, so he planned to kill Freeman. He was friendly with Freeman, knew his movements and had no trouble setting him up.

One night he waited outside Freeman's Yowie Bay house and, when Freeman pulled up, Muller shot him once in the head with a .22 pistol. He should have emptied the entire clip into Freeman's head. He didn't and Freeman survived and managed to rush next door to a neighbor's house and get help. Muller may have made a mess of trying to kill Freeman, but at least he tried to do something about his daughter, which showed he had plenty of go in him, much more than her husband.

Six weeks later Muller was killed. Freeman was conveniently out of New South Wales at the time. Another unsolved murder went on the books, another one that everyone in the country knew who'd committed. But no one wanted to solve it. [*George Freeman died of natural causes on 20 March 1990.*]

14
Doing Business

A dinner lubricates business
English jurist William Scott, 1791

[*From late 1981, when Neddy Smith was given the Green Light, his influence with New South Wales police soared. He was able to fix deals, and not just for himself and his close associates. Smith also worked on a commission basis, sorting out problems for criminals—and police. What follows is a series of incidents that illustrate different levels of corruption. In each case, Smith names the police involved.*]

Two months after Chris Flannery disappeared in May 1985, life started getting back to normal. People were making heaps of money again and everyone was happy, especially the police. They had missed their weekly handouts when the war started. The murders allowed the police to grab more power over the gangs by holding murder charges over their heads, keeping them in line.

I went back to being followed by the police. They had never let up on me for a minute. I was used to it; besides I was getting warned beforehand just who would be detailed to watch me for the day or week, whatever the case may be. Abo and I started getting out and about again, drinking ourselves into a stupor every day. One night we went to a regular spot, the Lord Nelson Hotel at the Rocks, where we had a few cool ones with Tex. It was pretty crowded, but quiet—that is until two detectives had a go at Abo and me.

Abo was having an argument with the barmaid, nothing serious, when these two young detectives came up, posing in front of the girl. They were definitely trying to impress someone. Anyway, the taller one said: 'Who do you think you are talking to?' I didn't bother answering him. I just whacked him on the chin with a left hook and he went out for the count. His brave offsider moved closer to the bar and called out to the girl they had been trying to impress earlier: 'Officer down, call for help.' That was as far as he got because Abo caught him with a beautiful right hand and said: 'Make that two now, cunt.' We both burst out laughing.

We enjoyed the rest of the night without incident. The next morning, when I woke up wishing I was dead from a hangover, it suddenly hit me what we had done. It didn't take the dogs long to smell a quid in the air.

[*A detective*] from the infamous consorting squad rang me. 'Hello Neddy, I think that we should meet and discuss this problem you are about to have.'

I asked him what the problem was.

'There is no problem at this precise moment, but we have to meet now to avoid there becoming one.'

He told me to meet him at the Royal Hotel at Randwick near the hospital. I got to the hotel ahead of time. [*The detective*] was a little late but turned up with another cop, a friend of mine, Detective Sergeant John Openshaw. He had a smile on his face a mile wide: 'Hello mate, been knocking out police officers again?' Then he went into hysterics laughing at his joke.

We got a drink and sat down. [*The detective*] started the conversation with: 'Neddy, you can't go around just doing as you please to police officers, they don't like it. Especially when it puts them on show in front of everyone.'

Openshaw said: 'These young guys never learn. They will know better next time, I bet.'

I gave them my side of the story, but they just said: 'You have to pay a fine for bashing two cops. Also for bruising their egos.' It was worth it just to get away with bashing the two fools.

'How much is the fine this time?'

The detective laughed: 'Well, Opey, what's the damage for a bruised ego these days?'

Still laughing [*the policeman*] replied: '$6000 should buy enough salve to fix their bruised egos.'

'That's the fine, Neddy. Can you get it now, or shall we make a meet for another day?'

I had deserved the fine for letting my own ego get the better of me. 'Okay,' I said, 'Give me 20 minutes and I'll get Abo to bring the money here for you.'

We continued drinking until Abo arrived with the $6000.

[*A policeman*] was having domestic problems: to put it bluntly he caught his wife playing up with one of his workmates when he came home early. He would get on the drink with me nearly every day and would get so drunk there were times that I had to take his gun off him to keep him from doing something silly. I often had to ring his girlfriend to come and get him when I couldn't do anything with him. Eventually she left him because of his drinking.

[*The policeman*] was a talker—and I'm a good listener when there is something worth listening to. He talked all the time, drunk or sober, about the different squads he'd been involved with. He would go into detail on how the different squads worked, their surveillance techniques and the vehicles they used. It took only a short time before I knew as much about the workings of the New South Wales police as any member of the force did. He would point out the places that the different squads congregated at, the pubs they drank at. That information was very useful. I would spend part of each day sitting off these places just observing who they were so that I would know their faces if ever they tried to sit off me. After a while, I knew most of their heads. He also showed me where they parked their undercover cars so I could take down the car numberplates. This proved invaluable to me many times over the years. It also helped other people who I passed the car numbers on to.

[*In the manuscript, Smith recalls how a meeting with a drunken policeman turned into a heated argument when the officer threatened to charge Smith and 'Abo' Henry with murder—a murder Smith said they did not commit. Smith was introduced to the drunken policeman by a more sober officer, who Smith knew well and had previously 'done business with'. The name of the victim has been removed to prevent identification of the police concerned. Otherwise, the events are from Smith's original manuscript.*]

[*The drunk policeman*] said: '$60,000. That's what it's going to cost you not to be charged with the murder of [*victim's name*]. Take it or leave it. I don't care one way or the other.'

He had to be kidding. 'You can shove your deal right up your arse. I will give the money to a QC and shove the charge right up your arse.'

[*The second officer*] was panicking. 'Look [*to the drunk policeman*]. I arranged for Ned to come to see you, so be reasonable. I don't want Roger after my hide.'

I pulled [*the second policeman*] up. 'I don't know what your go is, but I am not copping it off you or that fucking fool.'

He said: 'Look mate, he is keen to pinch you. He knows that he won't be able to make it stick, but he will get promoted over it. How about $20,000? Will you agree to that?'

I didn't want to do anything with a fool like this [*drunk policeman*]. I told [*the second officer*] that I would consider it. 'What do I get for the $20,000?'

'You won't have to front the inquest or the National Crime Authority. And you can go in to be interviewed and write your own record of interview. How's that?'

We walked back and the two police talked. They came back and said $20,000 would be OK.

'Listen [*Smith said to the second policeman*]. Abo hasn't got that sort of money.'

[*The drunk policeman*] again had to have his two bob's worth. 'Tell him to rob a bank; you have the fucking Green Light.'

[*Smith paid the money the following day. The day after Smith went to police headquarters for an interview, accompanied by two barristers.*]

When I got there, [*the now-sober policeman*] was all smiles. 'Ned. I am sorry about the other night, I was drunk. OK?' We all sat down and [*the now-sober policeman*] supplied us all with cans of Foster's and we got blind drunk while we made out the interviews. [*The two barristers*] were mad about the way things were being done. Once the 'interviews' were over, Abo and I went our own ways and left the lawyers to ponder on what had happened. The interview I made that day may have been made under unusual circumstances, but it was a true account of the facts. I told the truth about what happened the day [*the victim*] died. We were called to appear before the NCA a short time later. I heard no more about it after that day.

Abo and I called into the Palisade Hotel at the Rocks after one of our mad lunches. I had to see [*a policeman*] there. He arrived and we were starting our first drinks when Tex came in. He was worried. He told me there were two guys coming into the hotel who I didn't like.

I asked him: 'What's the problem? I don't like many people.'

He replied: 'They are from the opposition.'

The two guys walked in the front bar and sat down. I knew them both—they were drug dealers from the western suburbs. I knew the first guy, his name was Ray Lutton, a drug addict and dealer. The other one was a mate of Tex's. Now I knew why Tex was in a panic. He knew I hated the second guy because he was a boy molester. I hated child molesters and Tex knew it.

[*The policeman*] was worried. 'There isn't going to be any trouble is there?'

'No, not unless they start it.'

Lutton kept looking up at me, nodding. I ignored him. I wanted no part of him or his mate. He decided to walk up to me and put out his hand to shake mine. He started to say something, but never got the words out. I'd been brooding for 20 minutes and it all came out in me. I spat in his face and pulled out the flick knife I had in my pocket and stabbed him several times in the gut. He managed to stay on his feet. Then I pushed him outside into the street. The last that I saw, he was running down the street.

[*The policeman*] was looking for a way out: 'You shouldn't do that sort of thing in front of me, Ned. That will cost you, mate.'

Didn't it always?

If I had to pay for it, I decided that two was as cheap as one. The other guy was still sitting on the bar stool watching me. He was a big, fat slob weighing at least 20 stone. I didn't give him a chance to speak—I just hit him flush on the jaw with a left hook. The bastard didn't go down, he hung on to the side of the bar. So I put two more left hooks on his chin. That sent him crashing to the floor. Abo was laughing. He came up and we both pulled the guy's legs apart and kicked his balls in. He would think twice about molesting kids again. [*The policeman*] was waiting for me to say something. 'Ned, that guy may die. It will cost you a big drink.'

'Don't let it worry you. I will fix it myself, OK?'

Before he could reply, I handed him $2000 that I had in my kick and said: 'I am sorry for causing you a minor problem. This should fix it up. Don't you worry about fixing the blue, I will handle it myself.'

He pocketed the money, downed his drink, then left the hotel. On his way out he said: 'I will be in touch with you later. Stay out of trouble.'

Lutton did not die that time. He died a few weeks later from an overdose of heroin—self-inflicted.

Once again, my temper had got the better of me. I realised that it was so bloody stupid doing what I had done, especially right there in front of a cop. Oh, they didn't mind, as long as I could afford to keep on paying them what they asked. Sometimes I looked for stinks, but the majority of times they found me without any help from me.

I had a very charmed life as far as fights went. I had a clean record, not one defeat. Not too bad seeing as I am now nearing 50. There are plenty of young guys running around today that would love to have a crack at me, but they aren't game. They know that if, by some strange chance, they did beat me, I wouldn't cop it sweet. I would back straight up and I would eventually win, regardless of whatever I had to do. My pride is such that I could never accept defeat gracefully. Never.

People often ask me, 'Can I fight?' My answer to them is: 'No, but I can win.' That about says it all. I am not a trained fighter, but I know how to win when I have to. I always get the job done eventually.

[*A copper*], a mate of Roger's, was on suspension from the police force for [*criminal activity and was facing criminal charges*].

Roger brought [*the copper*] to the Iron Duke Hotel in Waterloo to see me about fixing his problem. This crim [*who we'll call 'Billy'*] was ready to get into the witness box and give evidence against [*the copper*], and [*the copper*] looked like going to jail over it, meaning he would lose his job and his super. I was asked if I could do something to help.

At the time, 'Billy' was serving time at Parklea Jail. As it turned out, I knew 'Billy' from when we were both at Bathurst during the Bathurst riots.

'Listen Roger, these jacks [*police*] have never done anything for me without charging me like wounded bulls. Why should I do him this favor for nothing?'

Roger went over and spoke to [*the copper*] for a few minutes, then he came back with him. [*The copper*] said: 'Listen Neddy, I have very little money at present but I give you my word that if I can ever return the favor in the future, I will do it.'

That was as good as money in the bank, so I agreed to help him.

The next Saturday I got Abo to visit a guy that he knew in Parklea Jail, so he would be able to see 'Billy' without signing in the jail register. I knew that 'Billy' always got visits on a Saturday and I also knew that the visits were held on a huge oval; all the prisoners mixed. This way Abo saw 'Billy' without any record being kept of the visit, just in case he might decide to drop Abo for pulling him up.

I am not sure exactly what Abo said to 'Billy', but whatever it was, it did the trick. [*The copper*] beat the blue and was reinstated.

[*One policeman's*] wife was having a problem; her employer was continually hassling her. I don't know why [*the policeman*] couldn't fix it himself, but he asked me to talk to the boss and stop him hassling his wife. I spoke to the guy and fixed the problem. It was only a small problem, but I mention it to show how things worked.

There were many cops that came to see me over their wives playing up on them. They wanted the blokes bashed or worse. No way I wanted any part of that. If they didn't have the guts to bash them themselves, then bad luck.

It was around mid-1986 when a guy I thought was my friend [*he ended up giving police information about Smith*] got in touch with me. He wanted to see me urgently. He had a problem and needed my help.

I drove to Sydney the next morning to see what I could do. We met at the Captain Cook Hotel at the Rocks, an early opener. His problem was certainly one I could help with. He had been doing a robbery on a warehouse belonging to a sporting goods manufacturer when the nightwatchman disturbed him and his gang. At the time, they were loading a second lot of tracksuits—they already taken one load away. (Greed had gotten the better of him and he had backed-up for the second time.)

He and his gang got away without anyone seeing them, but in their haste they left their fingerprints everywhere, including on the garbage bags they had been packing the tracksuits into. The truck was also traceable and was covered with the driver's prints.

'If you can do anything to pull the blue up mate, we will pay whatever the cops ask,' he told me.

I asked them where and when the robbery took place. He was in luck; it had been only the previous night [*and in an area where Smith knew the policeman in charge*].

'Yes, mate, I certainly can help, but I have to tell you, this cop is a very big asker and he always does a good job. It's strictly cash on result.'

He said that was not a problem as he had plenty of ready cash. I went to a public phone and rang [*the policeman*].

'How are you?'

[*The policeman*] started laughing. 'I didn't think that it would take you long to get in touch with me. I've been waiting for your call.'

(What was he? A fucking mind-reader or something? Apparently he had surmised that I would be getting in touch with him over this bust, but I don't know how he guessed.)

'Can I see you? I have a problem that you may be able to help me with.'

'That's what I am here for, lad. Meet me across the road for a bite of breakfast in an hour, OK?'

I drove to the meeting and when I got to the coffee shop, [*the policeman*] was there with another detective. He introduced me to the other cop and I sat down.

'What's the problem, Neddy? Is it your problem or are we going to discuss someone else?'

I went into great detail explaining to [*the policeman*] that it was for a close friend of mine. I gave him all the details except the friend's name.

'Come on, Neddy. You know me well enough to know that I don't do things without knowing who I am dealing with.'

I went to the red phone and rang the pub where my friend

was waiting for me to ring. I let him know what had happened and said: 'It's up to you, mate. I haven't told him who you are.'

Next thing I know, [*the policeman*] grabbed the phone from my hand and said: 'Listen. I don't do things this way. I like to talk to the man to his face if I am to do business. Get your arse over here and we will talk.' He handed the phone back to me and I explained just how to get here.

When he arrived we all sat down and discussed the details. How much he was going to charge my friend was worrying me: [*the policeman*] was a big asker. He was good at fixing blues, you got just what you paid for, but I thought he was going to charge him like a wounded bull. [*The policeman*] was a perfectionist as far as doing business. He hated slovenly people, and he always made sure that he left nothing to chance. He was very careful not to leave anything lying about that could come back on him at a later date.

[*The policeman*] went into great detail about how he would fix up the blue. He was trying to make a good impression on my friend. Instead of just wiping the prints off the garbage bags he would change all the bags. My friend could steal another truck and [*the policeman*] would let him change it over for the one they left behind. 'Now lad, that will cost you $2000. Is that OK with you, Neddy?'

I could not believe what I was hearing. I got him to repeat it just to make sure I heard right. 'I said $2000.' I was still in shock. I had told my friend that [*the policeman*] was a top asker—and here he was letting him off for $2000. My friend had brought $10,000 with him to pay [*the policeman*] so, in his relief at getting the blue fixed up, he gave it all to [*the policeman*]! He was impressed with the way [*the policeman*] operated. Now it was [*the policeman's*] turn to be surprised. He took the $10,000 and thanked him. 'You can come to me any time that you have a problem.'

I found out later that the shifty [*policeman*] ran a check on my friend with The Dodger and knew all about him. He knew he was a good payer: the $2000 was a feeler for [*the policeman*] to see for himself what he was like. This friend that I am referring to became so sweet with the police it isn't funny. He is terrified of anyone with the slightest bit of violence in them, and avoids violent people like the plague. We were good friends, but our friendship came to an abrupt end. I did the guy several big favors and there were times where I kept him from going to the nick. He later showed his appreciation by setting me up with the coppers.

I was always playing. My life consisted of good restaurants and the very best of food and wine, good clothes, expensive cars and women. I enjoyed my life to the fullest. I made every day count for something as I knew that my lifespan wasn't expected to be a long one. I knew I was not going to die in my bed of old age. This didn't worry me—and it still doesn't.

While I was staying in Sydney, I always had something going on or somewhere to go. I often used to go out with my friend Belinda, and her mother Jeanette. Both women are, and have been, my friends for a very long time. I can't think of two better friends that I have ever had in my life. We often got out on the drink and we had great times together. People can't understand me having two women as friends. They think men must have men as friends. Well, I can tell you, these two women were better friends to me than any bloke that I ever knew.

Belinda liked a stink and she was rarely disappointed when we went out on the drink together. Most times it wasn't my fault that a stink started. Mostly it would be some flip having a go at the way I dressed or jealous over the car I drove. Why should I worry about what they said? I had everything and they had nothing. I had the go in me to get out and get mine. Most of these shitmen had no go in them at all. They would bludge on the dole, too lazy to work and not enough dash to earn it any other way. They were just dreamers and that's as far as any of them would ever get.

We often played up a little and sometimes we would get out of hand, but I always paid for any damage that I caused.

We often drank at a hotel in Pyrmont, which was owned by a friend of ours. He was a top guy and a good friend to us. Nothing was too much trouble.

One night we were all drinking there, a big team of us: thieves, knockabouts and the odd squarehead was present too. Belinda and Jeanette were also there—they were welcome anywhere I went. This particular night, Rocky the joker—who had this habit of patting everyone down to check who was armed and who wasn't—got this girl's lipstick out of her purse and drew a target on the shithouse door. He then declared that no one could hit a bull in the arse with a bucket of wheat. This night everyone seemed to be armed up and Rocky's statement was worse than waving a red flag in front of a mad bull.

Everybody pulled out guns and started to shoot at the target. There were people ducking everywhere.

When the shooting stopped, someone said: 'I hope no one was in the shithouse having a crap.'

We checked the toilet for bodies, but it was sweet. Thank God for that. It would have been embarrassing if there had been someone there. The next morning the police arrived while the publican was filling up all the holes in the door and the walls. He gave them a drink [*some money*] and they left without any problems.

A few nights later I was drinking at the Lord Nelson Hotel with Belinda, Abo and a few others. We had quite a lot to drink. Belinda wanted to go to the disco at the City of Sydney RSL. We decided to go with her and box on drinking. I just can't help myself on the drink and this night was no different. Down I went, drunker than a skunk. When we got there the young bouncer refused to let us in. He was a big, young, fit guy—and cheeky, too. I started to tell him that I was going into the club regardless of what he said. Mistake!

The young fit guy threw himself back on to the wall and came bouncing back punching me right on the cheek. It was a good punch, but he was out of luck that night because he didn't hit me hard enough. I attacked him and flogged him senseless. Abo got stuck into the other bouncer and Mick, a mate of mine, started shooting at this black guy who stuck his head in. The black guy turned out to be Bunny Johnson, the ex-light heavyweight champion of the world. Well, he could have won the world sprint championship that night: he bolted up the street. It was over in a few minutes. They were all flogged and out on the ground. We left to go to the Quarrymans Hotel to continue drinking. I finished up with numerous fractures of the cheekbones and a black eye.

Of course, I wasn't to get away scot free. The usual thing happened. Early the next morning I got the customary phone call from The Artful Dodger telling me that my stupidity had earned me a call from [*a policeman*] wanting to see me as soon as I got showered and dressed. Roger told me where to meet them along Canterbury Road.

I got ready, then picked up Abo and we drove up to meet [*the policeman*] and The Dodger. I knew that it was going to be costly because of the shots being fired: he was going to make the most of the chance to stamp me.

We got to the hotel that Roger nominated and they were sitting in the bar. I introduced Abo to [*the policeman*]. Abo had never met [*the policeman*] before so he shook hands with him. [*The policeman*] started straight in on me: 'Neddy, you deserve to be locked up for being so fucking stupid. You know better than that.'

I wasn't at all impressed by the jail bit, but I said nothing. He read the riot act to me and finished by telling me that I had hurt the bouncer badly.

'This little excercise is going to cost you dearly. Think yourself lucky that you're onside.'

I thought I would get in first before he got too carried away and went in too high. 'Will $10,000 cover the bill for the damages?'

I placed the ten thousand on the table in front of him—there was no one else in the back bar where we were sitting. He smiled at Abo and us: 'Not bloody likely, Ned. That should cover the guy that you nearly killed. But put another two thousand there for my troubles and we will call this exercise over.'

We paid the two thousand with the other money, and [*the policeman*] scooped it up off the table and it disappeared from sight. But [*the policeman*] wasn't going to let me off that lightly, no way.

Later that day he rang me and said he needed to see me—now. Before going to see [*the policeman*], I organised to see the young guy I had bashed. I wanted a statement off him to say that I had not been involved in bashing him. I had a solicitor there to witness the guy's statement. The young guy was terrified—he wanted to help me any way he could. I got the statement, and got a friend to write one too, saying she was a witness to the fight and I was not the person responsible for bashing the young guy. Both statements were witnessed by a JP, then photocopied. I then headed to the meeting with [*the policeman*]. I knew he was about to come up with a story to stamp me for more money.

He could forget it. I had been more than generous considering the minor problem that I had caused. The $12,000 was plenty.

I arrived at the Showground gate and [*the policeman*] was sitting in his car with the door open. He had his serious look on his face so I knew my guess was right. It was another stamp.

[*The policeman*] tried to tell me that [*police*] weren't satisfied with the $10,000 they had received—they reckoned that I was a millionaire twice over and wouldn't miss it. I wasn't falling into letting [*the policeman*] stand over me, no way. I told him there was no way any cop was going to stamp me for another penny. Then I handed [*the policeman*] a copy of the two statements. He read through them and didn't know what to say. After a few minutes he said: 'OK Neddy, you have him [*another policeman*] over a barrel for now. Be very careful, though, as he may try and set you up.'

'You tell him he better get thoughts like that out of his mind, because I will not stand still and cop it. I will go straight to the internal affairs about him.' Just to stay sweet with [*the policeman*], I handed him another two thousand dollars for his trouble. He made out that he didn't want it but he soon snaffled it.

There was a murder. Four guys were charged over the blue and I was friendly with one of them. This guy got in touch with me asking could I do anything for him as he was cold [*innocent*] on the blue. The cops had just thrown him in for the fun of it, but he looked like getting fitted with it.

He was in jail, so I went to visit him, and I decided to try and help him. I went to see The Artful Dodger and explained the situation. As it turned out, he knew the guy concerned: 'Leave it to me and I'll get back to you on the matter soon as I can.' Again I visited the guy in jail and told him that I had seen someone and it looked as if it would be OK for him.

A few days later Roger got back to me and said he had seen a prosecutor. 'Here is what has to be done, and as soon as possible. Get your mate to get his lawyer to set up a lie-detector test. It won't reach court if he does what he is told to do.'

I knew that lie-detector tests couldn't be used in a court of law. 'But,' Roger said, 'it will be enough to ensure that your friend gets a no-bill [*the prosecution would drop the charge*] before the trial starts.'

Once again I went out and told the guy the conditions and he agreed. He got the test done and forwarded it to the prosecutor's office with an application for a no-bill to be filed on his behalf. As The Dodger predicted, the guy got the no-bill. The price of that little bit of business was only $10,000, quite cheap. I went with The Dodger to a hotel on the corner of South Dowling Street to pay the prosecutor the $10,000 for fixing the no-bill. This had to be paid three days before the guy was officially notified. I stood at the bar while Roger talked to the prosecutor nearby. I wasn't introduced to the prosecutor and I did not know him—never seen him before. I watched The Dodger hand him the $10,000 that I had given him and the guy handed The Dodger an envelope back. The prosecutor left the pub and The Dodger came over and gave me the envelope.

I opened it and read a copy of a letter informing the guy's solicitor that a no-bill had been filed and his client would not be required at court. The Dodger told me to go out to the jail and show the guy the letter so that he would know we had kept our word.

He was very pleased that he was going to beat the blue: he was not guilty anyway. He was officially notified the day that he was supposed to stand trial. I saw him when he got out of jail. He turned into another arsehole that I helped who shat on me. I never seem to learn from my mistakes. I guess that I'm just a mug that likes to help people out when they're in trouble. Maybe one day I will wake up to myself.

[*This officer*] had a bad problem: he wasn't sure whether he belonged in the police force or whether he wanted to be a crook. He became almost unbearable. He was always turning up at the same restaurants and pubs we went to. He started to dress like us and he drove a Mercedes, like most of us did. He even wore jewellery like we did. I believe that he changed sides without even becoming aware that the change had taken place. He was a frustrated crook.

One day I was drinking with Tex when in came [*the officer*]. He bought me a drink and started to tell me his problems. He had a teenage daughter who was going out with this guy who was a heroin pusher. He had gotten [*the officer's*] daughter addicted to heroin. [*The officer's*] marriage was on the rocks and he had plenty of problems. He had tried unsuccessfully to talk to this guy and he wondered whether I would talk to the guy and persuade him to leave his daughter alone?

'Do you think you could do this favor for me, mate? I will not forget it and I may be able to return the favor later on.'

I could see an opening for a bright lad here, so I took it head on. 'OK, old mate, your problems are over. Just let me have the guy's address and a description of him and I will do my best for you.'

He was all smiles. 'I will do one better than that. Here is a photo of the bludger.' He handed me a photo of a guy in his mid-30s.

Within a few days I located the guy at Coogee. [*The officer's*] daughter was with him, but I soon got her to leave us alone. I tried to talk sense to the guy at first, but to no avail. He was a shitman and a smarty. He wanted to argue about everything that I said. He kept reminding me that [*the officer*] was a cop—he thought that was reason enough to get [*the officer's*] daughter hooked on drugs. Finally, Abo and I walked him around the corner and gave him a terrible serve. Abo got carried away and went to town on the guy with his blade, stabbing him in the face half a dozen times. Then we kicked him unconscious and left him lying there.

The guy never bothered [*the officer's*] daughter again, but there were many more blokes that kept her involved in heroin over the years. But we left [*the officer*] to fix those himself.

I did plenty of business with all types of police for over 15 years. In that time, I never met one cop that wouldn't come to the party as far as copping a quid goes. There was the odd one that refused to do business directly with me for some reason or other, but they would do it for me, through someone else. They always came to the party. A few of the young guys just starting out in uniform refused to do business—I've always said it was easier to beat a murder blue than a drink driving charge—but most of them eventually weakened and gave in to temptation.

There were the stupid few that attempted to stamp me. They knew that I was making plenty of money and thought that they deserved a share of the profits. They never had any luck at getting any of my hard-earned cash. [*A copper*] was one that tried to stamp me. [*The copper*] had just taken over as the boss of [*a group of police*] and knew that I was travelling well at the time. He rang Roger and arranged to see him. Roger went to his office, where [*the copper*] suggested I was entitled to throw a monkey [*$500*] a week his way to stop him from loading me up with some bogus charge.

Roger blew up: 'You're the fucking big shot. Why don't you tell him yourself? He will tell you to go fuck yourself.'

[*The copper*] didn't like that one bit. He said: 'Tell your mate he won't last the week.'

Roger got in touch with me and related the message to me. I wasn't overly concerned. 'Has he got any go in him?'

'Not one bit, but the cunt will spear one of the younger guys in to load you.'

I made up my mind to get in first. I got Roger to fill me in on all of [*the copper's*] habits and movements, the way he operated and everything that he knew about him. The next day I fronted with [*a solicitor and barrister*] at the internal affairs branch and dropped the bucket on [*the copper*]. I told them exactly what he was planning to do about loading me up.

After seeing the internal affairs, we went to the police pub, the Wentworth Hotel in Wentworth Avenue. I knew [*the copper*] went there every lunchtime. I went in and spotted him at the bar, so I went straight up and asked, did he intend loading me up because I wouldn't pay him a bribe?

He just stood there dumbfounded. 'Well, here I am. Do you want to do anything about it or are you all talk?'

He stormed out of the hotel, raving and ranting on the way out. I stayed for an hour with my lawyers just to show the police that they didn't bother me. [*The copper*] was furious over me putting him on show, but I never heard from him again. Roger was too powerful for [*the copper*] to take the punt on backing-up and doing anything about me.

Another attempted stamp came from [*another detective*] who drove a Mercedes while he was in the police force—I don't know now he managed to explain it. He tried to stamp Tex for $5000 over a car that Tex had purchased. The car was owned by a convicted drug dealer, who wanted to sell it before it was confiscated. [*The detective*] had discovered this and tried to stamp Tex; he thought Tex had some connection to the drug dealer (he didn't). Tex was all for paying them the money. I soon put that idea right out of his mind. I didn't mind paying for something that you did, but I refused to be stamped by smarties for nothing.

I rang The Dodger and arranged for him to meet [*the detective*] and us at the Bunny Club. Tex nearly had a baby when he found out what I was up to. He wanted to just pay [*the detective*] the money. I arrived at the Bunny Club and explained the circumstances. Roger wasn't happy about [*the detective*] trying to stamp Tex. When the detective arrived, Roger had a word with him. I also explained that they were trying to stamp a friend of mine cold.

We all had a drink together and [*the detective*] told Tex he was sorry for the misunderstanding. Tex shat himself and tried to sling [*the detective*] $1000 for his troubles. He said to Tex: 'Don't even think about it, I have enough to worry about without Roger driving me mad.' [*The detective*] stayed for one drink only and left. He was later tipped from the police force on corruption charges.

15
A Spot of Robbing

'How does $750,000 sound to you?'

Friend to Smith

Abo and I were selling heroin for several different people. There was a lot of gear around at this particular time, it wasn't very expensive. Some of the gear was good, some not so good. We could afford to be choosy and take our pick. We had the connections and that's what counted. We had about 10 guys selling the gear for us. Abo would hand it out at the beginning of the week and we would come down to Sydney every Thursday and spend the better part of two days collecting the money that was owed to us. Each Saturday we would meet at the Star Hotel and pay our dealers. Normally, we would be finished and on our way back up the coast by Saturday afternoon. Abo was building a mansion near Lake Macquarie—he had purchased the land and started the building, but it was a mistake from the word go. The bills just kept coming in. Every quote from the tradesmen was bigger when the work was done, and it was then too late to blue about it. All he could do was pay.

Abo was married with three kids, two girls and a boy. I was godfather to his youngest daughter, Lauren. At the christening, Abo's wife Leslie was terrified that I was going to say something to the Catholic priest, like call him a poof. I was always having a go at Leslie about Catholic priests because she was forever saying prayers over me and blessing me all the time. Leslie had a bug about religion.

Meanwhile, there was a shake-up coming within the police force. They were going to put on another show of cleaning out the corrupt ones. Had they been fair dinkum, the police force would have been very short on staff to man the stations.

There had been a lot of suspensions already among the top cops, but they had to get more to try to regain public support.

It had to appear to the public that something serious was being done to try and clean up the New South Wales police force. In the early 1980s Merv Beck was given the job of cleaning up the gambling and SP business. It was a big task, but he seemed to apply himself to the task and managed to get plenty of results. Beck made dozens of arrests and he closed down dozens of small operations. He successfully closed me down. I didn't make too much of a fuss about it. I wasn't really all that interested in the SP business any more; the money was rolling in so fast [*from the heroin business*] I didn't worry about opening the SP again. The SP had served its purpose well while it lasted. It had been something for the police to keep under surveillance while I snuck around doing many other things.

I should have stuck to it, but I was getting lazy and slack, dropping my guard on the drink. Many people were telling me to get off the drink and keep my guard up. They told me that drink addled the brain; they weren't wrong. But I wouldn't listen, I knew better.

Lots of people came to me with different scams. They didn't have the knowhow or ability to do them themselves, and were prepared to settle for a spotter's fee. We paid 10 per cent of what we got to anyone who came up with a good go. It didn't matter what it was, as long as it could be done without violence. It sometimes turned out to be a nice little earn for them. Among those that came to us were plenty of greedy police. They always had information that a normal person didn't have access to—and their information was always spot-on. It didn't need too much checking.

The police had accepted me. They saw that I was good at what I did and I rarely made mistakes. I had the Green Light to do anything at all. I wasn't making enough use of it, though. I would have to liven up and get my act together. This Green Light wouldn't last forever. I knew this and my mind constantly wandered to people like Phillip Western and Butchy Burns who, years earlier, allegedly had the Green

Light, only to be killed by police when their usefulness ended. I had to take precautions to make sure that I controlled whatever I did with the police, and never let them get the upper hand with me.

I managed to stay in front for many years by having the situation reversed. They worked for me, not I for them. It worked out well. They got what they wanted (money) and I kept things in my court, doing things the way I wanted. Many times the cops disagreed with the way that I wanted to handle things, but I never weakened, even though sometimes their way sounded better. I had to keep control of the situation.

It was a Saturday. I was sitting at the Lord Wolesley Hotel in Ultimo having a quiet drink to pass the time before I headed home. All business was done and everyone was happy. Then a close friend of mine called; he wanted to see me urgently. When he got to the hotel he was all smiles, as though he had just won the lottery.

I bought him a drink and sat waiting for him to stop smiling and tell me the good news. He was excited about whatever it was he wanted to tell me, so I didn't spoil it for him. I let him take his time and savor the moment.

'Mate,' he finally said, 'have I got a deal for you.' He sounded like a car salesman. 'Are you interested in a big armed robbery? A very big one.' I sat waiting for him to go on.

'Mate, I know these three guys that are working together as pay clerks and they want to talk to you about your doing an armed robbery on the payroll.'

It sounded OK, but I asked why they had gone through him. 'Why didn't they come straight to me?'

'They are scared of you and they don't know you.'

I had plenty of money and I hadn't done an armed robbery for ages. There would be the money plus the break from boredom—not to mention the excitement of the actual robbery.

'I don't know, mate. What sort of money are we talking about?'

This was the moment he'd been waiting for. 'How does $750,000 sound to you?'

That was a nice little piece of change if he was correct. 'Are you serious, mate?'

'Of course. Now, will you meet them?'

I agreed. He wasn't wasting time, either: he had the three guys up the road waiting. He went and got them and we sat down and discussed the details of the robbery. They gave me a complete rundown on the pay office. It turned out that they were the only ones in the pay office when the money was delivered. Couldn't be better if I had wanted it to be.

It was a fortnightly payroll for the container terminal workers at Port Botany. The money was always delivered by Armaguard security vans on a Thursday morning at about 8.30am, I think it was. And here were the three clerks wanting to be robbed of $750,000. What more could I ask for?

I got every bit of information I could from them about the office, the timing and the movement of the guards. I told them I would look at the layout and get back to them. I thought about it for a while. Surely there had to be an armed guard with such a large payroll, even if only for insurance purposes. $750,000 up for grabs, it was certainly worth the effort.

That Saturday I drove home with nothing else on my mind except doing the robbery. All weekend I sat by the pool thinking it over. I worked out dozens of different ways to do it, but none of them meant a shit until I actually went and looked at the place. I was already organising people to do it with and I rang and made arrangements to see the police about getting permission. I had the Green Light, but I wanted to check that it applied to a go this big.

Thursday came and I was anxious to get to Sydney and look at the place. Abo came with me. I had not mentioned it to him as I was not sure he would want to be involved—he was earning plenty of money and didn't need the drama.

We got to Sydney very early so I drove straight out to the Port Botany container terminal. I wanted to know as much about the place as possible before fronting [*a policeman*] and his gang about doing it. I was sure they would want to know the details before allowing me to go ahead.

The place was huge. It was on more than 100 acres of land. There were security guards on every gate, except the one where the pay office was. I chose a spot on a hill overlooking the pay office to watch the armored car arrive.

It was a spot unlikely to attract attention from any gigs

[*nosey-parkers*]. Roger had told me all about the armed hold-up squad and how it operated, especially what detectives looked for from witnesss, like any cars with people just sitting in them weeks beforehand. I knew every plan the hold-up squad used and the routine it adopted when a robbery was reported. Roger used to laugh about the cops: 'They all rush to the scene of the robbery as if expecting the robbers to be still waiting for them.'

I used to always check things out very carefully. I left nothing to chance, I couldn't afford to. There was still the one chance in a million that some cop might take it into his head to buck the system and try to pinch me, so I took every precaution possible. For example, we left no part of our skin showing so it would be impossible to identify us [*from tattoos*].

From the hill, we didn't have a clear view of the office as there were trees in the way, but we watched the van arrive. I timed how long it took from the time they entered until they drove out of the gates. Six minutes exactly.

The van had dropped off two tins. When it left I drove in, passing the van as it came out. I drove into the office car park as if I was about to do the robbery. I wanted to see exactly what happened when the payroll arrived, what precautions—if any—they took, and how many people were in the area.

No one took the slightest bit of notice of us. There were about 60 cars in the car park so we didn't look out of place. I parked the car and walked casually towards the pay office. I had to pass quite a few people as I walked through the building. Still no one took any notice. We walked about 100 metres into the grounds and into the complex. There were plenty of offices, but I had no problem locating the right one. There was a worker's recreation hall just opposite the pay office, but it had only a few people in it at that hour of the morning.

I walked right up to the pay office and turned the door handle. The door opened straight away. I couldn't believe these people were so careless as to leave the door open. I looked into the office and, straight in front of me, were the three guys that saw me about doing the robbery. They were bent over their desks counting out envelopes and putting them in separate trays. It was so easy I could have done it then and there without even having a gun. The three guys looked at me and smiled.

I turned and walked back to my car. This was going to be one fucking easy go, that was for sure. Like going to the bank and asking for it to be withdrawn from your account. I decided this was for me. My adrenalin was already pumping madly—I was excited at the prospect of doing the robbery. It was then that I told Abo and asked if he was interested in doing it with me. Abo was very keen, so that was that.

We drove to my friend's place. 'It is definitely a go, mate,' I told him. 'Tell those guys that I'll see them on Saturday morning. I have a few minor details that I want to see them about, then all they have to do is sit back and wait to collect their money.'

Later that day I met Roger and explained what I wanted to do. He told me I would have to go through [*a policeman*] who ran that sort of business. I got in touch with [*the policeman*] the next day and told him what I had in mind. He said it was OK, but he was very explicit: no police were ever to be hurt. Not ever.

'You have the Green Light to go ahead. I will put you in touch with someone in the hold-up squad and you deal directly with him. Don't contact me yourself again. You will be watched once you start this type of thing. So leave it to the guy that I give you to contact me, OK?'

He obviously planned to keep a low profile and distance himself from me in case of some blow-up. That arrangement suited me fine. The less I saw of [*the policeman*] the better I liked it. He gave me the names of two detectives to contact regarding the armed robbery and doing the business. They were [*Smith names both officers*].

When I rang, the first person I spoke to was [*a police officer*]. He was expecting my call and we met at the Hoyts Entertainment Centre in town, where he told me the conditions and the percentage I had to weigh in out of each robbery. He said he would make sure there were police in the area covering me, and if anything went wrong they would make sure I was never charged. Their cut was to be no lower than $20,000. If the robberies were big ones, then they automatically got 10 per cent of the haul. When I left I was feeling great. It was all points go. Now it was up to me to work out a final plan. There were a lot of things to take care of such as clothing, guns, cars and how we would be disguised. A lot of little but very important things to take care of before we got off the ground.

I got into the swing of things pretty quickly and before too long, things were going along just fine. I always put a lot of work into robberies. I took them very seriously—it wasn't a game we were playing. I never ever left one clue that the police could follow through on, never made one mistake that could lead them to us. It wasn't as if I needed the money. I wasn't a kleptomaniac: I did robberies because I enjoyed them. Police would come to me and say: 'I've got one. Do you want to do it?' I couldn't say 'No', could I? Besides, if *you* could walk into a bank and withdraw as much money as you wanted without getting pinched, wouldn't you do it?

The van only delivered the payroll fortnightly, but we went over it every week to make sure that there would be no slip-ups. I decided the only way to get in and out of the building without anyone taking too much notice was to dress as security guards.

I got someone to rent a white panel van. [*Smith usually paid $500 for this service: he supplied a false driving licence and cash to hire a vehicle, and arranged for the 'hirer' to leave the vehicle at a car park. After the robbery, the hire-car was abandoned.*] I picked up the car and arranged for Armaguard signs to be painted on the doors, just the same as the real vans. It was perfectly done. With a little help from my friends—the police—I was able to get a uniform similar to those worn by the guards. The only minor problem I encountered was getting the security badges they wore on their arms, but eventually I got those too. We were ready to go, all was in order. And then the unbelievable happened. It couldn't have happened to anyone except me.

I was at the hotel, waiting for the three pay-office clerks to turn up, when my mate came in looking like his favourite dog had been run over.

'Mate, I have some bad news for you.'

It couldn't be that they had changed their minds. 'What the fuck's up?'

'You wouldn't believe it, but the three of them were killed on the harbor in a boating accident during the week.' He handed me a newspaper and there it was in black and white. According to the article, the three had just purchased a boat. They took it for a trial run and were all drinking. Apparently there was a gas leak on the boat, the three fell asleep and they never woke up—they died in their sleep. Fucking unreal. It could only happen to me.

I decided that it was just too good to let go. I was going on with it, regardless of them dying. There needed to be a few minor changes, nothing spectacular, just disguises. It was a real robbery now, so we had to wear false moustaches and sunglasses to try to cover our faces a bit. There was no way I could let the robbery go. I'd given my word to the police—they would think I talked through my arse if I failed to go through with it. It was either do the robbery or lose my credibility forever.

We were ready to go. It was payday at the Port Botany container terminal. Abo was a bit nervous at first. I suppose I was, too. Who knows whether they are nervous or not? All I was thinking about was the excitement and the money.

We had done everything. We had purchased a second vehicle, a kombi van, and done it up like a painter's van with ladders on top and cans of paint inside. It looked like the real thing. No one would give it a second glance, they would be looking for two men dressed as security guards racing away from the scene of the crime—not two guys in overalls in an old van with ladders and painter's signs on the side. It was in place and ready.

We drove to our position on the hill. I got out of the van and tore away the masking tape, uncovering the Armaguard signs. We were dressed in the uniforms and looking good. As we waited for the pay van to lob, another pay van passed by. As they went past they waved, a normal reaction for people from the same company when they see one another. Well, Abo shat himself. He nearly had a baby there and then. 'We are off mate, let's go, get out of here. Come on, mate, let's move it.' I couldn't stop laughing. Maybe it was nerves—I didn't know or care. 'Shut up, Abo. The only reason that they waved is because they saw the signs on the door and are letting us know they saw us. Calm down.'

I got him calmed down just as our armored van came into sight. 'Come on buddy, it's time to go.'

Abo was looking a bit off-color, but he started to drive

off slowly. He was going to be all right. Just as we drove in the gate, they came out. We were right on schedule. We pulled up outside the front door of the office so that the men doing the pay would notice the signs on the van. They never used the front door so we casually walked into the building and up to the pay office door. No one took the slightest bit of notice of us. I turned the door handle and—fuck, the door was locked.

Knock, knock. The door opened and this big guy said: 'What's up fellows, forget something?' I stuck my gun into his gut and pushed him inside with the other two guys. At first he thought I was joking, but he soon discovered I was deadly serious.

'Get on your stomach, now. Move it.' They moved very fast and lay down. Abo was supposed to lock the door to stop anyone from walking in on us. I was tying them up when I heard the door open behind me. This guy started yelling for help. Fuck Abo, he didn't lock the door. Where was Abo? I looked quickly around. There he was, looking through the vault for more money instead of minding me. I chased the guy, trying to stop him from raising the alarm, and followed him into a room full of wharfies playing pool and just sitting around the place. Christ, where had they all come from?

I got out of there fast and went back to get Abo. He was just coming out of the office carrying the money. We got to the 'Armaguard' van with dozens of people trying to follow us. We had no trouble with anyone as we got in and drove off. We reached the painter's van and changed over without incident. We were on time. That was good. As we changed cars and our clothes, there was this guy sitting in a truck watching us. Abo got behind the wheel of the van and off we went. Abo was a very good driver when he needed to be.

While he drove, I finished changing out of the uniform into shorts and a t-shirt. I got up alongside Abo in the front. He was struggling to get his shirt off so I helped him. We passed a police car parked by the road. As we passed, they waved us on. I returned the wave. For the second time that day, Abo nearly had a heart attack.

'We are off. They saw us, mate. What do we do?'

I had not told Abo that the cops would be in the area

minding us. I told him now. Boy, did he blow up at me: 'What?! Am I a cunt or something? Why not tell me? You nearly gave me a heart attack.'

'Just take it easy, mate. They are mates of mine and they are letting us through the gap before they block off the area.'

We drove to a prearranged destination. Abo then took the van to a place far away from where I was and I took the money and all the equipment with me. When Abo came back we counted the money while listening to the scanner to monitor how the police were progressing. The police were looking in all the wrong places, they never had a clue.

Counting the money was always the hardest part, ripping open all the pay envelopes and putting the money in the correct bundles. The whack-up was the main event. We had missed out on the $750,000. I was very upset as I thought that we had left it behind in our haste to get away, but later I found out from the police that there had been a strike and we had only got the overtime payroll. We finished with $100,000 for our troubles. I suppose it was better than a poke in the eye with a sharp stick.

We took out the $20,000 for New South Wales' finest, then expenses, and finally the money for the guys that painted the van. We got what was left—about $30,000 each. Not much. The following day I met [*the policeman*] and gave him the money. He was very pleased with the way the robbery had gone down. All was well because there had been no violence. Violence was a definite no-no with them, especially where police were concerned.

I always avoided violence when doing robberies. It was bad for business and brought too much heat from the media. I was curious about how we had missed the big money and [*the policeman*] explained about the strike. He said we were lucky to get the overtime payroll. How could it happen to me? First the guys died, and then the bastards went on strike. Abo and I decided to get drunk. That was the first armed robbery that I did for and with [*police*]. The first of many.

Abo began to get restless for another armed robbery. He was keen to make up for the blue he made leaving the door unlocked. It had been a bad mistake, possibly even fatal for me, especially if the guard had been armed—and he knew it. The chance soon popped up. It was only a small one, but it was a drink. One of New South Wales' finest came to me with the proposition: a payroll at Balmain. The cop gave me all the details and asked if I was interested in giving it a go? I told him that I would look at it and get back to him when I made up my mind.

I decided that it sounded like a piece of cake, minus the cream. I took Abo to Balmain to look it over and get some idea of the way they went to collect the money from the bank. There were three guys: they drove to the bank in one of their own cars, picked up about $70,000, then returned to the office. Sometimes they changed their route back to the office. But it wouldn't affect us because the last part of their trip was along a one-way street—they had to come that way.

We followed their movements for two weeks and decided it was a snack. They couldn't change that last stretch of road so the plan was to get them just as they neared their destination. I got in touch with [*the police*] and let them know when we would do the robbery. They knew there wasn't a great deal of cash and agreed to settle for less this time.

Using the old painter's van we still had from the Port Botany robbery, I decided to block the narrow, one-way street. I would get a driver to back out in front of them as they drove along, making out he was reversing from a block of flats. I would be in the back of the van, ready to jump out and get the money. Abo would be in another car, stolen of course. His job was to come up their rear and ram them, so as to shake them up and cut off any idea of retreating.

We got everything ready. The young team stole us a car—they were very reliable and not once did they let us down. The gear for the robbery was next on the agenda. We got dark-colored tracksuits, blue balaclavas and white cotton gloves. We always wore identical clothing so as to confuse any witnesses when they gave descriptions of us. Thus no two witnesses ever agreed on what happened or what the offenders looked like. There was always a difference in their stories.

Abo was watching for the car to come into sight. We kept in touch by walkie-talkies. At the same time we listened to a scanner that was tuned into the police bands. Everything was ready. Just a matter of waiting. Abo spotted them: 'Here they come.'

A Spot of Robbing

I told the driver to slowly back out as though he was reversing from the driveway. He began to reverse—I was in the back of the van, ready, masked and the shotty in my hands. As we backed out they stopped, not suspecting a thing until I jumped out and rushed them brandishing the shotty. They didn't get a chance to do anything as Abo rammed them right up the arse-end and slammed them against the dashboard. It was over in seconds. I grabbed the bag with the money while Abo jumped from the other car. He stood pointing his gun at them. We left the van blocking the street and took off in a third vehicle. We only went a matter of a 100 yards before we changed cars. Each of us went our own separate ways, meeting later to count the money and split it up.

I met the police the next day and gave them their little share. They were happy that it had gone down so easily without a hitch or any violence. It looked as though they might have been testing me with something much bigger in mind. A message got back to me that [*another group of detectives*] wanted a drink [*a cash payment*] out of the robbery. They dipped out. Just to be on the safe side we always burnt every bit of gear so as not to leave any clues for them to follow.

[*A detective*] came on the scene somewhere about this time. He was an eager beaver, hot to trot and he wanted to get involved in the action. But he had a problem. He was not one of the chosen ones in the inner circle. He approached me with a few really workable schemes, but I had to knock him back. [*The detective*] was not overburdened with brains. His mouth and his ego got the better of him at times. I finally decided to have a go at one of his propositions. He was doing heaps of research into different things and I thought that he was on to a good go. I got in touch with [*a policeman to seek permission*]. I told him that I was considering having a go at one of [*the detective's*] ideas. He wasn't impressed and told me to call him later that day. When I rang back I got a definite no.

I thought [*the detective*] had had a good idea. Next time I wouldn't ask [*permission*], I'd just go ahead and do it without telling them. What they didn't know wouldn't hurt them. When I saw Roger, I told him about [*the detective's*] plan being knocked back. Roger again told me: 'Always keep on top of things that you get involved with that they have a say in. Neddy, you are on top of things now, make sure you stay there. You tell them what you are going to do. Dictate to them and don't let them get the upper hand. Always remember that they are only human and they are more worried about you than you are about them.'

Roger always gave me good advice. He was all the time trying to further my education as far as the police force went. 'You have to understand how the fools think and then stay one step ahead of them.'

[*The detective whose plan was rejected by other police*] began promising different people the go at Kings Cross to sell dope. He was asking for trouble; the Cross was already spoken for. He was handed in by fellow cops for selling drugs at the Cross and received a big jail term for his trouble.

16
Broad Daylight

Liars ought to have good memories
   Algernon Sidney, 1622–83

[*On Wednesday 2 April 1986, Neddy Smith was run down in broad daylight in McEvoy Street, Waterloo, by a car that jumped the pavement and then attempted to reverse over him. The incident came less than 24 hours after Roger Rogerson appeared on Channel Nine's national current affairs program,* Willesee, *naming Smith as a police informer. On the program, Rogerson also told host Ray Martin that he had never taken a bribe nor, in the 27 years he'd been in the police force, had he known a corrupt police officer.*

The day after he was run down, Smith appeared on the Willesee *program to say that police were involved in the attempt on his life. It was an extraordinary interview by a man who previously had shunned publicity. Until then, Smith was known mainly because he was frequently named in royal commissions and in the New South Wales Parliament as a drug dealer and leading Sydney criminal, and because of his links to Roger Rogerson. One of Smith's main motives for appearing on the program was to deny that he was an informer—paid or otherwise—of Rogerson, or any other policeman. The television appearance produced a flurry of front-page newspaper stories and feature articles on Smith. Some of the reports focused on the possibility of a renewed gang war, but a new outbreak of violence didn't eventuate. Here, Smith gives his version of the attempt on his life.*]

I left the Iron Duke Hotel and started to walk the 100

metres to my car. As I walked across the driveway of Cambergs Carpet, where the trucks entered the factory, I suddenly felt an enormous pain. I was flung up against the wall. My first thought was that some stupid bloody truck driver, in a hurry to get in the factory, had hit me.

But I hadn't seen the car that mounted the footpath and slammed into me with the intention of killing me. A lunatic had been waiting for me outside the hotel. When I came out he had driven across the street, through traffic, mounted the footpath and slammed me into the wall. I was in shock and pain when I got to my feet.

It was lucky that I managed to stand up. I was just in time to see the driver trying to back the car over the top of me. This was obviously an attempt to get me out of the way. Instinctively, I tried to get my gun out of my pocket—it wasn't there. I remembered that I had dropped my guard and let Billy Duff talk me into handing it to him. Defenceless against this lunatic, I could only get out of the way as the car tried to back over me. I managed to get myself into a recess and I then saw the driver's face—for just a second we looked straight into each other's eyes—then it hit me like a ton of bricks: I knew the guy well and I realised I had been set up, set up by that mongrel Duff. The car reversed into a wall, then took off into the peak-hour traffic hurtling up and down Botany Road.

Somehow, I managed to make it back to the Iron Duke, where I collapsed. Abo was there and called an ambulance. I was rushed under heavy police guard to South Sydney Hospital. I had numerous injuries: my ribs, my left leg and my collarbone were broken. I also suffered injuries to my spine.

After regaining consciousness I saw police everywhere. I wasn't feeling too crash hot, but sick as I was, I wasn't having any of this police protection. I could no longer afford to trust anyone connected with the New South Wales police. I was well aware of the lengths they would go to if the need arose.

My wife arrived at the hospital and I signed myself out. I could barely walk, but I managed aided by my little wife, God love her. She had dropped everything when she heard I was hurt and come straight to Sydney, bringing with her a loaded pump-action shotgun to protect me if the need arose. I was lucky to have a wife like mine. You would be flat out finding too many blokes with as much go in them as my Debra had. She drove me home to Kotara.

Shortly before the attack, a friendly detective, a friend of Roger's, had warned me that [*certain police*] were going to kill me in the car park of the Iron Duke Hotel after the pub closed. The idea was to shoot me, then plant a gun on me. Their story would be that when they confronted me, I called out: 'I know you're Domican's men,' and then I pulled a gun. They would shoot me in 'self-defence'. I was the only one remaining alive that knew anything about the police involvement in the 'Gang Wars' and organised crime. Flannery had gone missing. So had his mate Prendergast. [*Laurence Joseph Prendergast went missing in the outer Melbourne suburb of Warrandyte in August 1985. His family claimed he had been killed, although an inquest in 1990 concluded that Prendergast may have staged his own disappearance.*] The rest that knew anything about the police involvement were either missing or in jail.

I hoped to fuck their plan by calling Mike Munro [*a journalist from the* Willesee *show*]. He came and did an interview at my home. After hours of filming, Mike decided that he had suffcent to go to air and he left promising to be in touch. [*The interview was done two days before Smith was run down. It was not broadcast.*]

[*Hours after Smith was run down*] Mike Munro contacted me. He wanted to put me on national television to tell my story. I agreed. Mike arrived at Kotara by helicopter with armed security guards to protect me. My wife accompanied me by helicopter to the Channel 9 studios where I went on television and had my say. The interview made headlines and brought the police into the limelight. It also achieved its intended purpose: to stop the police trying to kill me.

A few months after the interview, two cops fronted me and abused me. 'You have done the wrong thing by airing it in public. You should have kept it between us.'

I blew right up at them: 'You cunts are not serious, are you? You want to kill me and I'm supposed to just sit still and cop it. No fucking way!'

The police lived by a set of rules designed to suit them and them alone. Crims were expected to cop whatever the police did to them and their families and say nothing. That was all shit.

I am doing my best to fight back with the only means available to me.

Terry Ball and I grew up in the same district and used to run around together as teenagers. He was a great boxer and as a kid he won a few titles. He would fight at the drop of a hat. However, Terry was a nut case, and the most paranoid person I have ever associated with. He was also charged by police with running me over.

[*About a year before Smith was run down*] Terry was shot in the head as he was playing cards at a friend's place in Erskineville. Both Terry and the police claimed I was responsible. Believe me, the head is the last place I would shoot him. One would do better to just forget it as shoot him in the head. I had nothing to with shooting him, and I don't care whether the police or Terry believe me or not.

Anyway, a year or so later, I was run down. Terry Ball was big-noting that he was responsible, so the police arrested him for attempted murder. I had to appear in court as the police wanted me to identify him. I told the truth: I had seen the man who ran me over and it was definitely not Terry Ball. He was discharged from the court the next day.

Chris Murphy, his lawyer, took the credit for beating the charge, but it didn't take a genius to beat that charge as I turned him up. There were no other witnesses but me, so how could he be found guilty?

Another one to big-note about being responsible for the attempt was Tom Domican. Why he wanted to claim that I'll never know.

It was the reason behind me bashing Tom Domican in jail. He told Abo that he had run me over. When I fronted him over it, he tried to bluff me like he has been bluffing everyone for years. It didn't work with me. I tested him out and found out that he is all mouth and very little ability to back it up. [*More on this incident page 306–9.*]

[*Three months after being run down Smith began gearing up for another armed robbery.*] It was one that had been unsuccessfully tried a few years previously and resulted in one of the guys being shot in the head by none other than Roger Rogerson himself. Butchy Burns was the guy Roger shot dead. Butch had been on work release from Silverwater Prison, where he was serving a sentence for armed robbery. Police had been tipped off and sat off the place. When the gang tried to do the robbery, police moved in and shot Butch dead.

The takings of the South Sydney Junior Rugby League Club was the robbery [*the police*] wanted me to do. Roger had an enormous laugh at the idea. He even supplied me with more information than the cop who had asked me to do it. Every Sunday morning around 9am (they sometimes varied the time, but only by a few minutes) three men arrived at this bank. One stayed in the van—he was armed—while the other two got out carrying an old bag containing between 16 and 20 smaller bags, which were placed in the bank's night safe. I watched them for a few weeks. I was in no hurry to do it as things were going great for me; they had never been better. I also had an uneasy feeling about Butch being killed attempting to do the robbery. But in the end, I decided to do it regardless.

This one would need a complete surprise; we couldn't afford to give them the slightest warning. The best way to get close enough was to drive up alongside them. I would stand up in the back of a utility holding a pump-action shotgun. That way I could control the whole area while Abo, armed with a handgun, could grab the bag from the other two before they put the money into the night safe.

Again, I got the young guys to procure us a utility for the job. We got the old tracksuits on again, also the balaclavas and white cotton gloves. We needed a driver to stay behind the wheel on this one as Abo was going to grab the money. This was no problem as there were a few guys lining up to have a go with us.

I told the [*police*] that it would be the following Sunday and for [*a certain policeman*] to make sure he was working that day. If he wasn't on the day shift he would swap shifts so he could be there to look after us.

Sunday came around. We sat in a side street waiting for the van. I was in the back of the ute waiting anxiously. My adrenalin was pumping madly. I had checked earlier that [*the policeman*] was in position to mind us. The van passed us, they suspected nothing was wrong. We gave them 60 seconds, then came out of the side street and pulled up alongside them. They were so preoccupied with putting the money in the night safe that they didn't know what hit them. I had to bang the shotgun on the window of the van to get the armed guard's attention, while Abo rushed round the van and held the other two guys up and grabbed the money. There was no trouble. It was over within 60 seconds.

Abo jumped into the back of the utility and we drove away. We travelled a short distance, turned left into the first side street, then left again, and ended up behind the bank outside which we'd just committed the robbery.

We got out of the ute and into the back of a roller-shuttered truck I'd borrowed for the occasion. The driver got behind the wheel, while Abo and I changed clothes in the back of the truck. Once we pulled up at our destination we went inside to count the money. The driver took the truck back to the guy that owned it. We cut open the leather bags only to find $70,000 instead of the $100,000 we had expected. Of that, $20,000 went to the police. We divided the rest after expenses were taken out.

I met [*a policeman*] at the Regent Hotel the following Monday. He said everything went well except for one minor problem: we'd dropped two leather bags containing $12,000 in the back of the utility. We must have dropped them in our haste to get away. That was the first and the last mistake of that type I ever made doing an armed robbery.

Another robbery done without a problem. I was beginning to enjoy them. I had done most things in my time and these were something to kill the boredom that plagued me. I got this mad adrenalin rush to my body every time I did a robbery. I think it was excitement mixed with a touch of fear. I used to wonder if the feeling I got was anything like the feeling junkies got when they shot up dope. I was addicted to excitement. There was nothing in the world like it, except perhaps fear. Fear twisted my gut muscles into knots. It got me higher than a kite at times.

One night Abo and I were drinking at the Lord Wolseley Hotel in Ultimo. There was a big team of us there and we were all in a good mood. We were drinking whatever was going. A team of shoplifters was talking to [*a policeman*] about fixing up a blue. A couple of them had been buckled [*arrested*] that afternoon. There were a few bookies there, also on the drink.

This guy named Rocky, a shoplifter and a mad practical joker, was in fine form. He wanted to play a practical joke on Abo. I warned him that Abo may not appreciate it, but Rocky just laughed. Like everyone else present, Rocky knew that Abo always carried a pistol in the handbag he had with him at all times. Rocky's plan was for me to pull Abo's head [*get Abo's attention*] while he swapped Abo's gun for a banana.

Rocky positioned himself near Abo's bag, so I walked over and pulled Abo aside. I told him I'd seen the doctor that morning and I had cancer. Well, Abo came in like Flynn—he even got upset over it. Meanwhile, Rocky swapped the gun for a banana. He then signalled me. All of a sudden I jumped back from the window and yelled, 'Look out, mate.' I grabbed my gun from out of my belt, ducking behind a door.

It was hysterical. Abo dived on his handbag, ripping it open, thrust his hand in and came up with a banana. You should have seen the look on Abo's face. If looks could kill, Rocky would have been dead. Abo started screaming out: 'What am I? A fucking fool or something?' We were all laughing except Rocky—he was on his way out the door.

We were always pulling jokes, but not many people seemed to appreciate our sense of humor.

One Saturday Abo and I were at the Lord Wolseley drinking with this guy George. He owed us a large chunk of cash. We knew he would pay, but we decided to have a little fun with him. Abo pulled his head while I positioned myself behind George. Once behind him I put the sleeper-hold on him and he went straight out. While he was unconscious we picked him up and put him in the boot of our car. We left the boot up waiting for him to wake up. As soon as we saw he was waking up, we started talking about where we'd put the shovels. I wish that I'd had a camera with me. If I had taken a shot of the look on George's face I would have won an award, for sure. George leapt out of the boot and bolted. He paid us early the next day. And some people think we have a weird sense of humor.

Word circulated throughout the police force that I was active and to be watched at all times. I was put on the top of the Active Criminals list. That presented me with no problems as the police were onside—those that mattered anyway. Offers were pouring in from all quarters.

[*Smith says for his next armed robbery, at the Awaba Mine, near Newcastle, he was tipped off by a policeman.*]

Abo and I went over the area. It was in a good, easy spot to rob, out in the sticks. We got clothing the same as the miners and walked around without causing anyone to take any notice of us. We looked for the best way out of the mine, checked on police routines and timed how long it took the police to reach the mine once the alarm went off. On the surface it looked easy, but I still insisted on going over the place time and time again. The mine worked three shifts so I could look at any time, day or night. I chose the night because there was less chance of anyone spotting me.

On the day the armored van delivered the payroll we went for a final check. Nothing had changed. The van did exactly as expected. There were plenty of workers hanging around, but this didn't affect us because we would be in and out before they knew what had hit them. There were only two ways that the police could get to the mine and they both took four and a half minutes from the police station. But it wouldn't matter which road they took. We'd be long gone before they got close enough to cause problems.

Timing was the most important part of any robbery. It was essential to get in and out within four minutes. I would never hang around longer than was absolutely necessary, and I would strike hard and fast, throwing everyone into confusion, giving them no chance to think or start playing the hero.

I decided against stealing a car from the Newcastle area as I wanted the police to blame a Sydney gang, so I got the same team of young guys to 'rent' me one instead. They got me a Ford Falcon. I borrowed the same truck that I had used on the South Sydney robbery. It was a good truck and no one would ever suspect a truck. As I said, police always look for the obvious, such as a car speeding away from the scene of the crime. With the exception of the experienced armed robbery squad, most police had no idea of what to look for—they went by the textbook.

The adrenalin started to pump again. We were in the car watching for the van to arrive and drop off the money. It was on time. It pulled up, the two guards got out and took the tins to the pay office. They were in and out within six minutes. They got back into the van and, as they drove out of the driveway, we made our move.

We pulled up alongside the boiler house. We had changed the locks on the door the previous night so we could go through the boiler room and get close enough to the pay office without being spotted. We had to surprise them and eliminate any chance of them raising the alarm. Abo and I wore the same clothing as the miners wore (except we also had balaclavas and gloves). We got to the office without being seen. I moved inside with the shotgun ready. There was one man and a young woman there. The woman was eating an apple and tried to yell, but I pushed the apple into her mouth before she could get a sound out. Abo moved to get the money tin. The old guy just stood there frozen while Abo picked it up. He couldn't believe what was happening.

'Come on, let's move it.' Abo was moving too slowly. He picked up speed and we got back into the car in seconds. It took us 90 seconds to reach the truck—we'd hidden it where we couldn't be observed changing vehicles—and we were on our way. Abo and I managed to change our clothing and get into shorts and singlets. We were listening to the scanner to see if the police knew anything. They didn't know what happened, never had a clue what was going on. We headed back to the driver's house in Sydney and counted the money. Just under $100,000. It was equally divided after taking out $25,000 for [*the police*].

It was about this time that I decided to split with Abo and go my own way. Abo was getting too lazy and there was a lot of friction among two other guys and Abo. Abo was always telling them what to do and they resented it. They complained to me about having to do all the work themselves. The two guys, Trout and Mick, were good men to have working for me. I thought they were loyal men, although it turned out I was wrong about that.

[*Before Abo's departure, it appears Smith's heroin business had shrunk in size, partly because his main supplier, Danny Chubb, had been cut down during the 'Gang Wars'. Chubb's partner had taken over the importing business and had quickly come under police scrutiny, prompting Smith to take several steps back. So, instead of buying drugs, Smith began to concentrate more on stealing them from other drug dealers.*]

Dave Kelleher and his associate John Powch caught by surveillance cameras at Sydney International Airport.

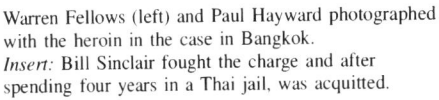

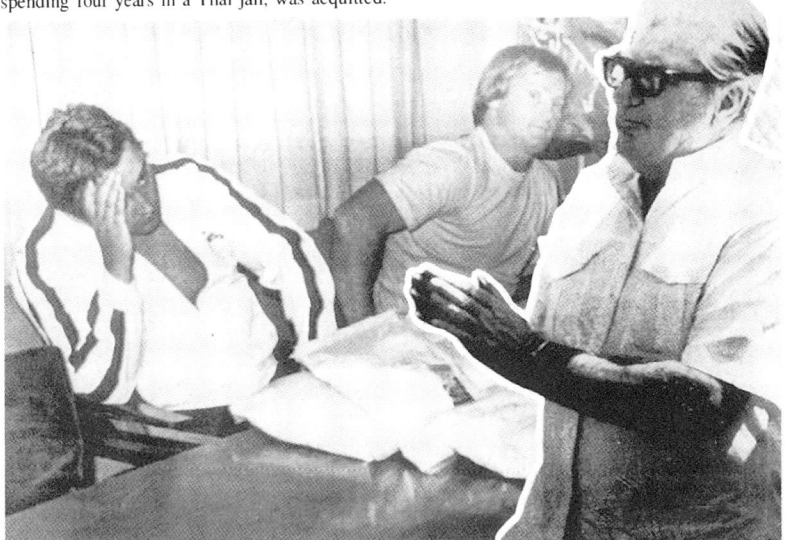

Warren Fellows (left) and Paul Hayward photographed with the heroin in the case in Bangkok.
Insert: Bill Sinclair fought the charge and after spending four years in a Thai jail, was acquitted.

Right: Abo Henry at home.

Below: Rex Jackson entering his 'new home' after being convicted for fixing early paroles, but not before getting Abo out.

Below right: My ex-lawyer, Val Bellamy and his client, Roger Rogerson, outside the Supreme Court. He was on bail pending appeal.

Home for six years, at Kotara, 200 km north of Sydney. Sturdy bars, closed circuit TV cameras, excellent lighting and two attack dogs ensured me against surprises. *Below left:* Daniel and me. Looking back a man ought to have quit crime while he was ahead and stayed home.

19 Henry Street, Sydenham. This is the first house we ever owned. Not bad for a boy from the back of Redfern.

After the Lanfranchi inquest, I took Debra on a cruise on the *Sea Princess*.

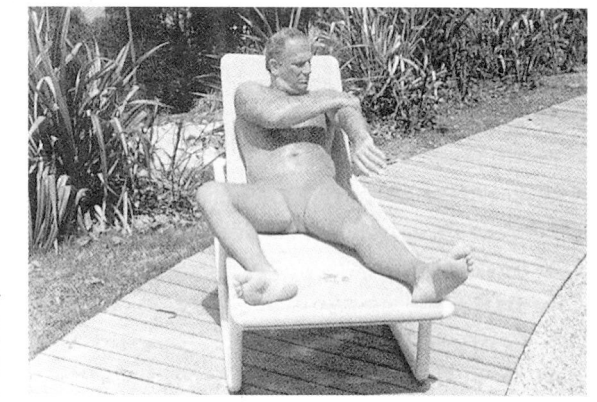

Home. It was great for a while, but I couldn't stick at it. The need for stimulation would pull me to town like a mug.

Not going anywhere on Lake Macquarie. Beats Long Bay for a place not to be going anywhere.

Christopher Dale Flannery, so called 'Mr Rentakill', couldn't resist this photo opportunity while on holiday at South Mole Island off the Queensland coast. The rope his enemies allowed him was, ironically, running out even then.

Chris pouring champagne over his wife Cath. It's only money.

Me and Debra at the Coachman with Tex and Wendy Moran. Tex was a bugger for a fight but guns froze him.

Top: Michael Sayers

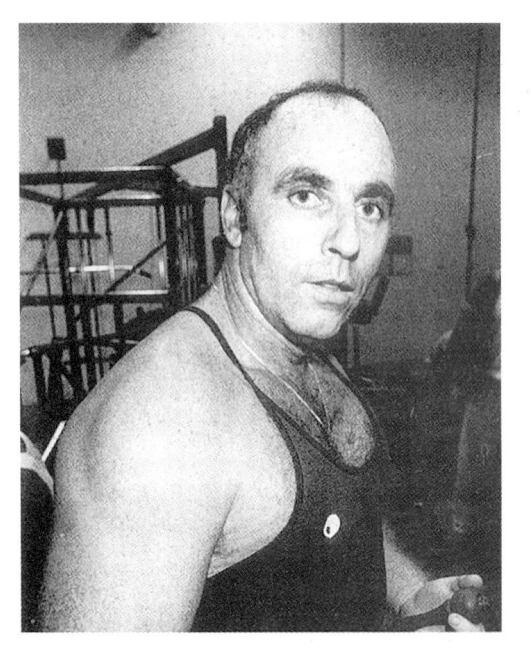

Above: Barry McCann leaves court.

Top: Tom Domican at one of his three-hour work-outs at the Canterbury-Bankstown Leagues Club. 'Who killed Laura Palmer? Tough Tom': jail graffiti.
Above: George Feeman talks to Lennie McPherson at the funeral of Paddles Anderson.

Above left: Tony Eustace
Above right: Danny Chubb

Below left: Chubb lies in front of his mother's house in Miller's Point, late 1984; McCann in the HJ Mahoney Memorial reserve, Marrickville, Christmas 1987 *(below)*; Sayer's body on the roadway in Bronte in 1985. *(bottom right)*

Green Light days. A few drinks at the Convent Garden hotel with Sgt Rogerson, girls and the kindly attention of a police surveillance squad. We hammed it up for their cameras: slapping each other with $50 notes, Roger taking his gear off . . .

Abo and I went our own ways. He wasn't happy over us splitting up. He tried to make a go of it, but had no luck for a long time. Without me and my connections he was lost. He kept on trying and eventually met two guys, legged into a few good earns and kicked on—it took him two years, though.

Abo was a good learner. He never forgot a thing and ended up with his own gang doing armored van robberies all over the place. He never changed over the years; he used to get the other two guys to do most of the work. It's great if you can get away with it, but I still liked to do most of the work myself. That way I controlled the situation from start to finish. When you have control you can work things your way. You are solely responsible for the outcome. And you can't blame anyone else.

I sort of teamed up with a guy called Warren. He was strange, but a very good earner. I made plenty of money with him. He used to have this thing about cop cars. As soon as he saw one, regardless of where he was, he would take off at 100 miles an hour and usually they would chase him. He once killed a girl accidently while escaping from police. We lasted until one of the charges he was on bail for came up and he was sentenced to a few years jail. We remained friends and I visited him a few times. This meant I was running on my own. I did really well. I was fortunate enough to be getting plenty of good earns and people were still coming to me with ideas, looking for their 10 per cent commission.

But I was in need of another guy, a partner to assist me in my business ventures. I needed someone who was willing, someone who could be trusted to do what was required. Not just a soldier, but a thinker. Soldiers were a dime a dozen, but thinkers that had enough dash in them—as well as brains—were like finding rocking horse shit. But I was fortunate. A guy I knew who had all the above requirements had just been released from the nick. He'd just finished a big one for a vicious armed robbery; just what I needed.

First, before I mentioned a word to him, I checked him out with The Dodger. He had no skeletons in the closet, he was solid. I knew this, but I'd been wrong before, so now I checked everyone out before I got involved. He passed with flying colours as I knew he would. I made it my business to bump into him a few times as if by accident. For the first few months he was interested in fucking women, nothing else. That wasn't a problem as I was in no hurry. He was fucking everything that moved and just generally having a good time. I had plenty of time, I had plenty of money and didn't mind having a rest.

It turned out that he ended up coming to me for work instead of me going to him. He was anxious to work at anything at all. He needed money fast and wasn't fussy how he got it. He had found out I was sweet with the powers that controlled all the major crime that went down in New South Wales and he wanted in. He was a willing young guy and we hit it off straight away. It was a strange relationship between us; we seemed to think alike. We would be looking at a job and would both speak at the same time, saying the same thing. We even came up with the same plans. Not once did we ever disagree over the way we would do a job. When we were working we never had to speak. We just knew what to do without communicating.

Before we started working together we went out a few times on the drink. He was a funny guy on the drink. All of a sudden he would take all his clothes off for no reason. It didn't matter where he was, he would just strip. Most places we went to took little or no notice of him, but we were barred from a few places. I trusted this guy with my life and my money, but under no circumstances could you trust him near your girl. He couldn't be trusted with your dog if it was a female. He had no principles as far as women went.

I never took Abo with me to meet the guys from the [*police*]. I was very protective of my connections and didn't share them with anyone. But I let my guard down with this guy. I always took him with me when I was paying them money, or even when I met them for a drink. He never met [*a certain policeman*], but he met nearly all the others that I was, at that time, doing business with. It was a big mistake.

I carried him longer than is mother did—she was lucky she only had to carry him for nine months.

These days he has lost any principles that he had. He thinks that he has fooled me and that I am unaware of what he has done. But I know.

17
Going to Work

'Work is much more fun than fun.'

Noel Coward, 1963

We will call my new partner in crime by the name of 'Harold', mainly to protect the guilty. It is quite obvious that is not his real name. I thought he was a very close friend and I would have been prepared to do anything for him. Again, my judgment of character was wrong.

Harold was, however, useful to have around. One night we were in the Covent Garden Hotel in Chinatown. It was crowded with loud-mouthed businessmen. I was standing against the wall having a drink with Harold and his mate when four loud-mouthed flips decided to have a go at us. At first we ignored them, but they got out of hand and started to carry on like they were something else. Just as I thought that enough shit had been thrown our way, Harold and his mate attacked the four guys. They gave them an unmerciful flogging. The one with the biggest mouth was struggling with Harold and Harold picked up a heavy glass ashtray and smashed him in the face with it. In the process of hitting him with the ashtray, the guy had put his hand up to protect his face. When he got collected with the ashtray, it cleanly cut off his little finger. The guy with the over-sized mouth fainted. Like all big mouths he had no go in him at all. Someone picked up his finger and handed it in to the barmaid to put on ice, so that there might be a chance to sew it back on again. She also fainted. We left before the police came and had a Chinese meal.

Nothing came of that fight. We stayed away from the

Covent Garden for two weeks before the owners asked us to return. We were their biggest spenders and the barmaids missed the tips we used to leave. We went back and the barmaids were happy again.

The Covent Garden was the main drinking hole for Harold and me. We also ate and drank at the best restaurants and spent heaps. We were constantly under observation by at least three different task forces consisting of both federal and state police. They combined because they couldn't put a squad together out of just state police and be sure I hadn't got some of them onside. Trusting souls, weren't they?

And they weren't wrong about that part of it. I had a good few state police telling me everything. I never had any Australian Federal Police onside in the taskforces.

Over the years I had nine joint state-federal taskforces and six state police taskforces investigate my activities. And those don't include the attention I got from police who were targeting other crims who knew me.

Sometimes the surveillance police would stand at the bar drinking, trying to look inconspicuous. They stood out like dogs' balls, drinking schooners and wearing desert boots. A very good disguise, seeing as how they were trying to fit in with us: we were wearing $200 shoes compared with their desert boots. It didn't bother me that they were watching me closely. I had grown used to them being around all the time.

Yet I was very careful what I did and who I spoke to. Just because I had the Green Light, it didn't mean I could trust the police completely. I committed every crime as though the police were trying to catch me. That way I kept my guard up at all times.

I knew I could lose the surveillance when I wanted to. I used to lose them every time I went to work selling drugs or committing armed robberies. Most police work by the clock. They start at certain times and they knock off at certain times. I didn't play by their rules. Whenever I went to work, I left home at about 4.30am: the police were all tucked up in their nice warm beds at that time. They didn't attempt to put me under surveillance until their shifts started at 6am unless they had specific information that I was definitely going to commit a crime. They had no hope of catching me by the methods they used. That's why the police have always used verbals to put crims away when they couldn't do it by the normal process of the law.

So why didn't they verbal me or load me up? First, they weren't game to. They knew I had plenty of money and the best lawyers money could buy on 24-hour call. I was always in contact with a solicitor, who I called every morning before I left home. I often rang him during the day and always at night, just to check in. On top of that, I was forever sending letters to different law enforcement bodies complaining of police harassment and declaring that under no circumstances would I ever talk to any police officer at any time without my legal representative present. That eliminated any chance they might have had of verballing me or planting something. Their hands were tied by police procedure and I knew it. I knew nearly every way that there was to tie up police and hinder their investigations. And I was taught by some of New South Wales' finest.

I was a very good learner when I needed to be.

The Australian Federal Police had more chance of getting me for some crime or other because I had no one sweet within their ranks. I could get the odd bit of information concerning any operation the Feds might have into me and what they thought I might be doing, but I had no one of my own in their camp. The Feds watched me regularly and closely on and off for many years. I committed many big crimes right under their noses. They were looking, but they weren't seeing the obvious.

Maybe, like most cops, they stereotype crims and think that we are all dumb and can't think for ourselves. It is a bad mistake if they do.

While they were watching me, expecting me to sneak around hiding in dark lanes and attending secret meetings with shady characters and talking out of the side of my mouth, I was blatantly doing the very thing they were spending millions of dollars trying to catch me for, right under their very noses. [*The use of the word* millions *by Smith is almost certainly correct; surveillance of any form, be it phone taps, bugs, or following someone, is manpower-intensive and thus a very expensive exercise.*] The Feds could have arrested me for any number of crimes both major and minor had they once bothered to search me or my car, or if

Going to Work 233

they took the time to wonder where I was when they were trying to put me under surveillance.

The Feds weren't all that dumb. Don't think I am bagging them. They were way ahead of the state police as far as observation and phone taps went. I just don't think that they were really keen on the idea of arresting me. I don't really know a great deal about the Feds. I confined my studies to the New South Wales police force. I had tried to learn all that I could about the way they operated. It was an obsession with me. To me, Feds were better suited behind a desk. They weren't streetwise, so to speak. I had some interesting but sometimes funny run-ins with the Feds over the years.

There was one time that a large team of us were drinking at the Fosters Hotel in the city. There were a lot of us, from different walks of life—we'd all committed some sort of crime. There were shoplifters, armed robbers, bust men [*professional burglars*]—there was someone from nearly every type of crime drinking there. We'd been drinking for a few hours when we spotted a team of Feds who had manoeuvred themselves in among us. They were dressed in suits. A lot of the men drinking there wore suits so they didn't stand out too much. We ignored them until one put a briefcase on the floor right in the middle of us. He put it up against the bar, then walked away and left it there.

He must have thought we were fools not to realise what he was doing.

This mate of mine called Les, a merchant seaman and not a crook, was standing with us. We told him what was going on with the briefcase, so he went up, got down on his knees and started to sing into the microphone built into the side of the case. I think he sang one of Al Jolson's old tunes, 'Swanee'. After that, we decided to move to the Lord Nelson Hotel at the Rocks. As we left, the Feds went into a mad panic. We were standing on the footpath for a few seconds when a group of people came pouring out on to the pavement. It was the Feds, looking everywhere for us. When they saw us standing there they didn't know what to do. So I decided to give them a hand: 'Listen fellows, no need to waste your time following us. We are going to the Lord Nelson Hotel. See you there.'

They didn't know what to do; they just stared at me. I could be a cheeky mug when I was drinking.

I drank at the Covent Garden Hotel just about every Thursday and Friday I was in Sydney. A sometime visitor was Midnight, probably the best shoplifter in Australia. She regularly came to have a drink and always had some nice piece of clothing to show me. She only stole the very best from the very best shops. I must have spent tens of thousands of dollars buying gear from her. She was a bit wild and you couldn't shut her up once she started to talk, but Midnight had a heart of gold. She helped everyone in need and expected nothing in return. But Midnight had one big problem: she was desperate to be a gangster. If she had been born a bloke there would have been no stopping her. Both federal and state police watched me purchasing clothing from Midnight. They took notes, but never once interfered with either her or me. Strange goings on. Midnight knew everyone who was anyone among the Sydney and Melbourne so-called underworld. She was well-liked by most of them. Certain cops would get me to order articles of clothing for their wives or female companions through Midnight.

It was getting close to Christmas 1986, a time of huge payrolls, nice earns for anyone willing to get off their arse and have a go.

Harold and his 'friend' were hot to trot. They needed money for Christmas, and so did I—my expenses were big. The cops would all be looking for their Christmas presents, because I always looked after certain police at Christmas. Not necessarily police I worked with, rather any officer I thought might come in handy at some time always received a little gift. Sometimes I would get something for his wife, depending on who it was. Not once was a present returned to me.

I knew that the armed hold-up squad would get a lot of overtime escorting payrolls over the Christmas period. They used to escort the pay vans until they dropped the payroll off, then they would leave, leaving the money there to be grabbed. I couldn't see the sense of the hold-up squad even bothering to follow the vans if they were going to watch them deliver the money, then just go and leave it there. Stupid, if you ask me.

All you had to do was watch the police and the van drive away and then go ahead and rob the payroll. I'm not blueing about it. It made my job easier, so why would I complain?

Going to Work

I got in touch with [*a policeman*] about some work. We met at the same old hotel, the Regent at Kingsford. I told him I wanted to grab a Christmas payroll and asked if there were any big ones within the next two weeks. He had several in mind but none to equal the Sydney City Council payroll. It would be delivered to a building in Clarence Street in the city, right across the street from the National Crime Authority [NCA] building. That made it interesting. ([*The policeman*] later told me that the NCA had spotted me hanging around outside their building and had filed a report saying they thought I was watching witnesses. They'd really seen me planning the council payroll robbery.)

I made arrangements with [*the policeman*] so he could make sure he was working that day, or had time to swap shifts with one of the other teams that may have been on. Everything was sweet with the police so I got Harold and we started to get the gear we would need for the robbery.

Harold wanted his mate [*we will call this mate 'Tony'*] to come in on this one. I was against bringing him, or any other stranger into the group—not to mention the opposition that I knew I would get from the [*police*].

I always had to clear it through the [*police*] if I wanted to bring in any new blood to work with me. But Tony presented a real problem. I spoke to The Dodger about Tony and he was against me using him. 'He is fucking bad news, Ned. I would advise against your using him.' Against my better judgment, I told Roger that I wanted to give the guy a go for Harold's sake.

There's a saying: 'Nurse a mug and he dies in your arms.' That's exactly what I did. I can blame no one but myself for what eventually happened.

This one wasn't going to be easy. It was in a bad position in the city. Traffic was a major problem. I had to take into account the fact that the street was a clearway. If we parked it would cause a traffic pile-up and attract attention. We couldn't afford that.

I ended up getting these two guys I knew to steal a few council signs used for detouring traffic. I intended to stop all traffic from coming down Clarence Street while we did the robbery. It was elaborate as plans went. We had to use more people than normal, but that was only to do minor parts.

To escape we would use a utility so we could jump into the back, thus have no difficulty getting into a car with the money. It would save time and enable us to get away much quicker from the area. We got someone to hire a HiAce van for the second getaway car. We would leave it parked on the overhead bypass ready to change into when we dumped the utility after the robbery.

We studied the payroll delivery: how many people carried the money, where they came from, where they went, and whether they were armed.

There were three men each carrying a briefcase in each hand, six cases in all. There were two other men, one on each side of them, plus a guy following up at the rear. He was the only one that was armed.

They came out of a side door in one building, walked across a short arcade, into a second building and up to some elevators. They then took the separate cases to separate floors to pay the employees from the different departments. We timed them, plus I had plenty of information from the police. It wasn't going to be easy, but we would do it one way or another. We would come away with the money.

We had a maximum of three minutes to get the money and be in the utility and on our way. We had to find the best way to get close to them without them seeing us. We finally decided that Harold and Tony, dressed as cleaners and carrying mops and buckets, would wait inside near the elevators, while I would follow them in to cut off any retreat. There was a harmless, unarmed security guard there. The only problem he could cause was if he had an alarm or was quick on the phone.

I went and saw [*the policeman*] and outlined my plan to him. He OKed it. He was a bit apprehensive about the NCA being just across the street from the robbery scene and the report they'd filed about having seen me hanging around. 'Don't give it a thought,' I told [*the policeman*]. 'I know what I am doing.'

On the morning of the robbery, these two willing young guys took the road signs to Clarence Street. They watched the armored car go by, waited 15 minutes, then put the signs across the street blocking it. Their timing was spot-on and the street was traffic-free when it came time to make our getaway. (The signs were left blocking the road for hours until the council removed them. It had taken the police some time to establish that they were not authentic.)

Harold and Tony were ready, dressed in overalls and wearing beanies on their heads ready to pull down over their faces. They positioned themselves near the lifts, even started mopping the floor. I waited outside, ready to tail the payroll in and cut them off. The traffic was diverted, the utility was in position. It was time.

The door opened—and only four guys came out. There were only two briefcases. What was up? The bastards had changed their routine because it was Christmas and the payroll was so big. What to do? I had no way of warning the others. My mind was racing. I wasn't sure just what to do: should we take the two bags or wait and see if they brought another lot up next time?

My mind was made up for me. I was tailing them in when I heard a shot. (It turned out Tony's gun went off accidentally as he tried to grab one of the cases). The door that I was about to go through shattered into millions of pieces. I was very lucky I hesitated just before rushing in.

Harold and Tony came out through the gap left by the shattered door. They had the two briefcases with them. They moved quickly to the utility, and I followed. We all got in, the driver went through the lights, turned left, then left again, and parked only a hundred metres from the robbery. We got out and ran up a small mound of grass, on to the overpass and into the HiAce van. It was parked there in case we ran into trouble. If anyone gave chase there was no way they could have driven on to the overpass. They would have had to drive miles to get on to it.

Off we went, changing on the move. We were all cursing them for changing their routine. It took us a matter of minutes to get to our destination and, once there, we settled down to the task of counting the money. Harold took $4000 off the table and went out for 10 minutes to give his girlfriend some money to buy a dress. I thought he was joking. When he returned we had the money counted. I had taken out the money for the police, and the rest was divided up. We didn't get a great deal, I think just over $90,000, so the council guys had outsmarted us.

Tony was reluctant to give the cops their whack. He wanted to lash [*renege on payment*]. We argued, I told him that we didn't want to commit suicide, and if he did, then he could do it on his own. I took the money for the police with me. That was the first and last robbery I did with Tony. He was sacked that day. I told myself that I was stupid not to have listened to Roger. We split up, Harold took his girlfriend to Queensland for a holiday and Tony took his girl somewhere too.

I propped in Sydney to pay the cops and make sure that everything was OK. I went to meet with [*the policeman*]. He took his money and he told me there was a minor problem. 'Your two mates have been identified by two guys that know them. They were seen loitering in the lobby of the council chambers just before the robbery.'

It was going to cost me another $5000 to ensure that the two statements made by the eyewitnesses would vanish. I thought this was a cold stamp [*a deceitful attempt to extort money*] and I told [*the policeman*] so: 'Listen, we have always gotten on well with no problems. Don't try stamping me.'

He was waiting for that. He produced two statements for me to read. I was shocked when I saw the names on the statements, because I knew one of them. I got in touch with Harold and told him what had happened. He was dubious at first—he probably thought that I was ripping him off. Harold contacted Tony and told him the news. Stupid Tony blew up and refused to weigh-in to pay the extra $5000.

Harold left the matter there and flew back to meet with me at the Regent Hotel at Kingsford. [*The policeman*] was waiting for us to arrive. We shook hands and had a drink while [*the policeman*] told Harold the story and gave him the statements to read. Harold couldn't believe it. He was mates with one of the guys that had identified him. There was little we could do, so we gave [*the policeman*] the $5000. We never heard another word about that robbery again.

[*In early 1987*] I spent some time at home because there wasn't much happening in Sydney. I enjoyed it, especially the time with my kids. I still went to Sydney, but not so often. I was sick of drinking myself stupid. It was madness. My wife used to give me the best spoil when I was in the house. I don't know why I ever went out. When I was at home I rarely ever went out the front door. I would lie by the pool just soaking up the sun and enjoying Debra's company. Sometimes I would do odd jobs around the house—mowing the lawns, cleaning the pool, washing the dogs—then I would lie by the pool recuperating from the previous few days drinking in Sydney. I rarely drank at home; on the odd occasion some cop came to my home I would have a few drinks at my bar downstairs, but never more than two or three. But it didn't take me too long to get restless. I think I went to Sydney for excitement—and I had no trouble finding it.

My wife and I were loners. We had very few friends, just a select few, and they were mostly in Sydney. We had each other so we didn't go looking for new friends. We kept the few that we had, and regardless of the shit publicity I've had, they remain our friends. Don't for one minute get the idea that I'm trying to make out that I was a perfect husband or father—I was not! Suffice to say that I love my family and they return the feelings ten thousand times over.

You will no doubt realise that I've played up with numerous different girls over the years—guilty on all counts! I refuse to go into that part of my life as it is of no interest to anyone. [*It is now a matter of public record that Smith kept a 'Sydney wife', as the woman involved described herself, for most of the 1980s.*] My wife has accepted me the way I am, knowing that I am far from being anywhere near perfect. She knows my indiscretions and just ignores them. My wife has stuck by me for nearly 20 years and continues to stick by me even now that I may be serving a life sentence in jail.

The worst punishment that a judge can give you is to take you away from the family you love, even though you sometimes don't realise it will have such a big effect on your life. The time that you spend alone in your cell at night thinking is the hardest time that a man can do. That is if you use your mind and you aren't a junkie. Enough of that crap—just a few home truths.

Harold was again keen to go to work, as we called it. He needed some money to keep the girls he was supporting with all the little luxuries they needed. I was ready to go again too, so I got hold of the [*police*]. Two of them turned up to meet me. We met at the Regent Hotel at Kingsford.

This was the first time that I had met [*the second officer*].

I was friendly with [*the policeman*], but I still took my time before I brought up the subject of doing another armed robbery. We were drinking and just passing the time of day when [*the policeman*] brought up the subject.

'Well, Neddy. Have you had a long enough rest now?'

I told [*the policeman*] that I was ready and asked if there was anything doing.

'Not right now, but I can promise you one within a fortnight. Is that OK with you?'

[*The second officer*] didn't have a great deal to say about anything much, he just sat there as though nothing was going on. I told [*the policeman*] that I would be looking around for something myself until he came up with one for me. 'That's OK, just take your time as there is no hurry for you to work is there?'

I assured him I would take care.

It was time to get out and about, time to find a nice juicy payroll. They weren't hard to find, you just had to look, take your time, be patient and relax. We needed a van that wouldn't stand out or attract attention. It would have to be one that people saw on the street every day, one that could remain parked with people sitting in it without looking out of place. We went out and bought a van at auction. I had a friendly spray-painter do it up to resemble an electrician's van, with signs on each side and ladders on top. It would pass. For authenticity, we dressed like electricians. We never had any trouble from people ringing up saying that we were acting suspiciously. We had a scanner installed in the van, not a hand-held one, but a large industrial Bearcat scanner that ran off the car battery.

The van had cost us $6000 before we even started to earn. We put that down as expenses: that would come off the top of the first earn. Every Thursday and Friday morning we went out bright and early, on the lookout for a likely candidate. Some days we parked near one of the Armaguard bases and followed different vans all over town, watching where they delivered money. We never got too close; we would stay a fair distance back and I'd watch them through binoculars—I wanted to see exactly where they went in and how many money tins they carried.

Other times we would check out large factories and see how many people the factory employed. We would walk in and do a rough count of the bundy cards [*staff cards put through a time-clock*] in the slots. This gave us a rough estimate of how many people worked there. Sometimes we would waste a whole day just sitting outside factories and nothing would happen. It could take between one day and two weeks to find a robbery worth doing.

It was a Thursday morning and we had been driving around all morning looking for something. We decided to pull up at a shop and get a few sandwiches. We were on our way down Harris Street, Ultimo, when we spotted an armored van parking outside a factory. We watched as two guards got out and took two money tins out of the side of the van. I pulled up on the footpath to watch—the road was a clearway till 9am. Harold jumped out of our van and walked casually over the road and tailed the two armed guards into the factory. They took no notice of him. Harold was an average looking guy, who didn't stand out or anything. He even had a chat to them as they walked into the place.

I sat back waiting, listening to the scanner in case there was any suspicion about our presence. There had to be at least $100,000 in the payroll; they usually needed two boxes for that amount. I was also timing how long it took the guards to drop off the money, get back to the van and move off. It was six minutes.

A minute later Harold got back inside our van. 'The pay office is 100 yards inside the complex,' he said. 'There is an office made of partitions and a lot of glass. You will have some trouble getting in there without being seen.'

I was interested: 'Can it be done?'

'Of course it can. We just have to put a little more work into this one.'

Over the next two weeks we spent a great deal of time going over every detail of the factory, Dairy Farmers at Ultimo. We constantly exchanged ideas and ways to get in and out without causing too much of a ruckus. Surprise was our main weapon. If we could get close enough to the office without being seen, then it was all over. The problem was the getaway. Harris Street was a clearway until after 9am, so we couldn't park in the street. The footpath was too bloody obvious; we could get boxed-in, unable to get away.

Dairy Farmers was working three shifts, so we went there one night to look over the place and try to come up with our entry and exit. To our surprise, we discovered that the door to the pay office was made of bullet-proof glass. While we prowled around looking for ideas, I discovered an unused lane at the back of the pay office. It was overgrown with weeds and grass—no one had used it for a long time. The lane led out on to Harris Street. Just what the doctor ordered for two smart lads. It would do us nicely to get in and out without being seen. All that was required was a pair of boltcutters and for us to put our own lock on the night before. We now had our way in and out, plus off-street parking that wouldn't look suspicious.

After discussing different ways into the office, we decided to knock the door off its hinges with a sledgehammer.

I rang [*the police*], a meeting was arranged, and everything was worked out for us to do the robbery the following week.

We got tracksuits again and balaclavas. I saw the young guys and ordered a panel van. I always paid them $1000 per vehicle. The night before the robbery, we decided to have one last look. It turned out to be a mistake. As I was looking in the pay office window, an employee saw me. I walked out quickly, but not before she got a good look at my head.

On the morning of the robbery we dressed in tracksuits and were masked up ready to go. Harold had a .357 magnum and, for a change, I carried a machine pistol. We had already cut the lock off the gate and replaced it with our own. The armored van was due to arrive at 9 o'clock so, at 8.45am, we removed the lock. Harold and I were dressed ready to go in the back of the van. The driver backed into the lane and parked where he could watch the street and see the armored van pull up. We were sweating in the back of our van. I hated the waiting. It drove me insane.

The van arrived. We gave the guards six minutes then pushed open the doors of the van and walked along the laneway to the small window of the pay office. No one had taken the slightest bit of notice of us. A guy was sitting at a desk with all the pay envelopes in front of him. The adrenalin was starting to pump in my veins.

Harold swung the sledgehammer at the door—and it bounced back. A girl in the office looked up, saw two masked maniacs with guns and a sledgehammer, and fainted. Harold gave the door another bash and this time managed to knock it off its hinges. We rushed in. The payroll clerk panicked and threw the tray containing the money at us, scattering it all over the place. Harold threw the silly old guy to the floor and we gathered up all the pay envelopes, put them in a bag and left the way we'd come in.

Four minutes had passed. We were behind schedule. We got into the back of the van, closing the doors. The driver didn't say a thing, just slowly eased out into Harris Street. We were stuck in heavy traffic waiting for the lights to change. I was watching the factory to make certain everything was clear when out on to the footpath came these guys asking if anyone had seen two robbers. They didn't even notice us and we were less than three metres away, getting changed in the back of the van. Then the traffic started to move and we were on our way.

We got to the roller-shuttered truck and got in the back. As we did we could hear sirens all around. I called out to the driver: 'Change the route, go straight there by the quickest way. Drive right through the guts of the police.'

He did as he was told and, the very next thing I knew, there was a young cop directing us through the intersection so we could avoid the police cars. Straight through we went without any problem.

Off we drove to count and share the proceeds of our day's work. Harold always wanted to shake my hand after a successful job, nerves or something. Anyway, we congratulated each other. We averaged about $100,000 from that one, after we took out the [*police*] share and divided the rest, less expenses.

I was lounging in bed on the following Sunday morning glancing through the paper when I saw a picture of me staring back. Shit. I jumped out of bed quickly. 'Debra, come here for a minute and look at this.' Here was an identikit photo of someone that had a striking resemblance to me. It *was* me. The woman who had seen me the night before the robbery had been able to give a detailed description.

Debra looked at it and asked: 'What were you up to while you were in Sydney this time?'

That photo had me bothered because the heading above it read *Wanted in connection with the hold-up of Dairy Farmers last Thursday morning.*

I got dressed and drove to a public phone booth to ring Roger to find out what was going on. I asked him whether he'd seen the paper. He laughed and kept on laughing. 'Yes, mate, I've seen it. You worry too much.'

That did it, I blew up. 'Fuck you, mate, that wasn't supposed to happen.' Roger kept on laughing. I didn't see the funny side. My face was in the fucking paper, not his.

'Listen mate, relax a bit, everything is all right. There was a small slip-up by one of the boys, nothing to worry about.'

No way was I going to be put off that easily. 'I will come down to see you tonight.'

Roger wouldn't have any of that. 'That's not necessary, mate, just take it easy, slow down.'

I wasn't satisfied. I wanted to know what had gone wrong with our deal. I got back home and Debra told me that Harold had rung and wanted me to get in touch. I knew he had seen the paper too. I couldn't be bothered going to the public phone again. Harold's phone was off [*bugged*] anyway, so it would have been senseless going to a public phone to ring him.

I rang him straight away and assured him that everything was going to be all right and not to worry. 'I'll meet you at the same place as usual.'

I spent an anxious Sunday worrying that the cops might knock on my door. I couldn't understand how [*the police*] could have let the photo of me get in the papers. They were getting very slack about business. What the fuck was I paying them for? This was no joking matter. I was going to have plenty to say to them when I next saw them.

The following day, I met [*two policemen*] and demanded to know what was going on. Apparently someone had given the photo to the press before checking. Fucking incompetence.

'What is going to be the end result over this picture?' I waited for an answer.

'Neddy, everything will turn out for the best, not a problem for you,' they said.

They were right. I heard nothing more about it.

18
The Life of Riley

Disgraced former NSW policeman Murray Stewart [Riley] has escaped again—by walking out of a British minimum-security prison.

News story, Sydney *Telegraph–Mirror*, 30 January 1993

Murray Riley was an old rogue and a likeable one at that. I had a lot of time for Murray. A few people have said Murray was an informer. I did millions of dollars of business with Murray and he never tried to harm me in any way. I can only judge people as I find them, and as I am treated by them.

Murray kept coming up with scams worth plenty of money. Not a lot of Murray's scams amounted to anything—hence his nickname, the 'Prince of Promises'—but when one came off, it produced huge earns for one and all.

One night Murray got in touch and told me to meet him at the Fosters Hotel. He had a scam worthy of my attention, he said. I was looking for another earn to refill the coffers, so I went go to meet Prince of Promises for a few ales.

Murray was always immaculately dressed and kept himself in good condition all the time. We drank and discussed his latest scam. He knew a guy who had six kilos of pure heroin that he had just imported into Australia. He had not arranged anyone to buy the gear, so he was looking for buyer that he could trust. 'Are you interested in ripping the guy off, mate?'

Me? Of course. I asked Murray who the people involved were, because I didn't rip off people I knew; that would be bad business. Murray told me all about them: I didn't know them, so it was sweet.

Murray said that the guy had heard of me and wanted

to meet me before he would discuss selling the gear. I wasn't at all impressed. I had a thing about putting my head on show, but Murray convinced me that the guy was not a cop and was genuine so I went to see him—and work out a plan to relieve him of six kilos of pure.

The meeting was arranged for the next day at the Star Hotel in Alexandria. Murray turned up with this well-dressed little Italian guy. We were introduced and he explained that he wanted to sell the gear in bulk. He didn't want to take risks that weren't absolutely necessary. That suited me fine. I didn't deal in ounces either.

I reckoned that I was entitled to a discount for bulk. He wanted to know how much I was interested in buying and when. We played the usual games with each other, then got down to the nitty gritty. He agreed to give me the heroin for $100,000 per pound if I bought in bulk. It sounded all right, but I told him I required a sample of the gear before I would commit myself. He gave me a sample straight out of his pocket. This was pure gear, he said. I would soon see about that.

I had it checked and it turned out to be pure as the driven snow—good for cutting twice without anyone knowing. I got in touch with Murray the next day and arranged a meeting. I wanted this guy's gear one way or another. I decided to buy the first pound of heroin from him, then rip him off for whatever I could get. But I still had not come up with a plan.

The next morning I met him in a car park. Murray was with him; they were sitting in the front of a car. I looked around for anyone acting suspiciously, saw no one, so I walked over and got into the back seat. Harold was sitting off me making sure nothing went wrong. I had no problems with him minding me; he knew what to look for and what to do.

I said hello to the pair of them and got the shit out of the way. 'Let's not fuck each other around any more than is absolutely necessary,' I said. 'I've checked the sample out and it looks the goods. I will pay you now cash for one pound. If it is the same gear as the sample, then I will be wanting a kilo more after lunch. That will be paid for in cash also. Let's get started on the right foot. You know me, Murray, I don't like fuck-ups. I will not cop anyone trying to dud me by handing me different gear than the sample. Let's do this business properly and we will all make money.'

Murray 'assured' me there would be no fuck-ups on 'his side'. Now we'd cleared that up, I asked them when I could expect the first pound to be delivered. The Italian wasn't in any hurry. He wanted to see the cash before committing himself. I told him to wait.

I got out of their car and walked across the street to the Star Hotel. I kept a lot of money in the safe in case I needed it for things like this. I got the $100,000, took it back to the car park and got into the back seat. All the time I could see Harold, but they had no idea they were under surveillance.

I threw the money on the front seat of the car and let the Italian check it. Murray was a little nervous, because he didn't have a clue how I was going to rip this guy off. To be quite honest, I didn't know yet either. I would just play it by ear.

I wanted the six kilos, or the better part of it, so I didn't want to rush into it and risk fucking things up. After the Italian was satisfied the money was all there, he said: 'Look, you're a genuine fellow, I can see that. Let's both not waste each other's time. I am prepared to give you one kilo straight away instead of the pound you asked for. I will take this money and you can pay me for the rest when you take the second kilo after lunch. Is that agreeable with you?'

It sounded like a good deal to me.

I told him I agreed and that he could take the money with him as a sign of my trust and I would meet him later to pick up the gear. I fixed it for him to drop the gear in the boot of a car that would be left parked in an arranged spot. I gave him a key to the car. There was no way that I was going to touch the gear or be within a mile of it.

Still no plan to rip him off had formed in my mind. No problem, though. We were going to finish with this guy's gear one way or another.

The car was in place. I had two men watching it; they kept in constant touch with me by walkie-talkie, giving me reports of everything that moved in the area. I had spent a fortune on all the latest surveillance gear [*supplied by a policeman*]. I hadn't got used to handling it all yet, but I was learning fast.

All went well. The Italian dropped off the heroin in the car boot as planned. The two guys waited for an hour before getting in the car and driving off. Harold and I went to meet them to check the gear. It was exactly the same as the sample. It was then that I decided how I would rip this guy off.

The heroin was sealed in a plastic bag with the Double U-O Globe stamp [*the heroin manufacturer's brand name*] on it. Harold opened the bag carefully, not leaving any prints, and removed the contents. He then cut [*diluted*] the heroin in half, producing two kilos of gear. He then filled the bag with the cut heroin and sealed it. This last stage posed no problem as we had our own sealing machine. They would never know that their bag had been tampered with.

I planned to take the bag of heroin back and get my money refunded. Then I would try to get more from the Italian guy. Either way, I would finish with a kilo [*of cut heroin*].

I phoned Murray and the Italian guy, who were waiting for my call. I made out to Murray that I was blueing over the quality of the heroin. 'You low cunt, you won't get away with trying to dud me.' I knew the Italian guy would be listening so I made it good. 'You pair are walking dead, fuck you both.' Murray tried to calm me down. He was a top talker and nearly had me convinced that he was fair dinkum.

'Neddy, calm down, son. Let's meet and discuss this like sensible men. If there has been some sort of mistake I'm sure that he will make it good.' We arranged to meet at the car park again. I got there ahead of them and placed Harold and two others close enough not to be seen until I wanted them.

Murray and the Italian guy arrived looking worried. I knew Murray would have told this guy stories about how evil I was. It was part of the way we worked these scams. They pulled up and as soon as they opened the car door I blew up. I should have received an Academy Award for my performance.

'Who do you pair of cunts think you are dealing with?'

I threw the bag I had with me at them in the front. Murray was playing his part perfectly. 'Neddy, please take it easy. Let's try to work out what has happened here before you jump the gun and do something silly.'

I was still going off my head at them: 'I warned you both

before we agreed to do this business that I wouldn't cop anyone trying to dud me, didn't I?'

The Italian guy was sitting there not saying a word.

'I want my money back or you are both dead men.'

The Italian guy looked at the gear then looked at me. 'Look, my friend, there is no way that either of us had anything to do with trying to dud you. There has to be an explanation for the mix-up.'

'Fuck you two,' I said. 'If my money isn't returned then you are both off.'

I'd arranged for Harold and the other two to come out where they could be seen after I had been in the car for five minutes. On cue, they came out where the guy could see them clearly. It had the desired effect.

'Now do you believe me when I tell you that I am serious about killing you?'

Murray convinced the Italian guy that someone in his own gang must have cut the gear without him knowing. The Italian guy agreed to pay my money back. He went and collected it and brought it to me at the Star Hotel. I had pulled off the first half of the rip-off. I had one kilo of cut heroin worth about $250,000 and my money back. Not bad for a morning's work.

I was all ready to propose another deal to the guy when he beat me to the punch. 'I would like to make up for the mix-up with the first lot. Can we try again to deal? This time I will personally give one kilo to you. That way there can be no mistake. Only you and I are responsible for the heroin.'

We decided that maybe it was worth the risk of me picking it up myself, just this once. (After all, a kilo of pure heroin doesn't come along every day.)

'OK, buddy. You go and get the heroin and I will pick up the balance of the money so that we can do the business all at once.'

I made arrangements to meet him in two hours. I told him it would take that long to get the rest of the money ready, but I really needed time to arrange a little protection from one of New South Wales' finest. So, while they went to get the kilo, I rang The Dodger to try and fix some police to be in the area to mind me in case something unexpected went down. Roger wasn't available, so I got on to Billy Duff.

'Hello Billy, can I see you now? It could be worth your while.'

He said he'd see me in 30 minutes and hung up. I waited with Harold until Billy turned up. He was anxious to get an earn. I didn't tell him exactly what was going down, just that I was doing some business and needed him to mind me in case of an unexpected turn of events.

'Just park where I tell you, keep your radio on and keep me in sight all the time. If a problem arises, come down fast and do whatever you have to do to get me out of the area. OK?'

'That's no problem, mate.'

'Before you go, there will be a $20,000 bonus for you after this.' He was rapt at the idea. 'Who do we kill, mate, and what do I do?' I laughed, but Bill Duff wasn't laughing one bit. He was deadly serious. Maybe I had offered him too much. I knew that he was not a big asker.

Duff positioned himself in the police car and waited. About 20 minutes later the Italian guy came in a different car. He was on his own this time, which made me a little suspicious. I waited, watching him for a few minutes. He called me over to the car by waving to me. I had my hand on a gun that was stuck in the back of my belt. I was not going to take any chances with this guy. I approached the car and leant in the passenger's window to speak to him. As I leant in, he moved quickly, leaning forward and reaching under the front seat. He never said a word as he moved. I wasn't waiting for anything to happen—I pulled my gun and stuck it straight up against his temple. 'Don't you fucken dare move cunt, or you are off tap.'

As soon as he saw me pull my gun, Harold came up quickly. He opened the driver's door and grabbed the guy by the throat, pushing his gun into his face: 'Will I kill the cunt now?'

'Slow down,' I said. 'Just take your time and grab whatever it was he was reaching for under the front seat.' Harold looked under the seat and started to smile. He produced a kilo of the very same gear as before. I could not believe that anybody would turn up a second time with the gear. There was one born every minute.

Bill Duff had arrived on the scene by now, wanting to know if all was well. I told him we had a problem about what to do with the guy. 'Let me lock the cunt up for you,' he said. There was no way I was going to have anything to do with locking anybody up, anywhere. The Italian guy was terrified. He realised that he had been got a second time, so there was no way we could get the remaining gear off him. Harold suggested the guy simply go missing in action, but that was not a go of mine. That was definitely out.

We ended up giving him a huge fright. I won't go into how we did it, but it worked because I never saw or heard from him again. We all went back to the Star and ordered a drink to celebrate our earn and I gave Detective Sergeant James William Duff his $20,000. That put a big smile on his face. He couldn't believe his luck.

Abo even turned up for a drink that day, but he had no idea what had gone down. I never told him, but he guessed that we had earned. He could smell money. He was unbelievable at knowing when someone had a bit of luck.

Murray Riley was just back from overseas, America I think—he had connections over there. He wanted a partner for lunch and a drinking session. Who better to ask? Harold and I qualified under the rules of hopeless drunks so we met Murray at the Le Sands restaurant at Brighton-Le-Sands. We were regular patrons, lunching there perhaps once a week. It was a beautiful restaurant, situated on the water, and it had the best seafood in town.

Murray was at the bar indulging in a cool beer when we arrived. He was in a cheerful mood, grinning. 'Hello, son,' he said, which was his usual greeting to everyone he liked.

I had a lot of time for Murray. People bad-mouthed him behind his back, but I couldn't care as they did the same to me. We enjoyed ourselves every time we got together and this day wasn't an exception. After consuming half a dozen beers we sat down for lunch. It was obvious that Murray had some sort of scam on his mind that included me. While we were eating, he started to tell me about his new scam. 'You are not going to believe what old Murray has for you, son!' Murray loved to hold the floor; he was a natural showman.

I couldn't help laughing. 'Come on, Murray, out with it.'

I was expecting another one of the impossible scams that he often came up with.

'Wait for it, son. I am getting to it. How does one million little pictures of the Queen's head sound to you?'

Murray was talking about one million dollars *cash*. I knew it was another pipe dream. If one out of 100 of Murray's scams was successful, it would have been terrific. I knew he had been going silly on the drink.

'Come down to earth, mate. Who has that sort of cash money lying around?'

He sat there grinning, as though he had won the lottery. 'Well, son, your mate [*a policeman*] has been in my ear to see you about this go. It is fair dinkum son, believe me.'

'[*The policeman*] is not a friend of mine. I hate the shitman.'

Murray cut me short: 'Now, now, son. [*The policeman's*] money is as good as the next man's. Agreed?' He had a point.

The scam consisted of ripping off a guy for 100 kilos of black hash [*cannabis resin*]. One hundred kilos could bring in $1.4 million if handled right on the street, but sold in bulk it would bring in only a cool $1 million. I wanted to know why [*the policeman*] had not got [*another criminal*] to do the job. Maybe I was being set up. I asked Murray what he thought about the possibility—that his mate [*the policeman*] might be trying to set me up. 'No way, son, I stake my life on it.'

'That's exactly what you will be doing, Murray old son, if something goes wrong.' That didn't exactly make him burst into song like he usually did after a few cold beers.

So Murray explained: the reason [*the policeman*] wanted me to rip the guy off was because [*the criminal*] had already taken the same guy for 90 kilos and lashed on him [*refused to pay*]. That at least proved the hash was there. This guy apparently had access to two tonnes of black hash and wanted to move it in 100-kilo lots for cash. That sounded reasonable. If you had that much gear you'd be stupid to hang on to it waiting around for top dollar. Get rid of it in bulk for a few dollars less and keep everyone happy by letting them all earn a dollar.

Murray said that he had already met the guy with the hash and the guy was keen to do business with me.

'Hold it right there a second, Murray. How did I come to get my name mentioned in this scam?'

'It's like this, mate. I dropped your name to him as a potential buyer of bulk. It's sweet, mate, I checked the guy out.'

I wasn't happy about my name being mentioned in a drug deal without first being asked. I gave Murray a piece of my mind. I decided to impose a fine on him when and if we got the gear from this rip-off.

I was in constant contact with Murray over this one. I couldn't let him out of my sight in case he decided to try and do it himself. I made a few inquiries around town to see what the best price for the hash was. As a seller, I could get $8000 a kilo all day long if I sold in bulk. If I sold 10-kilo lots, I could get $14,000 a kilo for it. I decided to accept $9000 a kilo for the 100 kilos in one deal. I thought that was the best way to get rid of it—all at once.

Murray had already told me the name of the fellow that we were going to rip off. I didn't know him, so he was allowed to be ripped off. Only friends were barred, but my friends were very few and far between.

Murray gave this guy a story about me being able to take 100 kilos every day for one week and that I was ready to part with the cash up-front after the first deal came off without a hitch. The guy seemed anxious to do the business with me. There's one born every day. Thank someone for small mercies.

This guy knowing my name meant I couldn't just rip him off blatantly. I would have to use a little finesse to leave him sweet for another go. For the whole week we went over at least a dozen ways of ripping this guy off without letting him become aware he had been got. As it turned out, he was the easiest guy in history to get.

There was only one way we could do it properly. New South Wales' finest would have to be in on the whack-up. I wasted no time in contacting [*a police officer*]. He came to lunch with myself and The Dodger. I gave him a set price for the job that I required him to do for me. Without even knowing what the job was, he accepted. After I told him my idea he was delighted and said he would get three other detectives that he was 100 per cent sure of to give him a hand.

My plan was simple. All that was required was for Murray to get this fellow to leave the 100 kilograms in the boot of a car and park the car in Centennial Park at the spot of our choosing. Then, with Murray and Harold, this guy would park across the street and watch me pick up the gear, to ensure nothing went wrong with the pick-up. But I would be 'arrested', along with a friend of mine, by the detectives led by [*the police officer*], who would handcuff us and take us away in a police car.

[*The police officer*] would drive off in the car containing the hash. Once around the corner, handcuffs would be removed and I would get into the car with the hash. [*The police officer*] would take my mate, who we'll call 'Peter', and charge him with some shit blue that he would beat later. The reason for charging Peter was in case this guy had some cop sweet who could check whether anyone was really arrested that day, or whether it was a bodgie pinch. We covered ourselves carefully. I told [*the police officer*] to make the 'arrest' look good enough to fool the guy watching the deal go down.

At last all was ready to go. I contacted Murray and told him to arrange it for the next day. I went over the plan with him again to make sure there would be no mistakes.

The next morning I went to Centennial Park to look the place over. It was sweet. There were no suspicious people lurking around anywhere. Then I called in to see [*the police officer*]. He was ready to go. Great.

Peter and I drove up opposite the main gates of Centennial Park and parked my Mercedes. We walked up the main road to make sure [*the police officer*] was still in position with his men. He was there waiting. I knew I could rely on him. Through the gateway we went. I could see the car containing the hash parked exactly where it was meant to be. I glanced over to see if I could spot Murray and the other two in their car. I couldn't miss them—they stood out like dogs' balls. They had rented a huge white stretch limo with blacked-out windows! Murray sure liked to do things in grand style.

As we walked along the laneway towards the car I was dying to glance over my shoulder to see if [*the police officer*] had entered the park. But I couldn't look because I was being watched from the limo. We reached the car; I was expecting a screech of tyres any second. But nothing happened. Where was [*the police officer*]? I opened the boot to make sure the goods were there. They were.

Now all I needed was [*the police officer*]. If he didn't come I would just have to rip this guy off blatantly. There was no way I was going to miss out. We stalled for maybe a minute longer, then I told Peter to get in the passenger side while I went to get in the driver's seat. At last, the long-awaited screech of tyres.

The cops pulled up and all got out with guns in hand, ready to go on with the charade as planned. To make it look good, I made out like I was trying to run away from them. One crash tackled me and, after a short struggle, he cuffed me. Then he stood me up against the police car and searched me. That should be enough to impress the guy watching me.

We were both handcuffed and placed in the back of the police car while [*the police officer*] 'searched' the car. He opened the boot and came over to the car and told the other cops to move off slowly so that those watching could get an eyeful. I knew only one of the other three cops. He was a mate of [*the police officer*] and The Dodger. Then one of the other two said: 'Well, we have finally managed to grab Neddy Smith after so long!' I had a bad case of nerves when he said that. I thought I really was being arrested. I knew that [*the police officer*] was very friendly with [*a policeman Smith did not like*], and I thought I'd been cleverly set up. They drove about a block or maybe two before [*the police officer*] pulled up on the side of the road. He told them to take off the cuffs and let me out. Was I relieved!

[*The police officer*] walked to the boot of the car with me and opened it to show me that the gear was intact. Then he said: 'Get in the car and go where you're headed. I'll follow you for a short distance to make sure you're all right. Just blow your horn when you're sure that you're sweet and I'll turn off. OK?'

'Thanks mate. I'll have your money next Thursday afternoon. I will meet you at the Covent Garden Hotel at 5 o'clock.'

I got into the car with the hash in the boot and headed towards Redfern where I was going to snooker [*hide*] the hash until I delivered it to my buyer that afternoon. [*The police officer*] followed me for a mile, then I blew my horn and he drove off. I doubled back the way I had come to make sure that I didn't bump into the stretch limo, then headed to Redfern.

They took Peter to a police station and he sat there for two hours drinking with the cops and having a bet over the phone. They charged him with goods in custody and let him out on bail. This was only to cover us in case someone ran a check on our scam.

I found out later from Murray and Harold about the guy's reaction to what he believed had happened to me and the 100 kilos of his hash.

When they saw the cops pull up and grab me, the guy had panicked. Straight away Harold went into his act. He produced a .357 magnum and pointed it at the fellow's head. 'You cunt. You have set Ned up to be buckled [*arrested*] over this gear. You're dead.' Harold made all sorts of threats to the guy, and to Murray as well. Murray was in the swing of it all and played his part well.

'Come on, old mate,' he said to Harold. 'Can't we talk about this for a minute?' They drove to the Lord Dudley Hotel at Woollahra to work out what to do about me and Peter being pinched.

[*Smith used a number of solicitors and barristers at this time. One of those legal advisers also had the seller of the hash as a client. Smith was well aware of this and used it to his advantage. The legal adviser cannot be named, so we will call him Jones.*]

I had already fixed it with Jones that he be part of the plan. He was waiting at home for the guy to ring him, then part two of the plan would come into action.

As they were sitting at the Lord Dudley Hotel, Harold was still threatening the guy. 'We have to get a lawyer for Ned as soon as possible.' He sat as though he was trying to think of a lawyer. 'Where can we get a decent lawyer on a Saturday?'

The guy came in on cue. 'I have my lawyer, Jones. I can ring him at his home now and get him to do something for Ned if you like.'

Murray and Harold got him to ring Jones, who was waiting for the call. They told him the story over the phone. He said he would go to the police station, find out what was going on and get back to them. Jones then rang me at the Woolpack Hotel in Redfern. I told him to come over so

I could explain what I wanted him to do. He arrived 20 minutes later, just as I was finishing my second cool beer.

I got him a drink and explained. 'Go back to them and say you have seen me at the police station. Tell them I am going off my head over the guy setting me up and give Murray a rev too. Tell him that I said he was off-tap too. Then, to make it look good, tell Harold that he has some explaining to do.'

Jones asked me how far he should go with the act. 'Go right on with them,' I said. 'Pull no punches with them. You have to make him believe the story. Then tell the three of them that the cops want $50,000 not to charge me and that they are keeping the stock as a bonus.'

Jones set off for the Lord Dudley Hotel. As soon as he walked in he was into the act. 'Murray, you're in plenty of trouble. The big guy thinks that you two set him up to be arrested and he's not what I would call pleased at all.'

Then he started on Harold: 'You are also in the shit with him for not doing anything to help him.'

Harold started telling the poor guy that it was his fucking fault. 'Listen to me, you cunt. If I get in any shit over this I will kill you.'

You can imagine the poor guy's thoughts at that moment. Then Jones threw in the bombshell. 'Listen you guys. The cops will do business. If you want Ned out on the street now, you are going to have to come up with $50,000 cash for them to let him go without any charges.' Jones explained that the other guy had to be charged with a lesser blue, but he would be allowed out on bail. What happened next took everyone by complete surprise.

The guy we had just robbed of one million dollars said: 'I will give you the $50,000 to give to the cops to get Ned out of trouble. One of you drive me to Double Bay to pick it up.'

Harold quickly offered to drive him to pick up the money. There were no flies on Harold. They came back and the guy simply handed the money to Jones and told him to pay the cops and get me released.

Harold and Murray didn't like the idea of Jones going off with the money, but they couldn't say a word about it. Jones came back to me at the hotel and when he told me the guy we'd just ripped off had given him the $50,000 to get me out, I couldn't believe it. How could anyone be so silly? Jones gave me the $50,000.

We sat drinking to our good fortune, while I gave Jones his whack. Then we went up to where I had left my Benz. We picked it up and went down to front the three of them. I had my act all prepared. They all knew what I was going to do—except the poor innocent guy we had just ripped off.

It was my turn to earn an Academy Award. In I went: 'You cunts let me get arrested.' I was quietly blowing up so the rest of the people drinking there could not hear me. I threatened Murray and the other guy. I gave them a good pay, then I went all quiet on them. The guy just sat there letting Jones do his talking for him. Jones was 'defending his client', and doing a good job of it, too. After 30 minutes of fake rage, I was buggered, so I let Murray and Jones calm me down and we got on to the next phase of the deal.

First, I told the guy how much I appreciated him putting up the $50,000 for me. 'Thanks a lot, but we have to work out a way to fix everything up so that you get your money back as soon as possible.'

He agreed with me.

We talked about ways to retrieve the losses he had suffered. I asked: was any more hash about that we could get hold of, so I could sell it and get him back the money he was down? 'If we could get hold of another 100 kilos then I could sell it straight away, without getting an earn myself, and I could get you square. You wouldn't lose a cent.'

He didn't hesitate for very long. 'If you can sell it straight away, I can get it. The only problem is that it will take me 10 days to get hold of the gear as it isn't in Sydney.'

We discussed the new deal and, after a few dozen drinks, we went our own ways, agreeing to meet in a week to finalise the deal. We all left the Lord Dudley separately and later met at the Woolpack to divide the balance of the $50,000 that the poor fool had parted with.

Murray wanted to know when he could give [*the police who came up with the hash rip-off scam*] their share. I told him they would get the first cash that came in. I wanted that arsehole [*the policeman who tipped Murray off to the hash*] out of the way as soon as possible.

Murray kept on about the sharing of the money. 'It has

to be whacked-up two ways, then you look after your gang and I will look after mine.' That suited me. I liked the idea, but the money wouldn't be shared until the cops got theirs off the top the way all expenses came off.

I told Murray that he would get his and the other bloke's next Thursday. Then Harold and I went to pick up the hash from where I had left it. We then delivered it to the bloke that was going to buy the lot in one go. There were no problems, so I went home to Kotara to my family.

It was always a relief to get home and relax with my wife and kids. I loved them very much and I now regret that I didn't spend much more time with them when I had the chance. I spent a lazy week at home, never leaving the house for a second. I lay by the pool all day without moving an inch, just relaxing. I never realised what I had—my home and my family—until I lost them. I tended to take them for granted. I didn't think I would ever be parted from them. It took being away from them to make me really appreciate them. I suppose that's the price I have to pay for leading the type of life I did. I have no one to blame but myself. I know this and accept it.

Harold and I never rang one another unless it was absolutely necessary. We were fully aware that the police taskforce was continuing its investigations into our activities. It was a certainty that our phones were monitored, so why make their job easier by ringing each other? Let the bastards earn their money.

I lay around the pool thinking what I could do to make my family happy and decided on another holiday, this time at Hamilton Island. I got my wife to make the arrangements for a week's time—I still had to pick up the money from the hash rip-off and pay everyone out.

When Thursday arrived, I was anxious to get to Sydney and into business. That's what I told myself anyway; if the truth be known, I was more than likely hanging out for a drink.

I used to leave home very early in the morning, making any police who followed me easy to spot. It also meant I beat the traffic. But my two good friends in Sydney, Belinda and her mother Jeanette, were another reason for leaving early. I would call in early for a coffee and a chat: I would get Belinda up at about 5am; I didn't have to get Jeanette up as she normally started work before then. Both good friends stuck by me all through my troubles, and still do today.

That morning I called in to see them at Belinda's. As I parked my car just after 4am, I noticed movement at a window in a factory across the street. It *had* to be Australian Federal Police—state police would never get out of bed that early. It was common knowledge that I often called in to see the girls when I came to Sydney, but it was unusual for the police to start watching me so early.

I decided to be very careful when I picked up the money that day—very careful indeed. I called and had coffee, staying a few hours to kill time, then left. [*A policeman*] had warned me that a taskforce had staked out a few places that I regularly went to. This was new. They were sick of tailing me and losing me, getting nowhere fast, so they decided to stake out several locations where they knew I would eventually turn up.

About 7am I drove around looking for tails. I couldn't be sure there were none because the police were getting better at tailing me. I satisfied myself there was no tail before I called over to a prearranged meet with Harold. We changed cars twice, then we changed again, this time into a van we had purchased only weeks before.

Harold and I had made up our minds to pay Murray and his team their share from the hash rip-off straight away. We also wanted to pay off the cops that helped with the 'arrest'.

I had made plans for another friend to pick up any money that was ready and for him to meet me at a place we'd arranged beforehand. Harold drove us to the meet. We counted the takings from the sale of the hash. There was just over $300,000: that was enough to get [*the policeman Neddy Smith disliked and distrusted*] off our backs.

We again changed cars, reverting to Harold's car, and drove to the Kauri Hotel at the back of Glebe to meet the Murray. We knew this hotel was on the list of places that were under surveillance. There was still no sign of any tail, so we went to the hotel to pay Murray and get him out of our hair. Murray was always punctual when there was money to be had. We wasted no time as there was a chance that the Feds were around.

'There is $300,000 there, Murray. You're paid in full.

The Life of Riley

That's equally shared, with [*the policeman's*] gang taken care of. Does that meet with what you expected?' We transferred the $300,000 to Murray's boot. Murray said he had expected a little more. I wasn't going to stand around going over figures with him at that time of the morning.

Then I saw some movement on the top of a silo across the road. 'Harold, don't look up, just walk down to the corner and make like you are looking up the road. Then glance up to the top of that silo and tell me what you see.'

He walked to the corner while Murray and I acted normally. You had to keep your guard up at all times with the Feds. They went to extreme lengths to catch people—and many crims just didn't realise how far they were willing to go. The silo was at least 70 metres high. I kept glancing at it to see what had attracted my attention. There was a sheet of metal missing from the wall and one of the cops was positioned there with field glasses and camera equipment to watch and photograph us while we passed over the money. Harold came back quickly. 'Shit, you're fucking right, mate. There's a guy up on top of the silo photographing us. Let's get out of here fast.'

We left quickly without appearing to rush. Luckily we weren't intercepted with the money on us. Harold couldn't believe that degree of attention. He had a lot to learn about the Feds if he wanted to remain free.

Later on, I contacted a friendly cop and found out that it was the taskforce that had been watching us. They planned to catch us the following day at the Kauri Hotel. The plan was to park a council caravan, like those used by workmen on site, outside the hotel. It would be packed full of cops who would wait for me to turn up to do business.

But we were not going to turn up again after having seen them.

It was time to get away for that holiday. That night I paid off [*the police officer*]. He was very happy to collect his money and pay off the other three.

The next day I headed back to Kotara, picked up my family and we went to Hamilton Island. Debra had said that a week away from all the shit would probably kill me, but I managed to last. We had a tremendous holiday and went on an unbelievable tour of the Barrier Reef. I have never seen any thing like it. My kids didn't want to come home.

But like all good things, it came to an end, and we headed home.

For the whole week away I kept thinking about all the drama and shit that I was forced to put up with. When I got back, it didn't take me long to get to Sydney and discover that things hadn't improved. While I was away, Murray had fucked up any chance I had of ripping off the guy for another 100 kilos—or more—of hash. He decided to go it on his own and rip the bloke off again himself. Now Murray is good when it comes to ideas, but he hasn't got the necessary when it comes to executing a plan.

Murray again used Jones, who was in on the plan, and [*the policeman who was involved in the first rip-off*]. This time [*the policeman*] did a raid on the guy's house using a false search warrant. During the search, [*the policeman*] produced two bags of white powder [*heroin*] from his kick and showed them to the guy. 'I found this substance in your bedroom, I believe it to be an illegal drug and I am charging you with the possession of it.' Then he read the poor guy his rights. The guy had his wife and kids there with him. He was terrified. He was sick in the gut. He vomited for 15 minutes straight. [*The policeman*] and the other cop gave him the treatment, really did a job on him. 'Before I take you and your wife down to be charged would you like to ring your lawyer?' The guy fell right into the trap—again.

Jones arrived on the scene and went on like he was seriously helping the guy. He pulled him aside and said: 'Listen, I know these detectives. I may be able to talk to them for you and do business for you. What do you want to do?' And what did he *expect* him to say?

'Yes, please, mate. If you can do something I will look after you, too.'

Jones went away and pulled [*the policeman*] aside and made out that he was trying to do business. What the poor guy wasn't aware of was that they had worked out what to say before they even got to his home.

Back came Jones: 'Listen, my friend, they are not real keen on doing business with you. They don't trust you.'

'Tell them I will give them anything they want.'

Jones went back for more discussions. He returned. 'They will do business with you, but they are asking for $500,000.

I told them that you can't come up with that sort of money, so forget it.'

The bloke started to panic: 'Tell them I have the money. I have $100,000 at my mother's. I will send my wife to get it now and I can get the remainder within 10 days, I promise.'

Jones reported back to [*the policeman*], and they came up with a plan to ensure they didn't get dudded. Jones went back again: 'This is how they want to do the deal. They will accept the $100,000 as a down-payment for services rendered. But to ensure that you don't lash after they let you and your wife go free, they want you to sign a statement admitting guilt to the two bags of heroin they say they found in your possession. They will hold on to the statement until you pay the balance—then the statement will be returned to you. That's the very best I can do for you.'

'OK, give me the statement to sign now and I will send my wife to get the money for you.' Jones was hiding a grin. The statement was prepared and the guy signed it. The two cops witnessed it formally to make it look good, but really, it wasn't worth a pinch of shit. Meanwhile, the guy's wife returned with the money, which the guy in turn handed to Jones. Then Jones and the police left, I suppose to celebrate, share the money and prepare for the next payment.

They were in for a rude shock. The guy became suspicious. He spoke to old Bill Sinclair, who told him that Murray was behind both rip-offs. He advised the guy not to pay the rest of the money. He took Bill's advice and there wasn't a thing that could be done about it.

When I got back from Hamilton Island and discovered what the 'Prince of Promises' had done, there was hell to play. Fucking fools. They fucked up a million or more dollars that we had in our palms. And worse still, Harold and I weren't included in the $100,000 that [*the policeman*] and company got from that rip-off. They left us out.

I evened the score 10 times over in the near future by leaving them out of three rip-offs that I did for more than six million dollars worth of hammer [*heroin*].

19
Stinks

Troubles come in not single spies, but in battalions
Hamlet, William Shakespeare

One night I was at a friend's nightclub in the city, a place where the clientele were half cops and half crooks. I was drinking with Roger, [*a policeman*] and maybe a dozen other cops. We were all enjoying ourselves, minding our own business. Abo and [*an ex-policeman*] were on stage singing a few songs for the boys when a shoplifter came in and told me that four cops on the landing were talking about us. They were saying they would bash us as soon as they got in the club. What a stupid thing to say: it was like waving a red flag at a bull.

In walked four big guys. I didn't know them, but Roger told me they were from the organised crime squad. They were well dressed and looked reasonable guys. I got the barman to take them up a drink. It was my practice wherever I was drinking to buy a drink for any cops that came in, just to let them know I was aware of their presence and that I wanted to be shown the same respect. The barman took up the drinks and said they were on me. Very loudly they said, 'Tell him to shove them up his arse.'

That did it. I'd shove the drinks right up *their* arses. I went straight up to them. They didn't expect me to do anything about their abuse, so they got a shock.

I knocked the first one straight out with a left hook—he never saw it coming until it was too late. Then I hit the second one on the chin and he was down and out too. The remaining two stood mesmerised. Into the third one I went, knocking him down, but not out. Abo and Tex came up and Abo started into the last one—Tex was terrified. As Tex tried to make his way out of the club, I caught him. 'Come on, mate, you aren't sneaking out like that.' One of the cops was getting to his feet so Tex hit him flush on the jaw: it was all over for him.

We stood back for a few minutes to let them get their heads together. One of them looked at [*the ex-policeman*] and said: 'You're one of us, mate.'

'Not any more, I'm not. All the guy did was to offer you a drink.' Abo got stuck into one of the cops again and threw him down the escalator. It was a wild night, that was for sure.

We were very sick the next morning when we realised what we'd done. The demon drink had worked its stinking tricks on me again. I resolved that I was going to have to see someone about my drinking problem. My memory was a mess. But I had no trouble remembering what happened the previous night. I wished I could forget it, but it stuck in my mind. I knew I was in deep shit this time. As always, when I had a problem, I rang The Dodger to find out what, if anything, could be done to break the blue down. Roger told me something was being done and not to worry about it.

Time passed and I heard nothing back from Roger, so Abo and I decided to stick our big heads in at the club to see what the atmosphere was like. We should be able to see how the water was lying if we put in an appearance. The manager was there. He seemed happy enough and didn't look too worried. 'Hello boys, want a drink?' (So much for getting off the drink.) I ordered one straight away. We drank the first one straight down, it didn't even touch the sides. While we waited for another, the manager said: 'Things look as though they will turn out OK over the stink. I got called into town today over it and the powers that be are none too happy with you pair. But there will be no pinch for what you did, because those guys came in looking for trouble and they shouldn't have been here in the first place. They were on duty.'

I must have been grinning because he told us not to look so smug. 'You are fortunate there were a lot of police present when it took place and a lot of them went into bat for you when they were asked to give their version of the incident.'

That was a relief and a load off my mind. He went on: 'The boss in town said to pass on this message to you: "If you so much as touch another police officer again you will hit the nick so fast your feet won't touch the ground".'

Who cared? We were out of the shit, so let's drink on. Madness, complete insanity on my part, but that was the way I was travelling. Downhill fast—and no stopping me.

One night, after Harold and I had pulled off the Waverley Bus Depot robbery [*described in Chapter 1*], Abo confronted me. He was drunk and so was I. Abo said he was still dirty that I sacked him. He also started to bag Harold to me. Then he got on to some story about being robbed of $20,000 while he was with me. I couldn't make much sense of it all. I told him to pull up and get fucked. He wanted to argue with me. Now, I refuse to argue with anyone at all. I cannot argue.

We got into a heated discussion about something or other and I had just had enough. We both had the same idea. Abo started to rise from his bar stool when I hit him flush on the chin. I didn't bother to even get off the stool. Down he went, but he got up quickly so I hit him again. Down he went again. Then we started trading blows. It was only a matter of a few seconds before he went down again. Only instead of getting straight up, he pulled a knife from his back pocket and started to open it. I knew what he was like with a knife so I took no chances. I picked up a metal stool and hit him over the head once or twice. I kept attacking him with the stool, but he managed to get to his feet and rushed out of the door.

When I woke up the next morning I was furious with Abo for pulling a knife on me. I drove home to Kotara, taking a machine pistol with me. I was intent on doing something about him and his knife. When I got home I told my wife about Abo pulling the knife. I told her I was going to do something about him. As usual, my wife showed better sense than I did. She talked me out of something I would regret later. And there was always the possibility that I may just get caught for it. After thinking about it for 24 hours, I calmed down and put it at the back of my mind for a later date.

Thank Christ there was someone around with more sense than I had to guide me, or I might have done something stupid. And for what? Over a silly fight. Despite our altercation, we remained close friends and still are today.

My drinking meant that only disaster could pull me up. I honestly didn't know why I was being so stupid. I was only shitting in my own face. Why? I had the best part of the police force on side and I could virtually do as I pleased without fear of going to jail. I was living the life of a millionaire, with everything I could possibly desire: the best clothing, cars and my own home, a pool, my kids were happy – what more could I want out of life?

Thinking back on these events I believe it was immaturity. I had come along too bloody fast and I couldn't handle everything that had been served up on my plate. But life went on. All my life I had dreamed of the sort of life I now had. And although I didn't realise it then, I was having problems handling it.

There were very few people in the world who managed to live the way I did. I spent money like it was going out of fashion, never thought about tomorrow, believed the money would never run out, never cared about *anything*. Except my family.

I made sure they came first in everything – they wanted for nothing. But they never really knew what I did for a living. I kept my wife and kids in total ignorance of my business. As far as they were concerned, I was in the SP business, nothing else.

The writing was on the wall for several members of New South Wales' finest.

Some had the misfortune of being photographed with me at lunch or drinking at pubs and the powers that be thought they had found a way to thin the ranks of suspected corrupt police, so there was a blitz on police who were associating with criminals. They soon had minor successes and managed to get rid of a few of the inner circle of Roger's gang. Roger was the first to go, then went *[Smith names six police officers]*. Many more were to follow, tipped for some form of misconduct or corruption.

[In 1986, Roger Caleb Rogerson was expelled from the police force after the Police Tribunal upheld seven of nine disciplinary charges against him, including the improper

association with criminals including Ross Karp and Dr Nick Paltos, revealing that 'Neddy' Smith and Lennie McPherson were allegedly police informers, and opening a bank account in a false name.

A year earlier, in 1985, Rogerson had been acquitted of attempting to bribe Michael Drury, a fellow officer. In 1989 he was acquitted of conspiring to murder the same man, after Drury had been shot and seriously wounded in June 1984. Rogerson had plotted with Christopher Dale Flannery and Melbourne heroin dealer Alan Williams (McLure) to kill the undercover drug squad detective because Drury rejected the initial bribe attempt, according to the Crown case.

Rogerson also avoided another criminal conviction in 1985 when he was acquitted on an assault charge.

So, for much of the time before he was expelled from the force in 1986, Rogerson was suspended. Yet during this time, and after he was kicked out of the force, Rogerson and Smith remained close—and in some ways acted as if nothing had changed.

But in March 1990, Rogerson was found guilty by a jury of conspiring to pervert the course of justice—hindering a police inquiry into the source of $110,000 in two bank accounts opened in false names by Rogerson and another man in 1985. He was sentenced to a minimum of six years jail. The sentencing judge, the District Court's Judge Shillington, said there was a clear inference that Rogerson had been involved in an important drug transaction (the Crown had argued the money came from a swap for heroin made at Sydney airport). A charge against Rogerson of conspiring to supply heroin was dropped after the conviction.

Rogerson appealed against his jail term and, on 11 December 1990, he was released from jail. But he lost his appeal and on 16 December 1992 was taken back to jail. His sentence, however, was shortened.

Roger Rogerson was released on parole on 15 December 1995.]

They were certainly thinning out the group of friendlies I had spent years cultivating—but it didn't matter a great deal because the police force was riddled with corruption and I had plenty left to fill their shoes. And besides, Roger and the rest of them had plenty of friends still active within the force. I was not finished yet. Not by a long shot. We just carried on. Business as usual. We still had the best part of the New South Wales police force on side, so why worry about a few sackings? As long as we could still operate as we had been doing, we would.

[*A policeman Smith disliked*] was smarter than most of the others. He had kept his distance from us, never going to lunches or getting on the drink with us in public. There was the odd time when he would have a drink with us, but he made sure we met in the suburbs where people were less likely to recognise us. [*The policeman is still serving in the New South Wales force*].

Things had been going along too well—I felt something might go wrong. I had expected the problem to come from [*the policeman Smith disliked*], but I was wrong. Treachery came from a different direction—[*another officer*] was the culprit. The low bastard rolled over on me. [*According to Smith, the officer was accused by his boss of complicity in one of the armed robberies. The policeman denied it and, to look good, came up with a theory that Smith was involved in a series of armed robberies. This led to a new taskforce being established to concentrate on the link between Smith and a series of armed hold-ups in New South Wales.*]

The taskforce, called Zig Zag or something similar, kept trying to catch me for nearly a year. They never had any luck. I had [*two policemen*] in the taskforce itself passing information to me.

Every cop I spoke to assured me there was no way the taskforce would load me up [*plant evidence*] or try to verbal me [*obtain a false confession*]. If that was true, then I hadn't a worry in the world. There was no way they would catch me fair and square. There wasn't one thing to connect me to any of the armed robberies—no hard evidence for them to even question me.

But even so, things were never the same again.

Before [*the police officer*] opened his big mouth, those people investigating me believed I was involved only in drug distribution. It served my purpose to keep them thinking like that; it kept them off my back, not looking for armed robberies. Now, they had no doubt I was involved in numerous hold-ups. Worse, some of my key police contacts were transferred. But that didn't stop the [*police*] from doing business with me. Greed kept them actively involved in the armed robbery business. But they did tighten up in several ways. They refused to get out on the drink with me or to meet me in person. [*A policeman*] was very toey about meeting me. He had no confidence in my ability to spot a tail. That didn't present a problem, because I used [*an ex-policeman*] as a go-between.

The taskforce was getting hotter every day. They stepped up their surveillance considerably and constantly took photographs of me and anyone with me. I couldn't find out why. Everything was hush-hush and no one was letting on what was happening. I certainly didn't like the attention. I had to be very careful collecting money and doing business.

The taskforce was unlucky. It failed to get us several times when we were vulnerable. If they had pulled me up on any number of occasions I would have been in deep shit. My luck was holding, although there were a few up-and-coming detectives looking to make a name for themselves by pinching me. So I knew I had to keep both eyes open—more so than ever before.

But I didn't. My vision was always clouded by drink. I was an alcoholic and wouldn't believe it. I was forever doing silly things on the drink, like bashing people for practically no reason. Friends told me to keep my guard up and slow down or I would end up killing myself—or someone might kill me.

Harold, meanwhile, took a long holiday with his wife and family. But his absence didn't slow me down one bit. I was running around with this bloke called Glen Flack. He was forever taking me to brothels for mad times. We started to take [*Jones, the lawyer*] and several cops and ex-cops to the brothel with us. We had some good times there. The only problem I had was that I had some problem aiming up at brothels. I just couldn't get to the mark at brothels, I don't know why, I just couldn't.

Glen was on with this young sheila called Priscilla—he used to spend a fortune on her. One evening we were at the White Horse Hotel when these young guys started having a go at Glen, saying he was her father or something similar. Glen didn't like them shooting their mouths off, so he attacked the young guy and it turned into a mad stink. The young guys got flogged and left the hotel only to return later to back-up [*seek revenge*] on Glen. The hotel was overcrowded when one young guy tried to sneak up and put a glass into Glen's face. I noticed the guy and grabbed him. There was little or no room to throw a punch so I did the next best thing—I grabbed hold of his hair, dragged him towards me and bit chunks out of his face. I got carried away and really chomped into his face, madly biting it to pieces. They ended up getting a cab driver to take him to hospital. It was madness.

Everyone kept telling me, including my wife, to get a grip on myself, to give the drink a rest. Foolishly, I took no notice of any of them. Every night I was in Sydney I drank myself into a stupor. I was riding for a big fall and couldn't see it. It wasn't long in coming.

Friday, 30 October 1987 started out as an ordinary enough day for me. A friend and I began drinking at the Lord Wolseley Hotel in Ultimo. From there we went to the Covent Garden Hotel for more drinks. Roger and [*a former police officer*] arrived and we went to a Chinese restaurant for lunch. We ordered four bottles of wine with lunch. When they were gone we got back on to the beer. We drank until about 4pm before going back to the Covent Garden. More drinking. Roger had us in fits of laughter with his jokes. We were enjoying ourselves and not annoying anyone. We noticed the usual teams of surveillance police there trying to look inconspicuous.

We stayed at the Covent Garden until 6pm then went to the Australian Youth Hotel in Glebe. There were five of us now and we were really giving the drink a serve. Roger was setting a heavy pace and I was having problems keeping up. It was around 8pm when we decided to go to the Coogee Sports Club for a meal and to listen to some entertainment. [*The former officer*] said he'd had enough and headed home.

I wish I'd followed suit.

Roger got into his car. Me and the other guy got into my car and I drove. Don't ask me how I managed to drive 10 metres in the state I was in. It wasn't long before the other guy told me to pull over and let him drive. The next thing I remember—and not too clearly—was the car stopping somewhere in Coogee Bay Road. There was a car behind us flashing its lights at us. My mate got out of my car and went back towards the other vehicle where a fight started between my mate and the driver of the other car. I remember a second person getting out of the other car. I got out too, I think with the intention of making sure the second guy stayed out of the scuffle. I had no intention of hurting anyone and I certainly didn't go to Coogee to make trouble—and I didn't know either of the guys from the other car.

The rest is a blur. The only reason I can relate any of it is because I have been through two court hearings, so I have pieced bits together, along with small flashes of my memory.

The other fellow and I started throwing punches at each other. I don't think either of us was doing any damage, just more or less pushing and shoving. I didn't see the guy reach anywhere, but suddenly he had some sort of iron bar in his hand. In my haste to get out of the way I tripped over as he swung the iron bar at me. We punched on again, neither of us getting very far, then I can remember my mate pulling me away and helping me get into my car. He drove. Before we drove off, or just as we were driving away, I heard a loud bang and the rear window shattered. We drove away with the other vehicle following us and trying to ram us. We got away, and drove to Belinda and Jeanette's house at Coogee.

My mate parked the car outside their flat. No one was at home but, as always, the door was unlocked. I went in and rang my wife, but she wasn't home. I fell asleep on the lounge. I don't know how long I was asleep for: I only woke up when Belinda began shaking me.

'The police have just towed Debra's car away from out front. Are you OK?'

'I think so.'

I couldn't remember where I was for a few seconds. I then remembered the fight. Something must have happened to bring the police into it. What? I asked my mate what had happened during the fight. He knew nothing—or so he told me. If he was telling the truth then I had nothing to worry about.

I washed my face then tried ringing my wife to explain about her car. I still had no idea what had happened so I rang [*an ex-policeman*]. He used to be [*in a position of high rank*] so I thought he might be able to find out what the problem was. He came to see me straight away. I explained about the stink and the car window being smashed—I asked if he would find out what the problem was. He left and, before long, came back. As soon as I saw the look on his face, I knew something was very wrong. He came inside. He was serious, which meant trouble for me.

'What's up, mate?'

'You are in very serious trouble, Ned. One of the guys that you two were fighting with just died of multiple stab wounds to the chest and stomach.'

I was shocked, I couldn't believe it. I knew that I had not been in possession of a knife. 'Who do they think did it?'

'They have no idea yet, but they are checking out the ownership of the car.'

I had to think straight, get my mind working on the best thing to do. I tried several lawyers but not one was available. I wanted to go into the police station and hand myself in, try and work things out before some gung-ho cop made a big thing out of it. I discussed handing myself in with [*the ex-cop*]. He advised against it until I found a lawyer to go in with me. He told me to go somewhere safe until he could fix the blue up, or at least arrange for me to hand myself in to someone.

He left, saying he would be in touch soon. An hour passed and I heard nothing. It was still early in the morning, so I rang [*another ex-policeman*] at home. I told him I had a big problem, asked him if he could come round. He came straight away and I told him what I knew. He left and returned 30 minutes later. 'It's not good news mate. You should have gotten on to me earlier. Word is out that you are responsible for the murder of one Ronald Flavell and all the top brass are out of their warm beds overseeing the running of the operation so they can make sure that no one tries to do anything to help you.'

I knew that this was going to happen.

'Tony Lauer [*a senior policeman, later to be police commissioner*] has personally taken charge of this investigation. He has spread the word that anyone who tries to help you in any way will be taken to task over it and dealt with very severely.'

I really had a problem with Lauer in charge of the matter. Worse, I still couldn't find a lawyer that was at home or in the office. It was as if some dark force was working against me.

I said to [*the ex-policeman*]: 'Listen, can anything be done to pull this madness up? Money is no object.'

[*The ex-policeman*] told me not to worry. The inquiry, he said, would 'be handled carefully and quietly'. He was wrong.

I went to my mother's place, then a friend's house, and phoned all over Sydney trying to find a lawyer. Several police and ex-police came to visit me and offer advice. Abo came down to Sydney and said he would try to locate Big Brother and arrange for something to be done. Even Roger dropped in and told me to relax.

Soon after he left, I looked out the front window and saw cops all over the street. The SWOS team [*the Special Weapons Operations Squad, a paramilitary-style group of police used for raids on terrorists and criminals regarded as dangerous*] were there as well. They surrounded the house and tried to break down the front door—it wouldn't give. They called out to me to open the door. Just as I approached the door to open it, one of the SWOS team dived straight through the bedroom window like a stunt man, rolled over a couple of times and came up with the biggest gun I'd ever seen in his hand. He screamed at me: 'Get on the fucking floor, now! Get on the fucking floor. Move. Now!' The door came crashing open and police came through in droves. They surrounded me, shouting. There were guns everywhere, all pointed at me. You would have thought that I had committed mass murder instead of just being involved in a scuffle that got out of hand.

I got down on the floor on my stomach. I had about three guns pushed up against my neck and head while they handcuffed me. I was then dragged to my feet by the officer in charge of the SWOS team.

'Hello, Neddy,' he said. 'Looks like your run has come to an abrupt finish, doesn't it?'

If it wasn't so bloody serious I would have laughed out loud. 'What's all this drama in aid of?' I asked. 'You know you don't need all this crap with me.'

The policeman started to laugh: 'Neddy, you are about to make your debut on TV. You are going to be a star.'

'Very funny. I have done nothing wrong and I refuse to talk to any police at all without a lawyer present.'

'Yeah, yeah, yeah. Take him out of here before he has me in tears.'

They took me out the front. There were TV crews everywhere. Maximum publicity. The police had planned this well. As I walked out I saw four federal police watching proceedings. That was strange, for the Feds to be involved in a murder charge. (I found out later that the Feds wanted to make sure I didn't slip through the net by doing business. They were watching the state police because they knew that I had slipped away many times in the past by paying my way out of trouble.)

I was put into a police car with three detectives and taken to Maroubra police station—reporters were waiting there too. It was obvious the police wanted as much publicity as possible. After the media had all the shots they needed, I was taken into the police station, interviewed and charged with the murder of Ronald Flavell. I was then put into the police cells.

Those cells do strange things to your mind—after a few hours on my own, I began to think of the shit I was in. The cells were having a bad effect on me. I couldn't get my mind straight. I constantly thought of my family and how they were going to get on without me. That first night in the cells was the worst night of my life. I thought that I had been left for dead by everyone. Where were all those people that I had helped out of trouble? Where were all the cops I had been working with for all these years?

The next morning I appeared in court and was remanded for seven days to appear at the Coroner's Court at Glebe. Bail was refused. My wife was at court and tried to talk to me, but reporters were all over the place and the low police wouldn't allow me to talk to her.

Later that day I was moved to the police centre. All the cops kept coming in to look at me. While they had all heard about me and Rogerson, few of them had ever seen me, so they came and stared at me all night long. After a while I was beginning to think I had two heads or some similar disfigurement. But some police from the old school also came to see me: they brought food and drink, and took me upstairs so I could ring Debra.

Then I was shunted out to Long Bay.

When I arrived at the Bay I got a shock: none of the sections would accept me! I couldn't understand what was happening to me. Shit, was I that hated? Apparently yes. Eventually, I was accepted into the remand section with the other prisoners, but not before I'd signed a document, at the behest of prison officials, that said I wouldn't hold the prison or its staff responsible for anything that might happen to me! (I found out a few days later that because of the publicity I was receiving over my relationship with The Dodger, the people from the prison's head office were listening to fools talking shit. Someone told them that my life was in danger, and they believed it.)

My priority was to get bail. It was essential I got out. When you're in jail people soon forget you, out of sight out of mind.

It was a long wait—five weeks—until my court appearance. I wasn't at all confident of getting bail—few people get bail on a murder charge. When the day arrived I was taken to the Supreme Court. Greg James, one of the very best QCs around town, was representing me, so I knew I was in with a half a chance.

Greg James proved his worth when it came time to cross-examine one of the arresting detectives. He quickly established that the detective had made three different statements about the events of the night of Flavell's death. Key facts in each of the statements were different—and worse, a number of those facts were inconsistent with the written evidence presented by the detective to the court. At this point the Crown withdrew its objection to bail and I was released on a $50,000 surety.

Debra was there with her sister to put up my bail. We went to a friend's restaurant for lunch. It was the first decent meal I'd had in a more than a month.

20
Losing Control

Every form of addiction is bad, not matter whether the narcotic be alcohol, morphine or idealism.

Carl Jung, *Memories, Dreams, Reflections*

[*Smith's primary aim on his release was to ensure he would be acquitted on the murder charge. He set the wheels in motion while on remand: $50,000 was paid to 'Big Brother' to work on one aspect of Smith's case, while another was paid to two others to tamper with evidence, fingerprints on cars and the like. Smith was to discover that the money had not necessarily been well spent.*]

Everyone was very careful about being seen with me once I got out, and Big Brother was no exception. He was very evasive. I finally managed to corner him one afternoon at the Lord Wolseley Hotel in Ultimo. When he saw me, he signalled me to meet him in the men's room. He always liked a lot of drama, so I walked in to hear his story. All I wanted to know was how things were going [*since he had been paid the $50,000*]. All he was concerned about was whether I'd been followed. 'Neddy, you are very tropical [*hot*] at the moment. I can't be seen talking to you.' He provided me with little reassurance that anything was going well.

[*Smith and Flack then went to see the two other police who had promised to fix certain evidence for him. He discovered that since they had been paid their $50,000, their enthusiasm had waned. They said they could make some arrangements for Smith—falling short of his expectations—but they needed another $20,000. The encounter, at the Convent Garden Hotel in Haymarket, was drunken and acrimonious.*]

I was far from happy with the way things were going, but at that stage I had little option but to accept their plan.

I agreed to pay the extra $20,000, but not before I had beaten the blue [*charge*]. No more money would change hands until I got a result. Payment on result; that was the way I did business. [*The two police*] weren't impressed one bit, but they had no option. I had grave doubts that the pair of fools would be able to handle their end of the deal. They just didn't seem to have the streetwise sense to do it properly. As it turned out, I was right.

Meanwhile, I had to get down to the business of making money to pay the bills that would soon accumulate: lawyers' bills in the vicinity of $5000 a day once my hearing began, the $120,000 for shithead and his mates, plus private detectives I wanted running around on my behalf to try and locate witnesses that may have seen the fight [*that allegedly led to Flavell's death*]. I even put ads in the local paper to try and locate any witness that might have been reluctant to come forward.

So I had to go out and earn the almighty dollar. No one was going to knock on my door and hand me money—I had to get it myself.

For a change, I had a stroke of luck. A guy I'd met in the nick came to see me about an armed robbery he had been planning. I'd never worked with this guy before, but I knew he had plenty of experience in armed robberies. I said I would talk to him about it before deciding whether to do it or not.

We met and he explained his plan: he wanted to rob an armored van in Newcastle. The idea was to snatch the payroll for the Hamilton railroad. He knew I was 'friendly' with the police and he asked whether I could get help on this one. I told him that I could probably arrange it if he thought it necessary. He did, so through [*an ex-policeman*] I arranged to ring [*two officers*]. I met [*one of the officers*] the next morning and went over the plan. He was keen, so I told him what was required. He was happy with the financial end of it, so it was on for the following week.

[*The officer*] was a bit concerned that the taskforce [*investigating Smith's earlier armed robberies*] was still watching me. 'They will fall on your house as soon as the robbery happens, you realise that, don't you?' I assured him it would work out. 'Just keep me well informed, and I will do the rest.' I told him that after the robbery he should pick up his money from [*the ex-policeman*].

The key problem with this robbery was that we had only one opportunity to do it. The fortnightly payroll was about to be converted from cash to cheque, so this was the last chance at the cash. This meant I wouldn't get a look at the payday action before we did it, but I agreed to the job because I had plenty of faith in the guy who'd spent months planning it.

We drove back up to Newcastle to have a look at the layout. We got into the pay office to check that out too. It all looked easy enough. The plan was to wait until the guards had delivered the money, then rush into the building, upstairs to the pay office and grab the cash. We got hold of clothing similar to that used by the railway workers; grey pants and shirts. Added to that were balaclavas, gloves and, of course, one pump-action shotgun and three .38 police specials.

I arranged for the young blokes to steal a car. We spent a lot of time planning our escape route. Minutes after our getaway—in a stolen car, of course—I planned to report on bail to the police station. (I had to report there regularly as part of my bail conditions on the murder charge.) That way I would have a near-perfect alibi. Who would expect a man who had just robbed a payroll to call into a police station?

My mate brought two other guys up from Melbourne to help out with the robbery. I didn't know them, but I knew he wouldn't have picked them if they weren't any good.

The day came quickly. We were all dressed identically in grey work clothes. Our balaclavas were rolled up to look like beanies on top of our heads, ready to pull down as soon as we moved. We drove our stolen car into the railway yard and waited. There were people all over the place waiting to collect their pay, so no one took any notice of us.

Waiting was the worst part for me, just sitting, waiting for the van to arrive. It came on time, but the guards didn't get out. I started to get impatient. The bastards were eating their breakfast or something. By the time they got out of the van, there were dozens of people there waiting to pick up their pay. We hadn't counted on so many people standing around. We quickly decided it would be too hard to rush up the stairs and grab the money from the pay office. With so many people hanging around, someone might get brave and try to be a hero.

So as the three guards got out of the van and began walking towards the pay office with two boxes and a briefcase, our car moved off towards them. We had 100 metres to cover before we would be close enough. Meanwhile, the guards were just walking along as though they didn't have a worry in the world. They were in for a shock.

We managed to get within 10 metres of them before the car pulled up. The guards had still not seen us. We rushed across a lawn and were on top of them before they knew what had happened. I got to the guards first and, pointing the pump-action shotgun, ordered them to lie on the ground. I told all the employees who were standing around to lie down too. Everyone went to ground except one guard, who went for his gun. He was quickly knocked down and relieved of his gun.

The two guys with me grabbed the money tins and the guns from the other two guards before moving quickly back to the car. Once they were safely inside, I backed away towards the car. A few guys looked, for a second, as if they wanted to be heros, but I made sure they had a full view of the pump-action shotgun. I got into the car and we sped out of the railway yards to the waiting van that we had parked just a few streets away. We changed vehicles and, as we drove away, I changed out of railway workman's gear into a pair of running shorts, singlet and runners.

Prior to doing the robbery I had told my wife that I was going jogging. I'd told her to pick me up at a park with her sister at a certain time. We drove to the park and I jumped out of the van and jogged to the car with my wife and sister-in-law in it. I opened the car door, said hello, sweating heavily and puffing. My wife handed me a towel and drove to the police station. We pulled up, and I went inside to sign the report book. As I entered my name, the police radio was blaring: 'Heavily armed men have just held up the armored van at Hamilton railway yard and escaped with the payroll.' A young female uniformed cop was staring at me while this was being broadcast.

I left the police station and Debra drove me to a friend's place. The other guys were waiting for me in his garage. They had already counted the money into bundles. We had scored just over $200,000. I took [*the police*] whack out first, then the $1000 for the car thieves, plus money for other expenses. The rest we shared.

After I showered and changed, I headed to Sydney to pay [*the police*] and have lunch. But there was a hitch.

Apparently the cop who had seen me when I reported to the police station had put in her report that I looked as though I was involved in something sinister and she described how I was 'sweating profusely'.

Her report led to me being asked to come in for questioning over the hold-up—and a serious interview for myself, Debra and my sister-in-law followed. It was the one and only time I was pulled in and seriously questioned about a robbery I did with the Green Light. The taskforce knew I was responsible for the robbery, but like all the others, they couldn't do a thing about it. They hoped that I might be too cocky in the interviews and my alibi might crack. No such luck.

The next time I went to the police station to report on bail, the young cop was on. She was staring at me. I couldn't help myself, I just had to say something.

'Listen love, next time I sweat, see if you can tell on me for something a bit lighter than an armed robbery, OK?'

She went red in the face and couldn't answer me. I walked out, laughing at her discomfort.

I had not worked with Abo for a long time when one day he dropped in to see me with a plan. 'Are you interested in a big go I've got on hold? It's not an easy one, but if you look at it, you might come up with an idea.' He told me the details of a big payroll for wharfies that was picked up by boat from a wharf at Hunters Hill. I went to have a look; I liked it as soon as I saw it. I asked Abo if he would cop a spotter's fee and leave the robbery to me. He refused, and I didn't blame him either—it looked like it would be a top earn. We agreed to give it a go and I spent a lot of time looking at it.

The payroll was delivered to the wharf by armored van. Just minutes before each fortnightly delivery, a police car would drive into the wharf area to make sure no suspicious-looking people were hanging around. Then the police would drive up and down the only street out of the area—one long road that went for about five kilometres. The side streets all led to the water, so a boat was the only way out.

I came up with the idea of dressing up as painters and making out we were painting the bus shed where the van always pulled up. By painting the shed we would be right on top of them when they arrived—surprise would be on our side. Once we had the money, we could either have a boat standing off the wharf waiting to pick us up, or drive a couple of hundred metres to one of the side streets that led to the water, and change to a boat there.

Abo was keen, but I wasn't in a hurry to do it. I wanted to take my time. Well, Abo had ideas of his own. He found two guys who were pretty willing and talked them into having a go at the payroll.

I was on my way into town one morning listening to the scanner when the police radio burst into life; four men had just robbed the payroll of $320,000 at Hunters Hill wharf. Abo had stolen my plan to dress as painters and used my idea of a boat to get away from the area. I cannot blue about it, as in that game it's a case of first-in best-dressed. Abo had pulled it right out from under my nose. Good one, Abo.

Roger was making headlines. Every time that Roger got a mention in the media, they would put my name right up alongside his. It was all I needed.

Not only was I getting hounded by the taskforce investigating the armed robberies I'd done, but the special branch [*the section of the NSW police that deals with political crimes, such as terrorism*] had taken an interest in me over a Chinatown bank robbery where they were alleging that up to $100 million had been taken, but that was just another example of the media printing shit. [*On 1 January 1988 police discovered that thieves had, in an overnight robbery, emptied 80 private safe-deposit boxes at the National Australia Bank in Sydney's Chinatown. Known as the 'Great Chinese Takeaway', the value of the haul will always be in doubt. Half the box holders refused to divulge the contents to police, probably because the Australian Taxation Office took an interest in the disclosures. Police said, at a guess, the value of the contents was between $20 million and $100 million. No one has been charged over the robbery.*]

It was all starting to take its toll on me. The strain and

stress of dodging the cunts for all those years was finally taking it out of me. I still carried on the same way, drinking myself stupid every chance I got. With Roger's help I managed to get blind regular as clockwork.

One night, Roger and I were drinking at the Covent Garden Hotel when I spotted three cops posing as drinkers at the far end of the bar. They couldn't take their eyes off us all night. Finally the lout came out in me. I went up to them and said: 'What the fuck are you cops staring at all the time? If you want something then don't be fucking shy, come right out and say so.'

They were a bit taken aback except for the youngest one, who started to abuse me. He said they were police from the special branch and he wasn't going to cop shit from the likes of me. They stayed there till the pub closed, getting more aggro as time went by.

Our team was staying back to drink on. These cops thought that they would stay too. I had other ideas about who was staying and who wasn't staying. 'Come on, you guys, the pub's shut. All out now, that includes you cops. Out.'

The next night they were there again drinking as though nothing was said. Roger and I got pretty drunk and decided to give these cops something to talk about. I had about $40,000 on me that I had won on the punt so I got it out—all in $100 bills—and started to slap Roger around the face with it. Roger laughed and went one better than me. He stripped off and he flashed his arse at the special branch cops. Next thing, he was running all around the bar in his underpants. I managed to get a few photographs of Roger in his underpants and one of me flashing all the money at the cops. I suppose it was our way of showing the special branch guys what we thought of their ability to catch us.

Roger and I used to play up if we saw any cops watching us or following us anywhere. One night after leaving the Coachman restaurant following a huge night on the drink, Roger spotted these Feds watching us and taking photographs of us. Well, he went over to their car and gave it a good kick and then started trying to rip off the front number plate. I had to pull him away from the car. We used to give them plenty if we got close enough to them. Thinking back on it now I can see that it was silly, but we didn't want them to get the idea that they had us worried one bit.

One evening I was having a few drinks at the White Horse Hotel with this mate of mine, an inspector of police, who I refuse to name. We'd been to lunch in Chinatown and I was in a very good frame of mind. I always enjoyed this particular guy's company. There was no shit about him. He would tell you if he didn't like you or didn't want to know you. He was a real man's man.

We were drinking by ourselves and having a good time, when a young detective came over and started talking to my mate. He completely ignored me—but that wasn't a problem as I was having too good a time. In fact trouble was the furthest thing from my mind when this young cop began to glare at me. For a few minutes I ignored him, but he kept on glaring and snarling. It was obvious he was drunk—but then so was I.

I looked at him and smiled to myself. This guy was looking for trouble. I continued to ignore him and I kept on talking to my mate.

But this guy couldn't help himself. He said: 'You're Neddy Smith, aren't you? You don't scare me one bit.'

'Look, fool, just have your drink and go bother someone else. OK?'

He wouldn't listen to me so my mate told him to fuck off.

'What are you sticking up for him for? You're one of us.'

I couldn't help myself. I had to pull this flip into gear before he got right out of hand. 'Listen to me, you halfwit, I don't need anyone to stick up for me, especially to a dickhead like you.'

He didn't take kindly to that and offered to fight me out the front of the hotel. That suited me fine. I was going to sort this fool out there and then. I started to walk out the front when my mate grabbed my arm. 'Hang five there, Ned. Look over there. See those big young guys standing waiting there?' He was pointing at six huge young cops watching us.

'Ned, this is a set-up to pinch you for bashing a cop. You are wide open since you bashed those cops up the other month. These guys have been sent especially to try you out and if you were silly enough to fall into their trap then they would charge you and then bash the shit out of you.'

My mate grabbed the young cop by the shirt, pushed him out the door and followed him. 'Listen to me, you arsehole, don't ever try that on any of my friends again, do you understand? If you had any go in you then you would fight the bloke and see how you went. Now grab those other shitmen and get out of here.'

The cop walked over to his mates and spoke to them. Soon after, they walked out of the pub. I had drunk enough for the night. If I had missed an obvious set-up like that, then I was in no condition to be out on my own.

I told my friend I was going and started to leave the hotel. Again he grabbed my arm. 'Wait a second while I get one of my team to take a look outside.'

I waited until his guy came back and spoke to him. My friend turned to me and said: 'Ned, give me your car keys and I'll borrow the Mercedes for the night. I am getting this young guy to take you where you want to go in the police car. He's sweet and will make sure you get where you want to go.'

'What's up, mate?'

'Don't worry about it. Those fucking louts are hanging about outside waiting for you to leave. They might try to give you a breath test. You will refuse to take it. That will give them an excuse to pinch you.'

I went with the young cop and, as I got into the police car, I could see the team of cops watching me. The young cop dropped me at the motel I was staying at—after making sure we weren't being followed by those shitheads.

Next morning I was brooding over that dickhead trying to set me up. I was not going to let it go at that, no way. He would pay dearly.

I showered, dressed and then caught a cab to see my mate and pick up the Mercedes. He told me the cop's name and I decided to fix the arsehole right up. He would be lucky to keep his job after I was through with him.

I knew that [*a detective*] was still following me as part of the taskforce investigation into the armed robberies. So I decided to kill two birds with one stone. I arranged for a solicitor to take down a letter to the ombudsman and one to the commissioner of police stating that I was aware that [*the detective*] was following me and was going to attempt to load me up [*plant evidence*].

The letter went on to complain of police harassment and, as the finishing touch, I said: 'While having a drink at the White Horse Hotel [*on such and such a night and time*], I was approached by [*the cop*] who had some information for sale about the taskforce that had me under surveillance. [*The cop*] then sold me the information about [*the detective*] and the taskforce.'

I signed the letters and they were both hand delivered. I thought no more about it until I heard from Roger that the cop had to face the police tribunal and looked like getting sacked from the force. Great!

About three weeks later I was on my own having a few drinks. I had only just arrived so I was still sober. I was talking to a girl behind the bar when two cops walked in. I knew one [*Smith names the policeman*]. I didn't know the guy with him. Both came up to me and I got them a drink.

[*The policeman*] introduced his mate: it was [*the cop*]. I hadn't recognised him. This was that low bludger that had tried to set me up. I was furious at [*the policeman*] for bringing him to see me and I blew up. 'Listen, you arsehole, let's go across to the car park now and settle this once and for all. You don't have six cops behind you now.'

[*The policeman*] grabbed me by the arm: 'Cool it, Ned. I brought him down to see you because he knows that he is in the wrong and wants to apologise.' The real reason for the visit soon became apparent.

[*The cop*] said: 'Ned, I know that I was in the wrong the other night, but you have caused me to front the tribunal over false charges. I will lose my job if something isn't done to retract the accusations before I front the tribunal.'

'I suppose that you expect me to retract the letter that I sent in to the commissioner and the ombudsman do you?'

'That's the general idea, Ned. If you would then I would be grateful.'

'No way will I retract the letter. You put your big head in where it wasn't wanted, so you cop it sweet.'

They both left the hotel and neither of them was smiling. Later, I thought that maybe I should have let him off the hook, but it was too late. I was becoming very unpopular with a lot of the police that had been drinking friends over the years. This incident was another example of putting some cops offside. Much of my problem stemmed from stupid decisions bought on by drink.

21
Betrayal

I heard some mention of Judas. I do not agree with that; it was not fair—to Judas, for whom there is this to be said, that he did not gag the man whom he betrayed, nor did he fail to hang himself afterwards

Prime Minister William Hughes, of Alfred Deakin

Through 1988, I went very quiet in the way of committing crimes. I did armed robberies on two hotels for friends to allow them to claim insurance money. I only got between $30,000 and $40,000, drinking money, out of them. I also did a jewellery robbery as an insurance job. It was set up by [*an ex-policeman*] who took only $10,000 as a spotter's fee (the jewellery was worth at least $600,000 wholesale). After that robbery we celebrated madly—I think every barmaid in town finished up with a nice piece of jewellery that night.

Yet I was being drawn back to the big cash hold-ups. It wasn't as if I needed the money. I was still ripping drugs off people and earning big dollars. There were so many fools around trying to give you the stuff, it was irresistible. Even so, I kept going back to the armed robberies. Perhaps I had a death wish. Perhaps I just loved the adrenalin buzz. And perhaps it was just because it was so bloody easy.

Sometimes I wondered whether some people wanted to be robbed. There were never any precautions taken to prevent people from just walking in off the street and taking the payroll off them. Nine times out of 10 when we went in after a payroll, it would be sitting there staring us in the face, begging to be taken. The most protection I ever encountered during a robbery was the one time the money was in a locked safe—but that didn't prevent us from getting it. Admittedly we always put plenty of work in beforehand.

We left nothing to chance and usually knew more about the place we were going to rob than the people that ran it. But, like everything else, no one does anything to prevent things happening until something happens to that person personally.

Even the armored cars were easy to do if you spent a little time and a few dollars. I'm not writing this book to encourage criminals to do armed robberies, but I must emphasise how slack police and security people are—and have been for years.

Most people in jail are there for petty crimes. Few, if any, have earned a really big dollar, enough to be independent and wake up knowing where the money was coming from. Most crims do things out of desperation, not greed. The real crims never hit the jails—they live the best lives the almighty dollar can provide.

I know simply because I ran with a lot of them over the years and I never saw one of them hit the nick. They usually bought their way out of any trouble they encountered along the way. They avoided violence: violence was strictly a no-no for them.

They are very smart and I respect them for it. These people will more than likely be the only criminals that will be dirty on me for informing on the police, because the time has come when they will have to get out and earn their money and take the same risks as little people. I am sorry it has to be that way, but you can't make an omelette without breaking a lot of eggs.

The magnet of armed robbery drew me back. This time it was the Johnson & Johnson factory and warehouse at Botany. I had spent weeks watching it and it only needed a few finishing touches before being ready to go. It would be worth the effort; there was around $200,000 for the taking. The robbery was a little more complicated than the previous dozen or so I'd participated in. It would be a good exercise to get me thinking again.

The factory entrance was guarded by four security guards who never left the front gate for a second during working hours. They thought it was the only way into the premises. Wrong. There was a back gate not 50 metres from the pay office. Perhaps these people thought that because a gate had a lock on it, no one could gain entry. Hadn't they heard of boltcutters?

I decided that to get in the grounds without attracting too much attention, we needed a van similar to that used by the guards. No one would think of challenging a security van with a 'uniformed' guard.

We bought a panel van and arranged for it to be painted the same way, and got some identical uniforms. The plan was for 'a guard' to drive through the back gate with us waiting in the back of the van. All we needed to do was remove the lock on the gate—and we planned to put our own on after cutting theirs off the night before. Once through the gate 'the guard' would chain the twin gates to the fence so no one could lock them on us if we were discovered. After that he was to drive straight up to the pay office as if checking on something. We would quickly alight from the back of the van, smash open the pay office door with a sledgehammer and, in no time at all, gather up the $200,000 plus and be on our way. Simple.

I contacted [*an ex-policeman was now Smith's link to corrupt police who sanctioned and received payment from armed robberies. We will call this man 'the go-between'*]. He was keen for me to do the robbery, maybe a little bit too keen. I told [*the go-between*] that the coming Thursday was the day. He later OKed the plan. He said it was sweet to go ahead.

On the day of the robbery we got there early. I was suspicious of [*a detective*] and [*the go-between*], so I wanted to spend a few minutes looking to see if anything was out of place. We watched for about 30 minutes: there were no suspicious people lurking, so we got ready to hit the place. We watched the armored van deliver two cash boxes. As it started to leave the grounds, we moved off towards the rear gate. I hadn't told [*the go-between*] how I intended to do the robbery. I just gave him the bare particulars, enough to let him know the place we intended to hit.

We set off. As I drove towards the rear gate I noticed two men dressed as council workers standing beside a big hole in the ground. Each man had a walkie-talkie under his jacket, watching the front entrance. They had not noticed us. It was a set-up to catch us. I'd been right. It wasn't just my paranoia at all. I called the robbery off and we drove away quietly without them knowing we had been there. We put everything away and went on as though nothing was wrong.

I had to see The Dodger. I knew for sure that he wouldn't have been involved in setting us up. I told him what had happened, but he refused to believe that [*the go-between*] had been involved in any set-up.

I went to see [*the go-between*] and confronted him with my suspicions about him and his mate [*the detective*]. He blew up, saying: 'What's up with you, mate, you know me better than that. I am your friend.'

I was still uncertain about [*the go-between*] but, with a mind dulled by drink, I accepted his story and went on working with him.

It wasn't as if I was broke or anything. I didn't have to do any more of these robberies. But I just kept right on doing the same stupid things and getting myself in deeper and deeper trouble. I told myself countless times to get away from the rat race for a while, give my mind time to clear. Drink wasn't interfering with my ability to plan and do the robberies—just my judgment of people and their shifty ways. I trusted people that shouldn't have been trusted with a dog.

Another armed robbery came to light. I'm not sure just who produced this one but I think it came from [*the go-between*] via another cop. All I know was [*the go-between*] said it was easy and worth about $100,000. I still had doubts about the loyalty of [*the go-between*]. I couldn't get the doubt out of my mind.

'How many people know about this robbery you are talking about?'

'Only me and this other guy that has one of the guards sweet. I won't be telling [*the detective*] a thing about it until it's over, then I will fix his team up with a drink [*payment*].'

I told [*the go-between*] that I would get back to him after I'd given it some serious thought. Harold and I discussed it for hours. We weighed up the pros and cons and both came to the conclusion that the things that we'd done in the past outweighed the likelihood of [*the go-between*] doing anything to harm us. He had always pulled his weight before and there was not one shred of evidence to say he wouldn't continue to do so—only my paranoia.

We met [*the go-between*] and told him we would do the robbery on the condition that he did not tell [*the detective*]

until after we'd done it. He agreed, then gave us details of
the job. It was on Duracell Batteries at Ryde. We spent two
weeks looking it over. As always, we went through every
minute detail. It was going to be a walk-up start.

It was a warm morning on 6 October 1988 as we waited,
sweating, in the back of a van for the armored car to deliver
to Duracell. The van drove in and roughly six minutes later
it drove away. They weren't even out of sight before we
drove into the front gate and pulled up out the front of the
building. Three of us jumped out—we were all masked
differently this time. I was the only one to wear a balaclava:
the others had on plastic masks. We were all armed to the
teeth as usual, scanners on our belts with the ear pieces
plugged into our ears to check police movements.

Up the stairs we went, moving quickly. We encountered
a guy in a suit walking up the stairs. We grabbed him and
ushered him up the stairs with us. We reached the pay office;
there were two girls behind desks and one girl in the office
with the money. Harold went for the cash while I kept my
eye out for trouble. We were in and out within 60 seconds.
Minutes later we were in the changeover cars and heading
home to count the money.

The robbery over, I still had to meet [*the go-between*] and
give him the whack for the [*police*]. He was pleased that
everything went down without incident, but had bad news
about [*a policeman Smith did not like*]. [*The policeman*] had
discovered that I had been leaving him out of the whack
over the last few robberies. He wanted to know why. Why
not? [*The policeman*] was complaining about how I was
supposed to have ripped him off over the hash deal [*which
Smith said was untrue*], so why wouldn't I leave him out?

[*The go-between*] was worried about [*the policeman*],
rightly so, too. It later became clear that [*the policeman*]
was out for promotion and wanted nothing directly to do
with me again. He was no longer an ally, but a danger.

Yet I still believed I was untouchable. No one could do
anything to me, not the police, not anyone at all. The
problem was times were changing but I was still living in
the past, living as though Roger and all those other cops
were still running things. I knew that Tony Lauer [*the new
police commissioner*] was now running the show but I
thought that I still had the numbers to hold out.

Life went on as usual for me. I kept on drinking and doing armed robberies. Roger and I still got together often for lunch or a drink. From time to time we got together with the rest of the suspended or sacked cops. I blame no one but myself for what happened to me. I picked my own company, chose my friends—and sometimes they left a lot to be desired.

I drank more and more and ended up in hospital with hepatitis A (not the contagious one). I went a funny yellow color and I couldn't move for a week or more. This was the first time I'd ever been sick or spent more than a day in hospital. The doctors said I'd let my body run down so far that my liver, kidneys and spleen had packed it in on me, all due to excessive use of alcohol and abuse of my body.

There was nothing the doctors could do to cure me; I just had to rest and try to recuperate on my own. I was put on a very strict diet of vegetables, no meat or dairy products at all.

I was shocked when doctors told me I was an alcoholic binge drinker. If I wanted to recover, alcohol was out. 'If you want to commit suicide quickly just have a drink now,' one doctor told me. 'It will be all over for you then, make no mistake about it.'

I spent a few days in hospital recovering. I couldn't handle being there, so I signed myself out and went home to my family for some tender loving care. I got plenty of that. My family looked after me until I was able to get up and fend for myself again.

It was hard not being able to drink. I'd spent the best part of my life drinking and going out to some place or other. What could I do now? Not being able to drink, I started driving my family mad with ravings about alcohol. Often they would have to leave the house to get away from me. I drove them insane for weeks until I learned to control my craving.

I began going to Sydney again. No drinking, but I still frequented the same hotels and restaurants as usual. But no drink. I had just realised that the drink had been my escape from reality. Reality was that there was more to life than running around getting drunk all the time.

Finally, a date was set for my trial on the murder. It was going to cost me plenty for this one. A QC charged anywhere from $5000 to $10,000 per day. Then you had to have a barrister and a solicitor. You couldn't have just the QC without the entourage.

There were a lot of lawyers that were bigger crooks than I was. The only real difference was that I wore a mask and carried a gun when I robbed people: they did it with a few words and a smile—and they did a much better job of getting *all* your money. Perhaps I should have been a lawyer, or a cop, or a politician. They are all basically the same underneath.

Being in need of ready cash to pay for the upcoming trial, I put in a few days looking again at the Johnson & Johnson robbery. We still had all the gear from a few months earlier when we'd pulled out at the last minute. I checked the delivery schedules—they were still the same. I decided to go ahead, so I spoke to [*the go-between*] about it, warning him not tell [*the detective*] about the robbery until after we'd done it. There would be the usual payment for the [*police*].

On the morning of the robbery I arrived early at our meeting place to look around, just being careful. I was walking from the house we were getting ready in—I had to move my car into a side street because the main road turned into a clearway at 7am—when I noticed a guy sitting in the gutter about 60 metres away reading a paper, or making out he was. He was positioned where he could see my car from any angle. Was it my paranoia again? No way. I'd been off the drink for months now. I got into my car and moved it to the other side of the main road where I could watch it and not get a ticket.

As I got out of my car, Harold was waiting for me.

'Listen Ned, when you were walking over to your car I saw this car cruise slowly past you and the four men in it nearly broke their necks looking at you as you walked up the lane. They never missed a step you took.'

Too much of a coincidence to let pass. We discussed it for 20 minutes, then went out and looked for anything unusual. There was nothing.

We decided to go ahead with the robbery as planned. Our 'security van' was out the back and had not been spotted by whoever was watching us. (It turned out the watching police had already gone to take up their positions at Johnson & Johnson, waiting for us to get there.)

Harold and I walked out to a van we had parked out the front. As we did so, we both picked up the same message over the scanners that we had strapped to our waists.

'Dog thirty-two, dog thirty-two, come in. Moving now.'

Then again it came in loud and clear: 'Dog thirty-two, where are you positioned?'

'This is dog thirty-two, we are at the intersection of Cleveland and Chalmers streets, waiting.'

That was where we were. Another 10 yards and we would be sitting on their laps. We were heading right into a trap.

We drove the van around the corner and dumped it there. We hurried back to the house so we could drop off the gear and guns.

We got out of our clothes and into shorts and singlets, walked to my Mercedes and drove away, watching the rear-view mirror to make sure that we were not being followed. The scanner was quiet, not a sound. They had slipped up badly by talking—someone's head would roll for that. After telling the two other guys in on the robbery—they had been waiting in the 'security van'—what had happened, we split up, having arranged to meet later.

I went for a coffee and a think. Was it a deliberate set-up or did they fluke us? It was too well organised to be a fluke. They were there in strength ready to fall on us the minute we looked like doing the robbery. [*The go-between*] was the only other person that knew about the robbery; it had to be him. But what I didn't know at the time was that a so-called 'friend' of mine had found out about the robbery plan and informed on us.

While watching the Johnson & Johnson factory, I'd spotted another payroll worthy of our attention. It looked very easy: two guards carried two extremely large tins into the pay office, stayed only a matter of a few minutes, then left, leaving one woman to protect the money.

Now this woman was a little bit security conscious. As soon as the guards deposited the money, she would check it and, while they were still there, would securely lock the payroll in the office safe. This may have eased her mind about the money being safer, but it made little difference to us. If she could put the money into the safe, she could just get it back out again and give it to us.

We discussed this robbery. Taking the money right out

from under the noses of the police appealed to both of us. We'd show those arseholes they weren't as smart as they thought they were. We'd take the payroll while they sat around the corner waiting for us to rob the place they were watching. Of course, the police would know beyond any doubt who'd done the robbery. So what! Didn't they know that I was responsible for well over a dozen other big armed robberies and what did they do about them? Absolutely nothing.

Their hands were tied by the fact that they couldn't or weren't game to load me up [*plant evidence*]. Without loading me they had to catch me actually doing the robbery in person.

The Davis Gelatin factory payroll was our target and on 3 November 1988 we hit it. We waited until the payroll had been delivered by Armaguard and, as they drove out, we drove in. This had given the woman sufficient time to put the money inside the safe and lock the door.

It was so easy. We got out of the back of the van masked up and armed, all ready to go. In we went. Harold's job was to take care of the woman with the key to the safe, get the money and leave the rest to me and the other guy. Our job was to gather everyone up and secure the rest of the premises. The only problem was that Harold had miscalculated the number of people who would be in the office. According to his calculations, there would be four people. By the time I finished gathering them up I had counted 30. I had them all lying on the floor when Harold came out of the inner office carrying two pay tins. So far so good. Things were going smoothly enough—until we got outside to the getaway car. There was smoke everywhere. The driver for this one was only new to the game and had revved the guts out of the car, nearly burning out the clutch. Still, we managed to get out of the area OK. But it wasn't over yet.

As soon as we got to the changeover car, the guy doing the driving had problems finding the key. Where had I found this guy? We were running behind schedule, especially with the cops sitting just around the corner all ready to go. It wouldn't take them very long to realise what had gone down and mobilise their squad.

The scanners were blaring about four men robbing the Davis Gelatin payroll at Botany and calling for every police officer in the area to respond. I was in a rage over this driver fucking up. He had put us all in danger by not doing exactly as I told him, but I was the one that had picked him for the job.

Finally he found the key and we were on our way. Everyone was a bit nervous as we sat in the back of the van waiting to see if they were on to us. I felt like blowing up at the driver, but I couldn't afford to as it might set the guy off into a panic. So I just sat there—and not too patiently at all.

After 15 minutes, we arrived at the safe house. My luck had held out once more. We all sighed with relief as the driver stopped the car and we got out. The scanners were still humming madly. Some cops had thrown discretion to the winds and were talking openly about the robbery and even mentioned us by the code names they had labelled us with.

Naturally, the driver was an out-of-work driver straight away. He never got another start with anyone. He retired from the rat race.

We may have escaped from the scene, but we had less luck with the takings. We discovered that we had hit them on an off week and one of the tins was empty. The money we finished with was only the overtime pay: after taking out $10,000 for [*the go-between*] we whacked up roughly $60,000 between four of us. Not a good day at all.

I saw [*the go-between*] and gave him the $10,000. He wasn't impressed with me one bit. The taskforce were going mad about me pulling the robbery off right under their noses. They knew it was me, and couldn't do a thing. They just had to sit still and hope that they would get lucky soon. [*The go-between*] was also getting very paranoid about me. He was aware that I was watching him closely because I didn't trust him any more.

Soon after the Davis Gelatin robbery, I noticed that the number of police watching me seemed to double. Everywhere I looked there were police—and they were not attempting to hide the fact they were watching me. That could mean one of two things. One, they were ready to pinch me and didn't want to risk losing me by not having enough cops watching my every move. Or two, they wanted me to see the extra surveillance in the hope that it would make me panic and do something silly.

Those were the only two conclusions I could come up with. But it didn't worry me. I still knew every move the taskforce was making. Or so I thought.

22
Back Inside

'You, in the back of the van ... Come out or we will commence firing...'

Police to Smith and accomplice

I met Roger, [*the go-between*] and [*an ex-policeman*] at a pub. I still wasn't drinking. We got talking and the subject of the Christmas holiday payrolls came up.

I had expected them to get around to this and was ready for it.

'What's happening for Christmas, mate? Anything going off or have you taken an early holiday?' That was Roger and his sense of humor again. He always managed to find something to laugh about no matter how serious the conversation was.

'Nothing special this year.' I refused to be drawn into the conversation. I wasn't telling [*the go-between*] anything. They ended up with the shits because I wouldn't confide in them. All I told them was that I would be working over Christmas, and there would be the usual drink for the [*police*] if I was successful.

As far as I was concerned I still had the Green Light. [*The go-between*] would pay the [*police*] and I would never be charged. It never struck me that the Green Light was fading: not even after the attempt to set me up by the young cops, or the fact we were almost pinched by the 'council workers' at Johnson & Johnson. I just didn't want to believe it, so I carried on regardless.

Days later, I was cruising around when I came across a van picking up a large payroll: two guards putting two wooden trays into a van. The lids were off the trays and the pay envelopes were clearly visible. It was the Botany Council payroll.

We had two weeks before the Christmas delivery; the fortnight's wages plus three weeks holiday pay. Yes Sir, that would do nicely.

I made the usual arrangement about cars. Harold was on holiday, so this time I was going in with two new blokes. One, Glen Flack, was very experienced, but the other, Richard, was a first-timer. He had never even broken the law before.

We got the gear we needed: identical tracksuits, balaclavas, gloves and scanners. Two stolen cars were used on this one: a stationwagon and a van.

The plan was to park the van outside the council chambers where the armored van pulled up. As soon as the guards took the money tins out of the van, we would jump from the back of the van and grab the payroll. Richard was to wait in the wagon across the street. As soon as we signalled him he would pick us up.

First, he parked the van with Glen and me in the back outside the chambers. Then he went to wait in the stationwagon, leaving what looked like an empty van: blacked out windows in the back meant Glen and I could not be seen. We kept in touch by walkie-talkie because our view from the back of the van was restricted, so Richard was our eyes.

But all the planning and all our modern gear was of no value to us this time. The police had been tipped off about the robbery. They were aware that we were listening to their transmissions so they sent false messages to confuse us. Whoever tipped them off (and I later discovered who it was) had told them how we did things—we never had a chance.

The armored van pulled up. The guards got out and started to get the tins. Just as I was about to pull the door open and take the money from the two guards—it would have been over in seconds—a voice called out: 'You, in the back of the van. It's the police here. Put down your weapons and come out of the van with your hands raised above your heads.'

I paused for a second. I couldn't believe this was happening. 'Come out or we will commence firing into the van.'

It was the worst feeling I had ever had, like getting caught with your trousers down, so to speak.

It wasn't fear I felt, but disgust at being caught. Trying to escape was useless. We were in the back of a van with no driver and no way out except through the side door—and outside the door were about 30 armed cops. We had little choice but to put our hands above our heads, get out and face the music.

I slid open the door, put my hands above my head and we got out. There were at least a dozen shotguns pointed at us. Guns were pushed up against our heads. One cop was nearly frothing at the mouth, he pressed his pump action shotgun up against my neck so hard. He was really uptight.

'You weak cunt, why don't you have a go so I can kill you?'

He was in a bad way.

We were thrown to the ground and handcuffed behind our backs. A shotgun was again pressed against my neck and my hands pulled up as far as they would stretch. Then one low arsehole started to kick me in the face. He was screaming at me all the time: 'You fucking maggot, now I've got you. It's taken me 10 years, now I've got you.'

The boss of the SWOS team came over and stopped the crazy cop from kicking me in the face. Then the police started going silly, hugging each other, jumping up and down, slapping their hands together and yelling: 'You fucking beauty, we have got Neddy Smith.'

That was a bit much, I thought. Who were they expecting? John Dillinger or someone?

(I found out later that some of them thought I only planned the robberies and didn't participate in them personally.)

I was also told later by [*one of the arresting police*] that they had been planning to kill me, shoot me dead. The idea was that once we took the guards, they would just knock [*kill*] us. Roger and [*two ex-policemen*] later told me the same thing: I knew too much, so I had to go.

I didn't know it at the time, but a council worker who brought his video camera to work to film the office Christmas party had saved my life. He filmed the whole arrest. The police had spotted him, so instead of waiting for us to grab the guards—so they could shoot us—they decided to get us before we got out of the back of the parked van.

Bad luck, guys. If I'd been killed there wouldn't be these problems. You fucked up badly and now it's payback time, time for you to lie in a cell alone at night wondering what your wife and children are doing, if they are being looked after, and if they have enough money to get by on. What goes around comes around. And you arseholes are about to go around!

I was driven back to the city. The police centre was like a zoo—and I was the only animal attracting visitors. The only difference between me and real animals was I didn't get any peanuts for my performance.

The police were continually photographing me. One fool of a policeman tried to get me to pose for a photo with him. He stood beside me, then went to put his arm on my shoulder. 'Fuck off fool, I'm not a fucking trophy.'

He didn't like that, but he did nothing.

Before long, my solicitor, Val Bellamy, arrived. But I knew I didn't need him, I was finally at the end of my road. There was no way I could get this blue fixed up, no way at all.

I was taken down to the charge-room and formally charged with the armed robbery, and several other offences. Glen and Richard were already in separate cells. They put me in with Glen and left Richard in one across from us. I felt sorry for Richard being one-out [*by himself*] at a time like this. You need someone to talk to on your first night in the cells. It is the lowest feeling in the world.

They kept us at the police centre for a few days. On Christmas Day I was transferred to Long Bay.

I knew what I was in for—I had already been in the state's toughest jails. But I was not going to let them get the better of me. Jail does funny things to a person's mind if you let it get hold of you. I knew I had to get my mind right or I would end up going off my head. I could handle it; I just had to withdraw into myself and mind my own business.

When I arrived at the remand centre I looked about me: same place, same people. Every time I came to jail, nothing changed. I knew that this place, or one very similar, was to be my home for many years to come. It was not a nice thought to ponder on.

I spent the next year going back and forth to court. I pleaded guilty to the armed robbery and was sentenced to 13 years with an eight-year non-parole period. I was happy with the result as it would not mean the end for my family. The Crown was far from happy and appealed against the leniency of my sentence. They were unsuccessful. Next, I faced the big one: the murder charge.

Despite being convicted of the armed robbery and the fact I was now a sentenced prisoner, I was allowed to remain at the remand centre. The conditions there were much better, especially visits. At the remand centre you get anywhere from two hours up to all day if time permits, rather than just the 30 minutes with your family that most other jails allow.

It is very difficult to keep a family together inside, so visits play a very big part in your chances of managing to do that. The visits were my only reason for wanting to remain at the remand centre.

I spent all of my time thinking. My mind was clear for the first time in years. The alcohol was almost out of my system and my thinking became very sharp. They had possession of my body, but not my mind. I would always have my thoughts to retreat to if the going got tough.

My spare time was spent reading law books. I still had a murder charge to front on and my solicitor, Val Bellamy, had been very conspicuous by his absence. He rarely came to see me, and when he did, he used to stay for only a few minutes each time. [*This was only one problem Smith faced in his preparation for his trial. His hope of employing the barrister Greg James fell through. Plans to employ another barrister, Patrick Costello, also collapsed. Smith sacked his next barrister. Finally, he employed a legal representative who saw the trial through.*]

My trial was a farce designed to get me out of the way for a long time, and they succeeded in doing just that. I should have been acquitted of the murder charge regardless of whether I did it or not. The Crown case failed miserably to *prove* I had anything to do with it. Everyone kept telling me I had won. The jury had other ideas. They were only out a short time when they returned with a verdict of guilty of the murder of Flavell. I wasn't the least bit surprised as I knew from the word go that I had no chance of a fair trial.

I may be down, but I'm far from being out and I will prove my innocence if it takes the rest of my life.

The rest is history.

I was sentenced to life. The judge put on a good show for the media when he passed sentence. Over the next few days the media gave me hell, printing any shit they could make up, none of it anywhere near the truth.

I was transferred to Parklea Jail in Sydney's western suburbs. Parklea was unlike any other jail I'd seen. Each cell had its own shower and you could cook your own food.

But Michael Yabsley [*the NSW Corrective Services Minister*] soon put a stop to that. He wanted to make a name for himself so he decided to put on a media show by confiscating all our private belongings. He certainly managed to stir up trouble at all the jails.

At first the trouble was only minor, like stopwork meetings. Then it got right out of hand. One afternoon I was returning to my cell from a family visit. As I walked across the square I noticed that it was deserted. That wasn't normal. Every visiting day a group of guys would hang around waiting for prisoners to come back from their visits—they'd grab them and search them for drugs. If they found any they would take them. It was a regular thing, every week.

This day, there was no one anywhere.

I continued on my way to the wing: all the crims were in their cells. Some were masked up and all were armed with iron bars or knives.

'What's going on? Who is going off?'

They all laughed nervously. 'Time to show Yabsley who is running this joint once and for all.'

They all sat there grinning. I went to my cell. I wanted no part of this. I'd had my share of rioting at Bathurst Jail. I put the TV on to watch the Grand Final. One of the young guys came to my cell: 'When the half-time hooter goes off, we go off too! We are going to wreck this joint. We'll show Yabsley who runs things here.'

I smiled at him: 'Listen mate, have you asked yourself how many of your mates will be there when the bashings start?' I'd experienced rioter solidarity before; I knew what to expect from the majority of the crims—they would shit as soon as the riot squad got there.

The half-time hooter went off and so did the jail. It didn't last too long as someone had warned the screws, but in the short time it lasted they caused millions of dollars damage. They did what they said they would.

The riot squad arrived, tear gas was fired in and the bashings began. It didn't take long for them to gain control of the prison again. They put us together in a small yard, then into cells, four to a cell. Each cell had only one steel bed, no mattress. The screws also hosed out the cells to make us more comfortable.

The screws then went from cell to cell smashing all the TV sets and electrical gear, no one was left out. We were kept locked up for a week, then I was transferred back to the Bay.

While I was back at the Bay, Graham 'Abo' Henry arrived. He had just been sentenced to eight years for stabbing Malcolm Spence, a police prosecutor. [*'Abo' Henry stabbed Sergeant Malcolm Spence outside the Lord Wolseley Hotel in Ultimo in December 1988, only days before Smith was arrested and charged over the failed armed robbery. 'Abo' Henry appealed against his subsequent conviction and sentence. In October 1992 his appeal was dismissed. According to a report in the* Sydney Morning Herald *by reporter Sandra Harvey, Henry refused to say during his original trial why he had stabbed Spence. But before the Court of Criminal Appeal, 'he revealed that he met Sergeant Spence to recoup a $50,000 deposit he claimed Spence had been paid to fix the murder trial of the notorious Sydney criminal Arthur Neddy Smith'.*]

While Abo and I were at the Bay, Tom Domican arrived from another jail. Abo didn't know him and I didn't really know him either, although I'd met him a few times. I wanted nothing to do with the man. He used to talk too much and always ended up getting himself, and whoever was in his company, emptied [*transferred*] to some other jail.

For the rumor-mongers, and just to put the record straight, I will tell the story about the confrontation I had with Tom Domican in Long Bay. [*Details of the fight, in early May 1991, were published in Sydney's* Sun-Herald.]

Tom came to see me and we talked. He seemed to accept the fact I didn't want anything to do with him and just walked away.

For a few days all was quiet. Tom was bothering everybody else except me. That suited me fine, until Abo got into Tom's company and Tom started to bag me to Abo.

After lunch one day, I was walking up and down trying to get the stiffness out of my limbs—that's the biggest problem I have, trying to loosen my muscles up. With this disease I have, I am always getting stiff muscles.

Abo came over to walk with me and started talking about Tom Domican. 'Mate, you should hear the shit that Tom is going on about. He's not a full quid.'

I told Abo to watch himself with Tom. 'You'll end up in deep shit hanging around with him. I'm telling you now, mate, avoid the man, he's bad news.'

Abo walked up and down once or twice, then said: 'Mate, I have to tell you something.'

I just kept walking. He said: 'Promise you won't repeat what I tell you?'

I had no idea what he was about to tell me, so I agreed.

'Ned, I was talking to Tom about the 'Gang Wars'. He reckons that you made a statement to the police about him trying to run you over.'

I blew up. 'What did you fucking say?'

I headed straight over to find Domican and front him. Abo followed me, saying: 'You promised that you wouldn't say anything. Come on mate, you will get me in the shit.'

I didn't care about any promise. I was going to put Domican on his arse for saying that I gave him up. I headed straight for him. He saw me and stood still, waiting. As I got near him I couldn't contain myself: 'Hey, you fucking big-mouthed cunt, get over here. I want to talk to you.'

He walked straight towards me, snarling. We met in the middle of the square and we were both ready to go on with it. Abo stood there waiting to see what happened.

Being the nice easy-going smooth-talker that I'm not, I cut into Tom right away. 'Listen here, you big-mouthed dog, did you tell Abo that I gave you up?'

He looked at Abo and said: 'You got it wrong, mate. I said that's what the police had told me.'

I was all hyped up. I was going to fight him regardless of what he said. I didn't like him anyway, and it was about time we saw just how good he was. If he was half as good as he thought, I was in for a tough treat.

'You're nothing but a big-mouthed dog.' I went to throw a left hook, but Abo was in the way blocking me.

Tom realised it was on no matter what he said. I just wanted to prove to myself and everyone that I had not told on anyone—and that Tom wasn't as tough as everyone thought he was. He had bluffed the whole prison system for too long with his boisterous ways and his shit talk about killing this one and that one.

'Get over to the wing, you dog. We will get two-out [*two people together*] locked in a cell and we will see just how tough you are.'

Tom wasn't the slightest bit worried. He must have believed all the shit he told everyone. 'We'll see who comes out of the cell,' he said.

Well, I must say, the guy had plenty of confidence. It was a pity he didn't have the ability to match it.

As we walked to the wing I was getting hyped up. I told myself that Tom was not coming out of the cell alive. Rage was building inside my guts.

When we got to the gate, Tom said: 'No way am I going in the cell. Let's do it here.'

I was standing with my back to him at the gate and the last thing that I can clearly remember is spinning around and knocking Tom flying. He hit the ground with a thud. The rest is a bit of a blank.

I've heard so many different versions of the fight that I don't rightly know what happened.

All I know is that he kept getting up and I kept knocking him back down. After about eight knockdowns he failed to get up. He never hit me once. He kicked me once, but that was the extent of it. They took him to hospital and patched him up.

There have been plenty of rumors about what happened that day. Tom said I king-hit him. Well, I did throw the first punch. Someone has to, don't they? And apart from that, all I have to say is that Tom sure had a lot of people bluffed for a hell of a long time without one ounce of ability to back it up.

I do expect that one day Tom may attempt to back-up with something in his hand. Good on him. I will have nothing but respect for him if he does, but let me tell him now: I won't just be copping it. We all bleed and he doesn't have a monopoly on backing-up or violence.

I will keep my eyes open. And maybe he should keep his mouth shut.

23
Payback Time

*'Neddy, do you realise what you are saying?
This is going to be huge.'*

ICAC officer to Smith

I ran into Roy Thurgar in the Bay. We had been on opposite sides during the 'Gang Wars' in Sydney—he was one of Barry McCann's minders—but that had been strictly business, nothing more. We talked and agreed that what had taken place outside should stay outside.

Roy was a nice guy, funny, but naive as far as the workings of cops went. He still believed that if you didn't commit the crime you would be found not guilty.

Roy had already talked to the Independent Commission Against Corruption [*the ICAC*], telling them especially about [*one particular police officer*].

We discussed his plans—and about what could be done about the low police. They had had everything their way for too long: they ran roughshod over us; they loaded us; they verballed us; they got other crims to give false evidence against us; they did whatever they wanted—and we were expected to cop it sweet. It was time someone did something about it.

For several months I'd been thinking about doing something myself, partly because the police had tried to set me up and kill me to keep me quiet, but also because certain police failed to help me beat the murder or the armed robbery blue. Sure, a few police came to see me in jail, but not to help me out—they just wanted to make sure I hadn't given them up.

But most importantly, they'd abandoned Debra. I'd been

running around with these guys for years, going to their homes. They'd been to my home. Our kids were friends. Our wives were friends. Yet not one of them asked Debra if she wanted anything, or whether they could help. None of them helped my family: they didn't give Debra two cents. When they were in trouble I'd kept their wives and paid their lawyers. They didn't even have to ask me. But now I was in trouble, there was nothing.

Roy Thurgar and I were talking over a cup of tea one morning when Roy said: 'Listen mate, you've had the Green Light with the heavy set for years, everyone knows that. You must know a heap about them that we can use to bring them undone.'

I agreed with him, but told him: 'You can't take these cunts too lightly, mate. They won't stop at killing you if you try to upset their little goes.'

I explained to Roy how dangerous it was to fuck with them, but he wanted to go on.

'OK, mate. I will think seriously about helping you and I'll let you know. OK?'

I went to my cell deep in thought. I had lodged an appeal against my life sentence and murder conviction. I was sure that my appeal was going to be successful. I wanted to wait until my appeal was heard before I did anything serious about the police. But I still wanted to help Roy. [*Smith's initial appeal was rejected, and he went on to help the ICAC. However, a subsequent appeal to the High Court of Australia was heard in June 1993. The appeal, Smith's last hope of overcoming his murder conviction, was rejected. 'Life', in Smith's case, will mean life.*]

Next morning I told Roy I was at least willing to talk to the ICAC. Roy and I wrote to the ICAC asking them to visit me as I wanted to talk to them. I stipulated no state police were welcome. The reason for the no-state-police clause was because I knew that if I was to have any success at all I would have to keep it quiet or it would be a waste of time—and probably the end of my life.

I heard nothing for more than a month, and thought they weren't interested in what I might have to say. (I've since learned that the ICAC are slow about everything they do.)

One morning the governor called me to his office. 'Neddy,

there are two cops from the ICAC here to see you. You don't have to see them if you don't want to.'

I thought: This is it. Are you going to stick your neck out, break all the rules that you have lived by all your life? The answer was Yes.

'It's OK, governor. I asked them to come to see me.'

I went into an office and saw two plain-looking guys standing there, looking nervous. I didn't know either of them. We introduced ourselves, shook hands and sat down. One was Tim Robinson (he always used to say to me: 'Trust me, Ned'). I can't recall the other guy's name. He didn't stay long on the investigation anyway.

Tim started the conversation: 'Neddy, we are here because you wrote to us. We are interested in anything you may wish to tell us.'

I'll bet you are, I thought.

'Listen,' I said. 'There are a few things I want to clear up first.'

Trust-me-Tim said: 'Like what?'

Here we go, I thought. It's now or never. 'First, what squads do you belong to and what is your position now?'

That was first on the agenda. Trust-me-Tim said: 'I was with the Australian Federal Police for years. I have been involved in several cases investigating your activities. I am now deputy director of operations with the ICAC.'

I nodded: 'That's fine.'

The other cop hesitated, before saying: 'I am state police, I was with the NSW homicide squad but now I am an investigator with the ICAC.'

I blew up. 'What's this shit? I stipulated no state police be involved with anything to do with me.'

I got up and left them sitting there. On the way out I said: 'If you still want to talk, come back without the state police.'

In the meantime I checked Trust-me-Tim out—and he had indeed been involved in several investigations into my affairs.

A few weeks passed before Trust-me-Tim put in his second appearance. This time he had a security officer for the ICAC with him who was also an ex-Fed. As it turned out, he too had been involved in several investigations into me.

At first, I'd planned to just help Roy by giving them some information on [*the police officer Thurgar had told the*

ICAC about]. Then I decided to tell them about the Flavell murder—I wanted them to reinvestigate it. And finally, I just decided, 'Payback Time'.

We sat down and I gave them a short run-down on what I wanted to reveal. I kept it short because I wasn't sure whether these two would continue the inquiry, or whether some other cops would take over.

They tried to make out that they were only slightly interested, but I could see the excitement on Trust-me-Tim's face. He knew this was going to be the biggest thing since sliced bread.

Trust-me-Tim suggested I talk to the ICAC director, Peter Lamb, in town at the ICAC offices. I agreed.

A week later I was taken to the ICAC headquarters to see Peter Lamb. He introduced himself and started what was obviously a prepared speech. I let him finish before saying: 'How long did that speech take to prepare?'

He laughed. 'Let's just skip the shit and get down to the fact that you want to talk.'

I nodded: 'OK, that suits me.'

'Now Neddy, Tim has given me a rough idea of what you claim to have. Can you back up what you are saying with any facts or proof?'

I told him I could. For the next three hours I talked about what I knew, and had done, with members of New South Wales' finest. Peter Lamb just sat there taking it all in. When I rested for a drink, he said: 'Neddy, do you realise what you are saying? This is going to be huge. I have to have time to digest it all. We'll stop for now and I will see you next week.'

I was taken back to the Bay, and once there I spoke to Roy about what had taken place.

It wasn't long before they had me back in town again. I had whetted their appetites somewhat.

Peter Lamb saw me again: 'Listen Neddy, I have checked out several things you said and found them to be true. We want to proceed with the rest of your story, but first, do you realise what you are getting into? Your family will have to be put somewhere safe in some secret location.'

I knew what I had started—and I was willing to go through to the end. As long as Peter Lamb kept his word, looked after my family and honored his promises.

Roy Thurgar was pleased that I'd moved against the coppers. We became good friends until he was released from jail [*in December 1990*] and murdered.

[*Five months after Thurgar's release, in May 1991, he was killed by one shotgun blast to the head as he sat in his car outside a laundromat in Alison Road, Randwick. He had opened the laundromat business with his wife six weeks earlier. Two men were charged with his murder and acquitted. The Crown claimed the pair murdered Thurgar because he planned to rip off $1 million of hashish; the key Crown witness was a police informer. During the trial, evidence was presented showing a letter written to the ICAC by Thurgar three months before his murder, in which he claimed police were planning to kill him and that he was the target of an alleged murder conspiracy headed by a Detective Inspector John Davidson.*]

I had many meetings over the next 18 months with the ICAC, and I revealed some startling facts to them.

It didn't take them long to realise how big this was. They gave me complete indemnity against prosecution [*of state offences*] on everything except murder. That didn't cause me any problem because I have never murdered anyone.

After 18 months of questioning I finally got to appear before the commission at a private hearing in front of Ian Temby [*the ICAC commissioner. Temby is a Queen's Counsel and former federal Director of Public Prosections.*] I gave evidence on two separate days, but only for very short sessions.

I didn't get to mention half the evidence I had given the ICAC investigators. Ian Temby kept the inquiry very quiet once the investigation started.

[*It was not until August 1992 that details of Smith's allegations became public. More than three months later, on Thursday, 3 December 1992, Smith made his first public appearance at the commission's hearings. It was to be the first of many that made front-page headlines. For Neddy Smith, however, it had been far from plain sailing.*]

I am beginning to regret having ever gone to the ICAC. They are the lowest group of unscrupulous people I have ever had anything to do with. They don't keep their word. What little confidence I had in them, I lost long ago. They are the most deceitful, dishonest team of people I have met in my lifetime.

My wife has been confronted by detectives while sitting at a bus stop with our children and threatened with physical violence if she didn't tell me to stop talking to the ICAC.

What did the ICAC do about that?

Very little. They upset my family's lives by moving them from motel to motel for months, but they did nothing about the police who had harassed my family.

The ICAC put hidden cameras around my house that took photographs of these people coming to my home. Still no action. Next, the walls of my house were painted with foul language: the ICAC did nothing except take notes.

So my family was put into the witness protection scheme. They were promised that my children's work and schooling would not suffer. My wife was told she would be compensated for loss of income. She was told the family would be looked after until they were independent or I was released from jail.

Not one of these things was done. My daughter missed out on sitting for her HSC. My oldest son lost his job, and was promised another job once he was relocated. Nothing. Debra lost her job and received no compensation at all.

But the worst incident was when my wife and family were leaving jail after visiting me. My wife and three kids were in one car with a federal policeman, followed by an escort car. They drove through the boom gate manned by four prison officers and, as soon as they turned into the road, a police car that had been waiting across the street tried to run Debra off the road and pull her up.

The federal cop driving Debra and the kids knew straight away that my family was in grave danger and took off at high speed with the cop car in pursuit. He got straight on to his escort car. The escort had seen someone trying to intercept my family.

The escort car eventually managed to force the cops on to the side of the road, allowing my family time to escape. When the two cops in the NSW police car discovered these men were Feds, they didn't know what to say. There was an inquiry into their behaviour and it was accepted by the federal police and the ICAC that the cops thought they had been justified in chasing the car containing my family because they had been under the impression that it was stolen. What a load of shit.

My family was then shifted interstate, but they could not cope with the treatment they got. My wife and kids were allowed to see me for only two hours once a month. Ordinary prisoners got two visits a week.

My wife and children decided, to hell with the police harassing them. Debra couldn't stand the thought of letting the police run her out of her home, so she and the kids left the witness protection program. They are still frightened of the cops, but at least they have friends to help them and they don't have to put their lives in the hands of the ICAC.

The ICAC reckon they're squeaky clean, but they've got no hope of competing with the state police who are streetwise and corrupt. They claim to be corruption fighters, but they lack experience—and many still have mates they went through the NSW police academy with. They leave things too late to check: they've lost so much documentation through leaving things until too late. And they've got a leak.

Meanwhile I am still helping them with their inquiry into corruption and organised crime in the police force, even though they are never content. It is gimme, gimme all the time.

And I'm giving because I'd like people to know what they've really got in this country. Most of the public are like sheep. They don't look up, they don't know what's going on—and they don't want to know. It's about time they found out.

One day in jail in 1991 Graham 'Abo' Henry and I discussed the ICAC—and I discovered that Abo was also talking to them.

We agreed that we were nothing more than a means for the ICAC to further itself, and that they had no feelings for the safety or care of our families, an opinion that I still have today. And I don't look like changing my opinion, ever.

The ICAC have stuck Abo and I in this shithouse of a place [*a segregated protection area in Long Bay Jail*] until the hearings are over, so that no crim can get at us and verbal either of us by saying: 'He told me such and such.'

And talking of crims, I want to say something to the crims out there: most of you have been crying about what the police have been doing all your lives, but you've done nothing about it. Abo and I are doing something, and all you want to do is bag us for doing what you guys haven't got the guts to do.

Regardless of what the media says about me, I am not giving *any* evidence about *any* crims in or out of jail.

The police are using the media to try and turn everyone against me, but it doesn't bother me one bit. I'll be there if any big mouths want to see me some time in the future. I have never walked away from any man and I never will.

Postscript 1

Smith is a very large man and is obviously intelligent although relatively uneducated. He is a man of strong presence and, to my eye, had a dignity about him which was not enjoyed by many of the other witnesses.

Ian Temby QC, ICAC Commissioner,
first report on corruption, February 1994

For more than a decade, Neddy Smith has been in jail, yet rarely has he been out of the headlines. In the months before this book was first published in mid-1993, Smith's revelations to the ICAC reverberated through Australia. He took to the witness box for days on end telling of drinks, bribes, bashings, drugs, robberies and corruption. Not surprisingly, much of his testimony was attacked as dubious by counsel for police, and dismissed. But in February 1994, any complacency evaporated when Ian Temby's first report – based on 146 witnesses who produced 12,857 pages of evidence – produced adverse findings against numerous police. Temby said police misconduct was "a lot worse than any of us imagined and a lot worse than any of us would be prepared to tolerate".

Temby said Smith's main allegation – that he was given police protection from 1976 and a green light from 1981 – was true. Barry Toomey, QC, counsel assisting the inquiry, said phone taps recorded by Federal Police backed many of Smith's claims and were very strongly corroborative and never contradictory.

But Smith had other problems. Within months of the ICAC findings, a police operation dubbed Taskforce Snowy began investigating more than a dozen unsolved murders – and Neddy Smith was the target. It leaked information to the media about a cell mate of Smith's, about the exhumation of Sallie-Anne Huckstepp's body, and the discovery of human remains on a beach. Smith was interviewed and ultimately charged, in

August 1995, with the murders of Lewton Shu (January 1983) and Bruce Sandery (April 1988).

Six months later, Smith was facing seven murder charges. The other alleged victims were: Danny Chubb (November 1984); Sallie-Anne Huckstepp (February 1986); Barry Croft (August 1987); Barry McCann (December 1987); and Harvey Jones (March 1995).

As the murder charges were laid, the rest of Australia discovered Smith's activities through the ABC television drama *Blue Murder*. The show won the 1996 Logie for best TV drama, and was screened in every state except New South Wales (and not shown until 2001) because Smith was facing murder charges and to broadcast it in NSW exposed the ABC to contempt of court charges.

In August 1996, four of the murder charges against Smith (Chubb, Sandery, Croft and McCann) were dismissed by a magistrate because of insufficient evidence. But in September 1998 a jury convicted Smith of the murder of Harvey Jones – a crime Smith still denies. In 1999 he was acquitted of Huckstepp's murder, and then the charges of killing Shu were effectively dropped.

Yet Smith was still linked to deaths. The NSW coroner heard allegations that Smith strangled model, cocaine dealer and gambler Mark Johnston, 36, in 1986, in the home of solicitor Val Bellamy. He was not charged. Again in 2000, Smith's name came up in relation to two deaths: the killing of former model Lyn Woodward in 1981 (a coroner was told she was shot dead by Roger Rogerson before Smith buried the body); and the disappearance of lawyer Brian Alexander. Again, Smith was not charged.

In June 2001, Smith's hopes of release from jail seemed to evaporate. He was refused leave to appeal to the High Court on the Harvey Jones murder conviction, meaning he faced two life sentences with nowhere, legally, to go. Yet Neddy Smith, who is sick with Parkinson's disease, is still fighting.

Tom Noble, August 2002

Postscript 2

"I will try my hardest not to die in jail but I might not have any luck in picking where I die."

Neddy Smith

Since I wrote this book back in 1993 my life has been one huge balls up. I have no one but myself to blame for the things that have happened to me.

My life began its downhill slide while I was writing this book and has gone from bad to worse over the past years. It is as if I was deliberately trying to self-destruct. I can't explain it, I don't know why, but nothing I did went the way it was supposed to. Every single thing that I undertook turned out bad. With no exceptions.

My first error of judgment was to become involved with the ICAC. I should never have approached them in the first place - and when I did I found out some of the mistakes they were making. I should have bailed straight out and left them to their own devices. They weren't really interested in exposing the corruption or cleaning out the crooked cops from the New South Wales police force. When I realised this I should have got out while I was still in front. But for some idiotic reason I hung in there hoping that they would prove me wrong and that all the shit I had copped in the media and the six years-plus that I spent locked away in solitary confinement wouldn't be a waste of time.

It didn't take me long to see that the ICAC were only really interested in getting as much mileage out of me and as much publicity as they could. They were a new law enforcement body, an unknown quantity, on trial to see if it would be worth the effort and the huge expense of keeping them going. They needed a big case first-up to show the government and the public that they were a force to be reckoned with. Well, they certainly got what they were after.

No amount of money could have bought the media coverage they got by cashing in on me and the investigation into the

NSW police. I was used up by ICAC and discarded like an old sock once they decided that I was no longer a good proposition and of no more value. It didn't take me long to discover that s\ome of those at ICAC had neither the experience or the ability for what was a huge investigation. They got off to a bad start, making the mistake of selecting people from the Australian Federal Police and NSW state police to investigate NSW police. I couldn't believe it. They chose men from they very same police force they intended investigating. How on earth did the ICAC intend to do the job asking police to investigate their friends or people they went to the academy with? That was their first mistake and they made many more. After two years the investigation came to an abrupt halt and the investigation was handed over to a royal commission on corruption. That was a move in the right direction.

But regardless of the ICAC and royal commission, nothing has changed as far as corruption goes. If anything, the only thing that has changed is that the NSW police have tightened their ranks and are refusing to let anyone infiltrate them the way I did. The corruption still goes on exactly like it has for decades. I doubt very much if anyone could ever get rid of the corruption in the NSW force.

While this investigation was going on I was placed in the special purpose centre against my will. They claimed that my life was in danger and I ended up spending just over seven years incarcerated in there. For practically the whole seven years I was in solitary confinement, never seeing or talking to anyone apart from prison officers, and my family on weekends when they came to visit me. The only time that I wasn't in solitary confinement was when they put me in a two-out situation with a registered informer who had just been brought down from Goulburn Jail to give evidence against another prisoner for murder. I knew that he had been deliberately planted on me by the police to find out whatever information he could. In fact, as soon as they moved me into the two-out unit I contacted (Smith names a law enforcement officer) who told me the guy was a registered informer and had been planted to try and find evidence about the information I gave to ICAC.

Straight away I let this dog know that I had run a check on him. He was under no illusions where he stood with me. After spending months with this dog I decided to feed him a load of bullshit, knowing that he wouldn't be able to help himself and relate to the cops all the bullshit I had been feeding him. This went on for months. The cops even started visiting daily to get progress reports. I was having a ball. But I outsmarted myself because the cops managed to get a special taskforce set up to investigate the crap I was feeding them and, to cut through all the crap, I was charged with seven counts of murder.

The hearing into the seven counts was heard by Magistrate Pat O'Shane, an honest magistrate. The hearing lasted for nine months and at the completion Pat O'Shane threw out four of the seven charges, and committed me to stand trial on three. It was an outstanding result. No one had ever had four murder charges thrown out by any magistrate in the history of the courts. The cops weren't happy and tried to have the director of public prosecutions overrule her decision but the DPP knew they could never get a conviction on the four that had been thrown out. They weren't all that confident on the three I had to face trial on.

I went to trial first on the murder of Harvey Jones. The trial lasted nine weeks and the jury took nine days to reach a verdict of guilty. The judge sentenced me never to be released. I was to die in jail. I later went to trial for the murder of Sallie-Anne Huckstepp and the jury took just over an hour to return with a not-guilty verdict. The last of the three charges, that of Lewton Shu, was no billed by the DPP.

I appealed the Harvey Jones verdict to the Court of Criminal Appeal but had no success. Then I took my case to the High Court of Australia but they refused to give me leave to appeal. That's as far as I can go with appeals but I am not out of the race just yet. I still have one more chance of proving my innocence but I won't mention what it is as I don't want to give the cops any start. They don't want me out ever again and would do anything to prevent me from hitting the streets again.

Will I ever be released from jail? Well, if I have any say in the matter I will be released within the next three years, maybe even less. But if it's left up to the government and the cops I will die in jail. Dying in jail is not a very comforting thought I might add, but dying doesn't bother me in the slightest. We're born to die. It's something that we have no say over so I just accept the fact that one day, in the not too near future, I am going to die and I don't give it another thought. When your time comes up you have no choice in the matter. You just have to go. I will try my hardest not to die in jail but I might not have any luck in picking where I die, so I'll leave that in someone else's hands.

My family has stuck by me for just over 14 years. My children never miss a visit, every weekend they come to visit me. My wife stuck by me for 13 years, she never missed a visit for the whole 13 years, but when I was sentenced to never be released I decided that she had given me enough of her life. Just because my life had come to a stop there was no need for hers to stop too so I told her not to come to see me any more and to make a life for herself. She stuck by me and was always there for me when I needed her. And she still is there for me if I ever need her. I applied for a divorce and, after 26 years married, it took only one month and one day for my divorce to be finalised. It was handed down on June 16 2001. We are still friends and we ring each other now and then, but I refuse to allow her to visit me because it would be too hard for me to let her go a second time.

These days my life is rather dull without going to court and fighting the corrupt cops for my freedom. I get up at five every morning and, after shaving and cleaning my teeth, I sit down and turn my laptop on and study the law, looking for a loophole or some precedent that will get me back before the courts so that I can try to have my case reopened and maybe get a new trial. My health isn't all that crash hot. I am still taking huge amounts of medication daily but it has almost got to the stage where it doesn't have any effect on me. Where each dose of medication used to give me some relief for around four hours I am lucky to get two hours relief. I can't complain about the medical treatment I get at the jail. The nurses do their best to help me but they can only do so much with the medication. Like me, their hands are tied and they can do nothing more than give me my pills.

I don't know how much longer I have before I die but regardless of how long it is, I will be fighting to prove that I did not kill Harvey Jones.

Neddy Smith, August 2002

A. S. Smith 156145
LMB 24
Matraville, NSW 2036

Two best-sellers in one

UNTOLD VIOLENCE

A rare look inside Melbourne's underworld, a place built on money, power and violence. "A better read that most crime thrillers and has one other major bonus. It's all true." – *Herald-Sun*

WALSH STREET

An instant best-seller that brings Melbourne's best-know criminal family to life in a plot involving drugs, murder, armed robbery and the killing of two police constables.
"As compelling as it is frightening."
– *The Sunday Age*

Available at good bookstores $22.95 including GST
Distributed by Tower Books